THE LOST RELIGION OF JESUS

THE LOST RELIGION OF JESUS

Simple Living and Nonviolence in Early Christianity

Keith Akers

Lantern Books
A Division of Booklight Inc.

2000
Lantern Books
One Union Square West, Suite 201
New York, NY 10003

Printed in the United States of America

Library of Congress Cataloging-in-Publication Data

Akers, Keith
 The lost religion of Jesus: simple living and nonviolence in early Christianity by Keith Akers
    p. cm.
 Includes bibliographical references (p.) and index.
 ISBN 1-930051-26-3 (pbk. : acid-free paper)
  1. Jewish Christians—history—Early church, ca. 30-600. 2. Ebionism.
  3. Christianity—Origin. 4. Christianity and other religions—Judaism.
  5. Judaism—Relations—Christianity. I.Title.

BR195.J8 A5 2000
273'.1—dc21   00-048739

For my parents

The author gratefully acknowledges permission from the following to use material in their control:

Unless otherwise noted, all scriptural quotations are from the Revised Standard Version of the Bible, copyright 1946, 1952, 1971 by the Division of Christian Education of the National Council of the Churches of Christ in the USA. Used by permission. All rights reserved.

Oxford University Press, for scriptural quotations from *The New English Bible With the Apocrypha* (Oxford University Press, 1970).

Linda Hess, for the poetry of Kabir in *The Bijak of Kabir*, translated by Linda Hess and Shukdev Singh (San Francisco: North Point Press, 1983).

Scholars Press, for the quotations from *The Precious Pearl*, a translation from the Arabic by Jane Idleman Smith (Missoula: Scholars Press, 1979).

Koch, Glenn A. *A Critical Investigation of Epiphanius' Knowledge of the Ebionites: A Translation and Critical Discussion of* Panarion 30. Ph. D. dissertation, University of Pennsylvania, 1976. *Diss. Abstr. International* 37 (October 1976) 2253–A. Quotations used by permission.

TABLE OF CONTENTS

ACKNOWLEDGMENTS

THE LIFE OF A BOOK OFTEN BEGINS IN CONVERSATIONS, and numerous people have given me advice or encouragement along the way. These people, in approximate order based on the time the help was given, include my friend Charles Vaclavik, Steve Kaufman, Charles Patterson, Kay Bushnell, John Simcox, Heather Young, Amie Hamlin, Meredith Robbins, Peter McQueen, Larry Grimm, Justina Walls, Judy Miner, Tim Liston, Bruce Friedrich, Sue Giovanini, Bernadette Sonefeld, Regina Hyland, F. Stanley Jones, Richard Schwartz, Bill Shurtleff, George Pelton, Susan McKee, Sue Tiezzi, Sharon Dryden, Norm Phelps, Roberta Kalechofsky, Carol Adams, Patti Breitman, Lewis Regenstein, Howard Lyman, John Robbins, Alex Pacheco, Tom Regan, Dan Dombrowski, Victoria Moran, Rachel MacNair, John Swomley, and Walter Wink, and any others whom I may have overlooked.

Thanks also to the people at Taylor Library in the Iliff Theological Seminary in Denver, where I did almost all of my research. Thanks to my editor, Martin Rowe, for his persistence in believing in the book. Thanks to the long-departed pastor who baptized me, Dr. Edward Galloway, for telling me that God really had given us the straight story right at the beginning. Thanks to my parents, the first people to give me a Bible I could read. Thanks to my dear wife, Kate Lawrence, for her own support in both my spiritual and literary development.

FOREWORD

HAVING FOUGHT ON THE LOSING SIDE OF SO MANY struggles, I have begun to be suspicious of the growth of the Christian church as it swept into a gentile world. Three decades ago I began to discover "Jewish Christianity." It is not that brand of Jewish Christianity that we find in the modern world, which simply means Jews being converted to Pauline Christianity, but that Christianity of the first few centuries that remained Jewish and rejected Paul outright. These earliest Christians identified with the poor, espoused nonviolence and vegetarianism, avoided alcohol, and rejected the virgin birth and bodily resurrection. Their nonviolence led to repudiation of both animal sacrifice and human bloodshed, so they condemned both Temple sacrifices and participation in war. Since they held fast to the Law of Moses, they had to explain its advocacy of both sacrifice and warfare. They did this by a theory of "false insertions." Moses, they argued, never said these things, so they must have been added by "the lying pen of the scribes."

Other scholars have explored this field, and several significant studies have been published, but none of them have the impact this one has. The author, in marvelously lucid prose, has succeeded in presenting this "heretical" branch of Christianity with a judiciousness and balance that is commendable, and in a manner accessible to the average reader. But more important, Keith Akers challenges Christians today to reconsider who the real "heretics" were and who the "orthodox." For Akers presents nothing less than an entire recasting of Christian origins, as well as a whole new conception of Christianity that he feels is deserving of serious consideration as an alternative to the theology and practice of the "Great Church." How appropriate, then, that the author is neither an academic nor a specialist in biblical studies, but an independent philosopher with vegetarian convictions.

These "Jewish Christians" lost, having been successively shattered by the War of Jerusalem, the Bar Cochba revolt, and persecution by both Jewish authorities and gentile Christians. But Karl Popper reminds us that what we learned in school was not "world history" but the history of power politics. This is nothing but the history of international crime and mass murder, in which some of the greatest criminals are extolled as heroes. This is even true of the "God acts in history" school of Christian theology. It assumes that worldly success judges what was good or evil, rather than our own active moral consciences. The doctrine that "history will judge" is simply the assertion that future might makes right. [*The Open Society and Its Enemies*, 2:259–280 (Princeton University Press, 1966)].

What Popper suggests is that the losers may deserve more serious consideration than the winners; that the keepers of the tradition may have been more faithful than the accommodators to Roman society; that the revelation given by Jesus was not otherworldly or mythological, but an uncompromising ethical demand that asked everything of those who followed.

Walter Wink
Professor of Biblical Interpretation
Auburn Theological Seminary, New York
January 2000

INTRODUCTION

MOST SCHOLARS, WHETHER LIBERAL OR CONSERVATIVE, assume without argument that modern Christianity began with Jesus and moved outward to become a world religion on that basis—perhaps elaborating on or modifying the teachings somewhat, but retaining this basic structure. I believe that this view of history, and consequently most historical Jesus scholarship, is fundamentally flawed.

Even a cursory analysis of the historical evidence shows that Christianity was filled from the very start with internal controversy over basic issues. The differences between those claiming to be Christian in the first four hundred years after Jesus' birth were *greater* than at any other time in history—greater even than that today. Regardless of what view we take about Jesus, we must acknowledge and come to grips with these schisms—trying to understand all sides as best we can—before we can understand Jesus. These early Christians may not have understood Jesus, but they were closer to him than we are.

At the basis of all these schisms is the first and most divisive question in the first centuries of Christianity: What is the relationship between the followers of Jesus and Judaism? Early Christians answered this question in different ways. In broad terms, there were three schools of thought in early Christianity as to what this relationship should be:

- Jewish Christians, who wanted to retain a full link between followers of Jesus and Judaism. For the Jewish Christians, Jesus was the prophet predicted by Moses who had led the people back to the true law revealed to Moses but forgotten by the tradition.

- Gnostics who wanted a complete break between the followers of Jesus and Judaism. Many gnostics thought that the God of Jesus and the Jewish God who created the world were two different gods altogether. This led the gnostics to reject the world, because it was a botched creation of a lesser god. They believed that knowledge ("gnosis") of the highest God, the father of Jesus, led to salvation after death in a spiritual realm independent of this world of suffering and death.

- The orthodox, who wanted a smooth transition from Judaism to Christianity. Like the gnostics, they wanted Christianity to have a fundamentally different basis from Judaism. The orthodox considered the basis of Christianity not to be the revelation of God's law to Moses on Mt. Sinai, but rather the revelation of God himself through Jesus—a revelation that superseded that law. But like the Jewish Christians, the orthodox worshiped the same God the Jews did and saw in Jewish history the prophecy of Jesus' revelation.

All these views were differing ways of coming to grips with a fundamental problem: that Jesus was born a Jew, lived a Jew, and died a Jew. Yet in the years after Jesus, the number of gentile Christians came to far surpass the number of Jewish Christians. Christianity came to consist less and less of those who continued to acknowledge their Jewish roots by remaining loyal to the Jewish law, and more and more of those who believed they had no allegiance to the law of Moses but only to the revelation of Jesus and the church he founded. Eventually, Christianity came to regard *any* allegiance to the Jewish law, unless subsequently validated by Jesus or the church established in his name, as a heresy. This book is a re-examination of the history of Jewish Christianity and its implications for understanding the historical Jesus.

For the Jewish Christians, Jesus was a loyal Jew who preached the law given to Moses; but upon examining this law, Jesus reached radical conclusions. To the Jewish Christians, it was Jesus' ethics of simple living and nonviolence, rather than a new theology, that distinguished him and his followers from other Jews. They believed that Jesus' preaching was first and foremost about simple living, pacifism, and vegetarianism and that he never intended to create a new religion separate from Judaism. I believe that the Jewish Christians understood Jesus better than any of the gentile Christian groups that are the spiritual ancestors of modern Protestant, Catholic, and Orthodox churches.

History has given the Jewish Christians an unusually bad press. Paul portrayed them as narrow-minded, the later church condemned them as heretics, and modern scholars have ignored them. These assessments, however, are not justified. Jesus lived and died a Jew; most of those who heard his message were Jewish; the initial leadership of the church was Jewish; Jewish Christianity is of the highest importance in understanding Jesus. When the larger gentile Christian church drove out Jewish Christianity, I will argue, it also lost the core of Jesus' teachings. The values of simple living and nonviolence became increasingly marginalized in a church that came to accept the very materialism and violence against which Jesus had protested.

Modern Christianity, whether Protestant, Catholic, or Orthodox, has thus misunderstood the message of Jesus. By the fourth century, the Nicene Creed had stripped simple living and nonviolence from the center of the message of Jesus altogether. In the place of Jesus' new way of living was a complex and convoluted Trinitarian theology that spoke of the virgin birth, of rising from the dead, and of the final judgment, but nowhere of the message of Jesus. Instead of a call to change our lives and our relationship to God and the world we have an all-powerful Messiah without a cause.

Understanding Jesus' message is as important for the modern world as for the historian. Many today are concerned about the environmental crisis and the pillaging of the earth's resources by rampant consumerism, the spiral of escalating violence, the victimization of the world's poor, and the slaughter of animals for food. Perhaps Jesus' message of simple living and nonviolence is relevant for today's world—even though it has been lost from most of modern Christianity.

Part I
THE MOTHER OF ALL SCHISMS

1 BROKEN THREAD

FACTIONS IN THE EARLY CHURCH

I N THE BEGINNING, JESUS AND ALL HIS FOLLOWERS WERE Jews; in the end, the church condemned the Jewish Christians as heretics. Until we resolve this paradox, we cannot hope to understand Jesus. The first and greatest division in the early church concerned the relationship of the followers of Jesus to Judaism; it shaped everything that was to follow.

Jewish Christianity consisted of those early Christians *who followed the teachings of Jesus, as they understood him, and also remained loyal to the Jewish law of Moses as they understood it.* The qualifications are important, because the Jewish Christians were eventually rejected both by orthodox Judaism and by orthodox Christianity.[1] *Their* understanding of Jesus was not that of orthodox Christianity (as it came to be), and *their* understanding of the law of Moses was not that of orthodox Judaism (as it came to be). Jerome's celebrated comment in the fourth century summarizes this dual rejection: "As long as they seek to be both Jews and Christians, they are neither Jews nor Christians" (*Letter* 112).

The Jewish Christians considered Jesus to be the "true prophet" who would lead the people *back* to the eternal law that commanded simple living and nonviolence. The law had been given to Moses; indeed, it had existed from the beginning of the world. In sharp contrast with the gentile Christian movement, which emerged in the wake of Paul's teaching, Jewish Christianity strove to make the Jewish law *stricter* than the Jewish tradition seemed to teach.

Jewish Christianity is the blind spot in virtually all accounts of Jesus. Everyone agrees that Jesus was a Jew and that his initial followers were Jews. Yet of the thousands of books written about Jesus, almost none acknowledge the central importance of Jewish Christianity. There are many who are eager to focus specifically on the Jewishness of Jesus, until they get to the point of examining those of his followers who, like their teacher, were also Jewish.

The "Jewishness" of these early Christians does not refer to their ethnic group or nationality, but rather to their *beliefs*. Paul was at one time a Jew, but he also preaches freedom from the law and therefore explicitly rejects Jewish beliefs. Paul, and some of the other Jews who became Christians, renounced the law of Moses and, therefore, were *not* part of Jewish Christianity.

When we turn the pages of history to the second, third, and fourth centuries, however, we find several groups that fit this definition of Jewish Christianity. They shared Jesus' approach to the law; they dissented from some of the teachings of Judaism, but attempted to remain within what they regarded as the highest ideals of that path, as articulated by Jesus. There were also during this period a large and growing number of gentile Christians who did not think of themselves as Jews, who believed that God had condemned the Jews, who did not see themselves bound by the law given to Moses, and who viewed Jesus himself—as the incarnation, according to them, of God—as a higher authority than anything given to Moses. It is certainly *possible* that these later gentile followers of Jesus had a better understanding of Jesus than the later Jewish followers of Jesus; but it is very unlikely. One has only to ask this question to see that there is a significant problem here. Without understanding Jewish Christianity, we cannot claim to have understood the history of the primitive church; without understanding Jewish Christianity, we cannot claim to have understood Jesus.

Factionalism in the Early Church

Factionalism was an important aspect of the history of the early church. The traditional Christian understanding of its own history—and the implicit understanding of most scholars—is that Christianity was a gradual or incremental evolution from its starting point. It may be that the later church modified or added to the tradition, runs the argument, but it started with the teachings of Jesus as the basic structure. Most modern "historical Jesus" researchers, whether liberal or conservative, begin with this (unstated) view of history and the assumption that, if we can just identify what was added later and strip it away, we will see the "historical Jesus."

The history of Christianity that this book presents, by contrast, is *not* one of incremental development. It is of a succession of crises that confronted Jesus' followers—*crises that caused fundamental alterations in Christian doctrine and perspective.* Coming to grips with these crises is essential to understanding the teachings of Jesus, because *it is through these crises that the church filtered its awareness of Jesus.* The source of the murkiness and contradiction of early Christian history lies neither in our lack of information nor in our own inability to understand this history—as if the teachings of Jesus are irretrievably lost to history or concealed in manuscripts hidden deep in the Vatican. Early Christian history seems so contradictory because it *was* "contradictory"—so many people were saying so many different things at such an early stage of Christian history.

The evidence for diversity in early Christianity is widespread and comes from the writings of early church leaders, from historical accounts, and the New Testament itself. The literature of early Christianity is often strongly polemical, and the bitterness of the attacks on other followers of Jesus who are "misrepresenting" Christianity is quickly apparent.

- Paul describes an angry confrontation he had with Peter in Galatians 2. Accounts of other bitter disputes can be found throughout Paul's letters.

- Ireneaus (second century) wrote a lengthy work *Against Heresies*.
- Hippolytus (third century) wrote *The Refutation of All Heresies*.
- Origen (third century) comments that "many" Christians had differences of opinion with each other on "subjects of the highest importance" (*De Principiis*, Preface, section 2).
- Tertullian (third century) wrote five books *Against Marcion*, in addition to less lengthy polemical works such as *Prescription Against Heretics*, *Against Hermogenes*, *Against the Valentinians*, and *Against Praxeus*. He describes heresy as widespread (*Prescription Against Heretics* 1); however, he himself joined the Montanists, who were themselves declared heretics.
- Epiphanius (fourth century) wrote the *Panarion*, a lengthy work directed against heresy in which he outlines the views of eighty groups and denounces each one.
- Theodoret (fifth century) wrote the *Compendium of Heretical Fables* in which he describes and attacks sixty heretical groups.

Early Christianity was not at all stable. "Stability" is in fact a characteristic of *later* Christianity, beginning about the time of Constantine and the council of Nicaea (in the year 325). After Constantine and the controversies raised at the council of Nicaea, there were still serious disputes, but they had a much narrower focus and did not occur nearly as frequently. In fact, there were only three truly great heresies after this point. The first was the monophysite controversy, which concerned whether or not Christ had one or two natures; later there was the split between Roman Catholics and Eastern Orthodox over the authority of the pope; finally, there was the greatest heresy of all, that of Martin Luther and others, which launched the Protestant reformation.

For over 1600 years following Constantine, controversy over doctrinal matters—while it did occur—was the exception rather than the rule. But during the first four centuries after Jesus, Christianity was even more doctrinally divided than it is today. Moreover, these disputes did not involve political questions of church authority, nor obscure theological points that most ordinary Christians had difficulty understanding; they involved the very nature of God, Jesus, and salvation.

In Christian history, these early crises were both admitted and denied. Eusebius' fourth-century *Ecclesiastical History* portrayed the schisms the church faced as just bumps on the road of history, due to the sorts of misunderstandings that were bound to arise as any message was carried forward. For Eusebius, the followers of Jesus established a church and wrote down the teachings of the Christ. They faced opposition, persecution, and even setbacks. But in general the gospel gained increasing numbers of adherents as time progressed. Three hundred years after the death of Jesus the Roman Empire embraced the faith. Eusebius portrays Christian history as the record of revelation gaining increasing acceptance over time.

This idea has a powerful hold even among "liberal" scholars who are otherwise skeptical. If we are committed to this "incrementalist" view of history, early Christian diversity becomes an insoluble puzzle; for the earliest period of Christian history should be the period with the least amount of later elaboration and revision. Yet as we go further back in time in Christian history, the dissension and diversity actually *increases*. It is no wonder that some scholars, seeing this vast diversity, conclude with Albert Schweitzer that the historical Jesus is an enigma hidden from us—better an object of faith than a subject of historical inquiry.

Christianity did *not* emerge as a gradual development from the teachings of its founder. Rather, this book will argue, a series of severe crises shook the primitive Christian church, permitting broad schisms to develop, and fatally weakening the leadership of the early church. The thread connecting modern Christianity to Jesus was decisively broken by these crises.

The Controversy Over Gnosticism

By the second century, Jewish Christianity was not even the most important heresy. Another and even greater heresy arose to oppose what was to become orthodox belief. It was known as gnosticism, and it engaged the church in a desperate life-and-death struggle for the soul of Christianity. Scholars disagree on what exactly "gnosticism" is, but in this book we will define it very broadly as any Christian view that rejects the creator God of Judaism and despises the physical world he created.

In the year 140, a man named Marcion appeared in Rome, putting forward a dramatic view of Christianity: that the God of the Christians and the God of the Jews *were two different Gods altogether*. The God of the Jews was the God who actually created the world; but he had botched the job, with the result that we have a universe of pain, suffering, and death. The God of Jesus, by contrast, stood above the world and would save us from it if we would only *know* him. The God of Jesus was a *stranger* God, a stranger to this world of woe. Those who knew Jesus and the true Father God of Jesus would, like Jesus, escape from this world at death and be saved eternally.

Since Marcion (and other gnostics) maintained that the religion of Jesus had *nothing* to do with Judaism, gnosticism was in many ways the polar opposite of Jewish Christianity. The attractiveness of gnosticism was due in part to its straightforward answer to the perplexing question of the relationship of Jesus to Judaism. The gnostics cut this Gordian knot by severing the relationship completely.

Marcion's belief in two gods instead of one was rejected by orthodox Christianity. Marcion was thrown out of the church at Rome and a bitter struggle ensued. *Nevertheless*, Marcion's view had wide appeal in early Christianity. He quickly attracted a large following and his views were only suppressed after several centuries of struggle. The writings of the church fathers from the second and third centuries reflect a strong preoccupation with Marcion and other gnostics. The church fathers wrote literally volumes about heretics generally, and the gnostics in particular. It is clear from just the volume of writing and the desperate viciousness of the diatribes against heresy that they felt there was a real possibility that some version of gnosticism might triumph in the struggle with what we now know as orthodox Christianity.

While Marcion lost his struggle, the influence of gnosticism on Christianity was nevertheless very significant. To begin with, one of the themes of gnosticism was that the creation of the world was less than perfect, a product of an evil—or perhaps merely incompetent—creator God. This belief was indirectly reflected in the tendency toward asceticism among many early Christians, in an effort to "escape" from the world. Some Christian ascetics engaged in bizarre and self-punishing behaviors, such as self-flagellation and spending years sitting on a pillar. The whole idea that this present world is a world of woe, rather than (as in Judaism) the very good creation of a loving, all-powerful God, is a "gnostic" view. How, after all, could it be that the loving, merciful God of Jesus would also have been the creator of this world of suffering?

Marcion also had a strong influence on the New Testament. Indeed, when Marcion preached his gospel, there *was* no New Testament canon. Individual gospels existed, of course, as well as the letters of Paul and letters of various revered figures in Christianity; but no one had identified a collection of sacred writings as definitive for any of the followers of Jesus. Marcion *did* have such a collection: his canon contained a version of the gospel of Luke plus ten of the letters of Paul. Marcion was also the *first* to use the term "gospel" to refer to writings about Jesus.[2] Gerd Lüdemann states, "Without Marcion there would have been no New Testament; without this heretic, no letters of Paul."[3]

It is certain that Marcion could not have had such an impact unless early Christianity was highly diverse and lacking in stable leadership. It is as if, a century after the death of the Buddha, a strong heretical form of Buddhism arose that denied one or more of the four noble truths. It is as if, a century after the death of Mohammed, a strong heretical form of Islam arose that maintained that a secret and superior version of the Qur'an existed of which this sect alone possessed a copy. Such serious heresy at such an early stage in the history of *any* religion could not have been the result of a stable and strong central religious authority; rather, it would be convincing evidence that something had gone awry at an early stage.

"Heresy" was not a single point of view by any means. The Jewish Christians differed sharply from Marcion and other gnostics. While Marcion presented Paul as a hero, perhaps as the only apostle who truly understood Jesus, the Jewish Christians detested Paul, whom they regarded as an apostate. They believed that the God of Jesus was the God of the Jews; they also believed that Jesus was a prophet who came to reform the Mosaic law—to return the people to the original law of God, which had been given to Moses but then distorted by those who followed after Moses.

The controversy over gnosticism shows how deep the divisions in Christianity were in the second century and how fragmented Christianity was at this early stage. If Christians just a century after Jesus had this much trouble in understanding the basic teachings of Jesus, then how can we, standing two millennia after Jesus, hope to do any better?

The New Testament

The problem of the divisions in early Christianity raises a further question: why can't we just turn to the New Testament to resolve outstanding issues which were confusing in early Christianity? This is the instinctive reaction of many Christians, especially Protestants. Isn't the New Testament precisely such a guide for anyone needing clarification?

There are several reasons why doing this does not work. First of all, the New Testament itself displays a wide variety of contradictory viewpoints and agendas; the writings themselves are not historical records as much as advocacies for different audiences within the early Christian communities. Secondly, it leaves out a number of viewpoints and ancient gospels. Thirdly, it was subject to extensive editing and modification. All this could be overlooked, perhaps, if early Christianity were otherwise a unified, coherent movement; but early Christianity was anything but unified and coherent, as we have already seen.

The New Testament can easily be invoked for support of countless mutually contradictory explanations of Jesus. As a result, even those seeking to interpret the Bible literally often come to a completely different understanding of what that literal interpretation is. On the basis of the Bible, some Christians are pacifist, while others support war; some support capital punishment, others oppose it; some accept alcohol, while others do not; some allow divorce, some allow divorce only in cases of adultery, and some do not allow divorce at all; and so on. Each viewpoint can cite its favorite verses or interpretations. Fundamentalists may object that the New Testament is complete and consistent and provides a reliable guide for life and religion; but if this is the case, it is hard to explain all the contradictions among the fundamentalists themselves.

There are numerous discrepancies, both major and minor, in the New Testament accounts: the names of the twelve apostles, the location of Jesus' post-resurrection appearances, the completely different genealogies in Matthew and Luke, for example. The synoptic gospels (Matthew, Mark, and Luke), called "synoptic" because their pictures of Jesus are similar to each other, are sharply different from the gospel of John. The letters of Paul, in turn, present a very different picture of Jesus than that found in the synoptic gospels. Sometimes there are even contradictions: for example, Jesus affirms that he has come to fulfill the law and condemns those who violate even the least of the law's commands (Matthew 5:17–19); but in his letters Paul says that Jesus annulled the law and says that his (Paul's) own adherence to the law was "so much garbage" (Ephesians 2:14–15, Philippians 3:8).

To the impartial reader it is obvious that many different ideas are at play; centuries of exegesis designed to harmonize the New Testament writings cannot overturn the problems that lurk there. John Dominic Crossan, author of several books about Jesus, points out that we can construct almost any picture of Jesus we want to by selecting the "right" texts. Jesus can be shown "to be for or against legal observance, for or against apocalyptic expectation, for or against Gentile mission, for or against Temple worship, for or against titular claim, for or against political revolt, and so on."[4]

But even putting this aside, the New Testament would be a poor guide to historical reality. The New Testament is highly selective; gospels that did not meet with the approval of the early church were eliminated. Due to the twentieth-century discoveries at Nag Hammadi, we now know what the New Testament might have looked like if history had turned out a bit differently. As diverse as the New Testament is, it pales in comparison with the diversity of the range of views held by significant numbers of the followers of Jesus just within the first century after Jesus. It should not be necessary to repeat the statement of Hans-Joachim Schoeps that the New Testament "must surely be regarded as a tendentious, contrived product of the second century,"[5] or Robert Funk's conclusion that the New Testament is "a highly uneven and biased record of various early attempts to invent Christianity."[6]

Moreover, it may be next to impossible to fully reconstruct what the original texts of even the "approved" New Testament books said. Helmut Koester reminds us that the oldest known manuscripts of parts of the New Testament are over a century later than the presumed original versions; and it is precisely in the first century when the most serious corruptions of the texts (changes, additions, and deletions) are likely to have occurred. Koester concludes that "textual critics of the New Testament writings have been surprisingly naive in this respect."[7]

Even within the sphere of the orthodox there was disagreement as to which books should be included. The Muratorian canon, based on a manuscript thought to originate as early as the third century, fails to include Hebrews, I Peter, II Peter, one of the letters of John, and James, all of which are in the modern New Testament; it does include, however, the Apocalypse of Peter and the Wisdom of Solomon, which ultimately were not included. Some writers even attacked the Gospel of John in reaction to the Montanist heresy, a heresy with strong apocalyptical and pentecostal elements.[8] It was not until the fourth century, with Athanasius, that someone mentions the exact twenty-seven books that now constitute the New Testament. But Eusebius, who lived about the same time, describes the books of James, Jude, II Peter, II John, and III John as disputed[9], indicating that even at this late date there is still some considerable debate going on. Even as late as the Reformation, Martin Luther objected to the inclusion of the letter of James in the New Testament; and Catholics and Protestants disagree to this day over the Apocrypha.

This book is *not* a detailed attempt to determine either what the canon should have been, or to determine which of the sayings of Jesus from the canonical or other gospels are "authentic." Our task is both more humble and more fundamental. It is more humble, because evaluation of all New Testament and other texts for authenticity is completely beyond the scope of this book. But it is more fundamental, because it establishes the framework within which any discussion of the historical Jesus must take place: the history of Christianity. For if we do not understand the basic context and history of his teaching, how can we hope to ever understand the exact words?

The New Testament provides important evidence about the historical Jesus and the history of early Christianity. However, it cannot be taken simply at face value: it is a highly edited, inconsistent document put together to support the viewpoint of a single party in early Christianity, namely the victorious party. It is the *outcome* of early Christian history, not just a record of it. The starting point of historical Jesus research is history; we must first establish the historical context of Jesus' mission and message. We believe that this book can establish this historical context: it is Jewish Christianity.

History and Revelation

"But how do you know?"

It might seem from the foregoing discussion that we are trapped in relativism: we are faced with equally plausible but contradictory interpretations of Christian records. Jesus as gnostic teacher, Jesus as military revolutionary, Jesus as social critic, Jesus as dying savior—with countless equally possible interpretations, how can we decide for or against any of them?

We propose a simple criterion for evaluating any theory about Jesus: *Does it make sense of Christian history?* "Christian history" means, of course, the life of Jesus (most Jesus theories do a pretty good job with this); but it also includes later events as well. The mission of Paul, the destruction of Jerusalem, the controversies over gnosticism in the second century, and the council of Nicaea in the fourth century—all of these need to be included.

Pick up any book on the historical Jesus, whether written two hundred years ago or yesterday, and you will most likely find no substantial discussion of Marcion and his role in second-century Christianity, no mention of the destruction of Jerusalem in the year 70 and its effect on Christianity, no mention of Jewish Christianity, no discussion of the other countless schisms in early Christianity,[10] and no discussion of the council of Nicaea. With a few exceptions, most books on the historical Jesus pass all of this by. A few pages, a few paragraphs, or even a few footnotes are all that you will see on key historical issues. "Let's concentrate on the New Testament texts relating to Jesus," they seem to be saying, "and let the later history of Christianity take care of itself." The texts "float in the air," outside of time, space, and history.

We cannot understand Jesus without *first* understanding early Christian history. The very records that we invoke for the understanding of Jesus were themselves decisively shaped by later events. We must, therefore, turn to these later events to understand the earlier records. The history of early Christianity is exactly what shaped the text of the New Testament—and any criterion of what the "good" and "bad" texts are must rely on *some* idea of that history. Most scholars, if they are tempted at all to go down the path of Christian history to understand Jesus, quickly turn back after encountering the demons of schism. But it is precisely these demons we must confront.

In this chapter we have sought to establish a very rough outline of a "road map" for the history of early Christianity. We have also proposed a framework for understanding who Jesus was: the history of early Christianity. Early Christianity was highly schismatic, and this fact complicates our knowledge of Jesus. We do not yet want to take sides, or say that someone was right or wrong; we simply want to see the problem and work our way back to the original question that led to the confusion: Did the followers of Jesus see the Jewish law as a guide for their lives?

Conclusions

The idea that Christianity developed gradually from its beginnings, based on the teachings of Jesus but perhaps making certain additions or changes as the tradition developed, has a powerful hold even among the most liberal of scholars. Christianity did not develop this way, however. Rather, there was wide discord in early Christianity—something that was actually to Christianity's advantage, since in the rapid growth of Christianity, those features that had more appeal to the people of the Roman Empire would spread more rapidly and ultimately define what Christianity was. Had the followers of Jesus uniformly remained a Jewish sect, Christianity very likely would *not* have become the religion of the Roman Empire.

These schisms in early Christianity were not concerned with matters of detail of the Christian message nor with obscure questions of theology. They cut to the very heart of what Christianity was and is. They were the material of the repeated crises that dotted the landscape of early Christian history.

It is against this backdrop that we consider the history of Jewish Christianity. Were followers of Jesus those who followed a new path, a new religion, transmitted directly from God through Jesus, and that superseded everything in Judaism that was not in consonance with it? Or were the followers of Jesus simply Jews following the prophet who sought to return to the true and original law of God, revealed to Moses? Or was the relationship even more complicated than this, or something else altogether? This was the issue that continually faced Christians in the first four centuries. The final resolution of this by orthodox Christianity was that Christians had no allegiance to the law of Moses as such, but rather first to Jesus and the church he founded, which replaced the law of Moses. This resolution created a paradox: in the beginning, Jesus and all his followers were Jews; in the end, the church condemned the Jewish Christians as heretics.

2 THE FOLLOWERS OF THE TRUE PROPHET

WHO WERE THE JEWISH CHRISTIANS?

W HO WERE THE JEWISH CHRISTIANS, WHAT DID THEY believe, and how do we know anything about them at all? Jewish Christians in the broadest sense of the term— those following the law of Moses and following Jesus as well—existed from the very beginning of Christianity. They appear in both favorable and unfavorable contexts in the New Testament. However, the most striking evidence for Jewish Christianity is found outside of the Bible: from the descriptions of church writers who knew about Jewish Christianity and attacked it, and from two early church documents written predominantly from a Jewish Christian point of view—the *Recognitions of Clement* and the *Clementine Homilies*.

These writings give a clear picture of Jewish Christianity. There were a number of Jewish Christian groups, all largely similar to each other, the most important of which was known as the *Ebionites*. The Ebionites thought of Jesus as a prophet—in fact, the true prophet predicted by Moses in Deuteronomy 18:15–18. In Deuteronomy, the people tell Moses they are so afraid of God that they don't want to hear the voice of God again, and God agrees not to speak to them—but with the proviso that a future prophet of truth, a prophet like Moses, will someday be sent to them. The Ebionites got their name from the Hebrew term *ebionim* meaning "the poor"; they believed in simple living, were pacifists, and were vegetarians. The Ebionites, therefore, had both similarities and differences with what we know of other Christians living in the first four centuries after Jesus.

Because the Ebionites represent an *independent* tradition of what Jesus said and did outside of the New Testament and the orthodox churches, and because of their practice of following the Jewish law, they have a special claim for our attention—just as much, or more, than the claims of the faction that formulated the New Testament. Wasn't Jesus a Jew himself? Even in the New Testament, doesn't he follow the law and teach others to do the same? Wouldn't the Ebionite tradition, in this case, have a better claim to represent the views of Jesus than the tradition of those who rejected the necessity of keeping the law?

Jewish Christianity in the New Testament

The New Testament is not as helpful as one would like on the subject of Jewish Christianity. There are numerous references, both pro and con, to ideas that the Ebionites held—for example, on the question of keeping the Jewish law, on vegetarianism, on pacifism, on baptism, and on the temple. These passages will be dealt with at length during the course of this book. There are only a few passages that refer directly to Jewish Christians, in Acts and in the letters of Paul. They are not particularly flattering to Jewish Christianity and they are confusing and sketchy.

- In Acts 11:2, Peter is criticized by "the circumcision party" (presumably, Jewish Christians) for meeting and eating with gentiles. Peter explains that he had a vision in which it was revealed that there must be a mission to the gentiles as well as the Jews.

- In Acts 15, there is a lengthy account concerning a controversy started by some followers of Jesus who are Pharisees. These Christian Pharisees insist that gentile converts be circumcised. After lengthy discussion, the views of these Christian Pharisees is rejected; gentile converts, it is ruled, need only adhere to four points relating to the law.

- Acts 21:20 portrays James as telling Paul that there are many thousands of Jews who have converted to Jesus and that they are "zealous for the law." Paul agrees to go to the temple to make a sacrifice to appease their feelings.

- Galatians 1–2 relates several disputes that Paul had with the early leaders of the church. The church leaders agree that circumcision is not necessary; however, they do not agree over some food issues (which Galatians does not elaborate on). This brings Paul into an angry face-to-face confrontation with Peter—a dispute in which James, John, Peter, and Barnabas all oppose Paul.

In these passages, which will be explored in more detail later, we see important evidence for factionalism in the early church. The accounts in Acts give a distorted view of Jewish Christianity: they imply that the Jewish Christians are only concerned about highly legalistic matters such as circumcision and making sacrifices in the temple. The view expressed by the so-called "Christian Pharisees" in Acts 15:1—that only those males who are circumcised can be saved—was a view held by only a minority of Jews in the first century. Thus, these Christian Pharisees would have been considered reactionary even by most other non-Christian Jews. This is certainly how the later church wanted to portray Jewish Christianity—as a reactionary Jewish group that for some reason claimed to follow Jesus.

There are more reasons for being suspicious of the descriptions of Jewish Christianity in Acts; most importantly, Paul's letters conflict with Acts on several key points. In Acts, Paul compliantly circumcises Timothy (16:3); in Galatians, he indignantly refuses even for a moment to make a concession to the "false brethren" by circumcising Titus (2:3–5). In Acts, Paul is appointed by the church to meet the apostles (15:2); in Galatians, he goes not from any human directive but "by revelation" (2:2). In all his letters, Paul indignantly rejects the idea that it is necessary to follow the law of Moses in order to be saved; but in Acts, he goes to the temple to make a sacrifice! It is not absolutely impossible to reconcile these accounts, but the character of Paul is so strikingly different in them that it must be deeply troubling to any objective reader.

From Paul's letters, we know he had opponents. They are loyal to the law, deny Paul's right to be called an apostle, and are ethical vegetarians. The later Ebionites were loyal to the law, despised Paul, and were ethical vegetarians. It is indisputable, therefore, that the germ of Ebionite ideas—even though the "Ebionites" as such did not yet exist—already existed in the first century, among the very first followers of Jesus. It is also indisputable from Galatians that Paul's opponents at one time included not just a reactionary faction of conservative Jews in the early church, but the leadership of the church itself—liberal leaders who acknowledged that circumcision was not necessary for salvation: James, Peter, and John.

The New Testament gives us only one side of the story, the side given by the faction that assembled the New Testament. The Jewish Christians gave a very different account. They described Paul as a traitor to Christian principles—most likely because Paul watered down the original radical principles of Jesus, which had nothing to do with "legalism" surrounding circumcision but rather with the principles of simplicity and nonviolence.

Jewish Christian Literature

Much of our knowledge about Jewish Christianity comes from three early Christian writings: the *Recognitions of Clement*, the *Clementine Homilies*, and the *Panarion* of Epiphanius of Salamis.

The *Homilies* and *Recognitions* are the only surviving documents of any size containing Jewish Christian writings. These third-century documents were purportedly composed by Clement of Rome, an early church leader. It's conceivable that (in some earlier version) they really were written by Clement, though most scholars believe they were not; thus they are often referred to as the "pseudo-Clementine" literature. For our purposes it is not important whether or not Clement wrote them, just that they contain a lot of Jewish Christian ideas. Both the *Homilies* and *Recognitions* share a lot of material, seeming to be different versions of one original work. About one quarter of each document is undoubtedly of Jewish Christian origin and refers to Jesus as the "true prophet" predicted by Moses in Deuteronomy, a characteristically Jewish Christian theme. The rest of these books contain a religious romance telling how Clement was miraculously reunited with some of his lost family members and how they all converted to Christianity. The passages of most interest to students of Jewish Christian origins include the account of James in the temple (unique to the *Recognitions*) and the debates between Peter and Simon Magus.

We know that the *Homilies* and *Recognitions* contain Jewish Christian ideas because of the remarkable and extensive description of the Jewish Christians by Epiphanius. He is the fulcrum upon which much of our knowledge of Jewish Christianity rests. Epiphanius wrote his most famous work, the *Panarion* or "Medicine Chest" (medicines, that is, to be used against the "disease" of heresy), in about 380 CE, over a half century after the Council of Nicaea.

Epiphanius is an excellent source for several reasons. First, he is an eyewitness to history. He has talked to individual Jewish Christians and has copies of their literature—which he quotes from—in front of him. Second, he is a hostile source: he despised Jewish Christianity, thus he cannot be accused of manufacturing evidence favorable to Jewish Christians. If there was any "dirt" on Jewish Christianity, Epiphanius would have it. Epiphanius describes a number of broadly similar Jewish Christian groups; he gives the best and most vivid description of the Ebionites, the most important of the later Jewish Christian groups. He also describes Ossaeans, Elchasaites, and Nazoraeans, as well as a Jewish group called the Nasaraeans, all of which are very similar in their beliefs.

There are remarkable parallels between the Ebionite beliefs that Epiphanius attacks in the *Panarion* and the ideas in the *Recognitions* and *Homilies*, summarized in the Appendix (see page 233): the description of Jesus as the "true prophet"; support for vegetarianism; attack on animal sacrifice; simple living (or poverty) as a virtue; the conflict with Paul; and the rejection of "false texts" in the Old Testament. Even though the *Recognitions* and *Homilies* have been known since ancient times, for our understanding of early Christianity they are as significant as the Dead

Sea Scrolls, the Nag Hammadi manuscripts, or any of the other early church writings we have.

Many of the Jewish Christian themes in these documents are *also* described in the New Testament—such as attacks on animal sacrifice, the virtue of simple living, hostility toward Paul, vegetarianism, and allegiance to the law. In all these various ancient texts, we see reflections of a dissident Jewish Christianity—a Christianity that, as I have suggested, has a stronger claim to understand Jesus than the gentile Christianity which was the ancestor of the Protestant, Catholic, and Orthodox churches of today.

Ebionite Beliefs

The Ebionites saw in Jesus the "true prophet" predicted by Moses who would restore the now-forgotten laws that Moses received on Mt. Sinai. In basic theology, therefore, they were no different from other Jews; unlike the trinitarian gentile Christians, they did not seek to put Jesus on an equal footing with God the Father. However, their views on the content and nature of the law was different from that of orthodox Judaism. It was a transformation in lifestyle, not a new theology, that for them set Jesus and his early followers apart from other Jews.

Ebionites had the following characteristic beliefs:

- **Jesus is the true prophet.** The Ebionites based their belief in Jesus on Deuteronomy 18:15–18, when Moses predicts a future prophet due to the people's reluctance to hear the voice of God. For the Ebionites, Jesus is this prophet, the prophet of truth.

- **A simple lifestyle is desired by God.** If anything, "simple living" is insufficiently radical to describe what the Ebionites had in mind. The name *ebionim* means "the poor" in Hebrew; the Ebionites traced their "poverty" back to the time when all the followers of Jesus held all their possessions in common (Acts 4:32–35).

- **Jesus condemns animal sacrifice.** "I came to abolish sacrifices," says Jesus in the Ebionite gospel, "and unless you cease sacrificing, my anger will not cease from you" (*Panarion*

30.16.5). One of the chief purposes of the true prophet in the *Recognitions* and the *Homilies* is to show the Jewish people that the practice of animal sacrifice must be ended.

- **Jesus teaches vegetarianism**. Epiphanius describes the Ebionites as vegetarians, and in the *Recognitions* and *Homilies* vegetarianism is strongly connected to the rejection of animal sacrifice and is required of all the followers of Jesus. When Epiphanius questions a Jewish Christian as to why he was a vegetarian, the Jewish Christian responds simply: "Christ revealed it to me" (*Panarion* 30.18.9).

- **Alcohol should be avoided**. The Ebionites used water instead of wine in celebrating the Eucharist. The *Homilies* has Peter attacking alcohol and attacking paganism because of its drunken worship (*Homilies* 11.15).

- **God has one law for everyone**. The distinction between Jew and gentile is abolished for the Jewish Christians just as it was for Paul (Galatians 3:28), but with a different result altogether—everyone should follow the universal and eternal law (*Homilies* 8.10) revealed to Moses (*Recognitions* 1.35). In this respect the Ebionites were traditional Jews who sought to convert the world to their version of Judaism.

- **The law has been distorted with false texts**. This is a highly unusual doctrine, heretical both to orthodox Jews and orthodox Christians: that the Jewish scriptures have been distorted, with the result that not everything in the scriptures can be trusted. Specifically, the Ebionites thought that laws relating to animal sacrifice were later corruptions, though there were a number of other distortions as well.

- **Warfare is condemned**. Epiphanius does not mention pacifism, but several passages in the *Recognitions*, undoubtedly of Jewish Christian origin, espouse pacifist principles. In *Recognitions* 1, when Paul before his conversion tries to murder James, the Christians offer no violence in return because of their pacifist principles. Later, Peter announces opposition to war (*Recognitions* 3.42).

- **Christ has already appeared many times**. The Ebionites felt that Jesus' life was neither the first nor last appearance of the Christ. According to Epiphanius, the Ebionites thought that Christ was "in Adam" and appeared, as Adam, to the patriarchs. "Christ" usually refers to Jesus, but is sometimes used by the Ebionites as a title meaning "the anointed one": the *Recognitions* implies that all believers are anointed as "Christs" (1.45).[1]

- **Baptism is important for salvation**. The Ebionites believed that baptism was important—it replaced animal sacrifice (*Recognitions* 1.39). However, baptism is described in contradictory ways, sometimes as a one-time ritual conferring salvation, sometimes as a daily ritual—like prayer.

- **There is only one God**. The Ebionites were not only monotheists but also strict unitarians who denied the orthodox doctrine of the trinity. For the Ebionites, God does not appear in three persons; Jesus is the prophet of God and the Messiah, but is not the same as God.

- **Paul was an apostate from the law**. The Ebionites didn't like Paul at all, considering him "an apostate" from the law. In the *Recognitions* and *Homilies* there is no direct attack on Paul, but when Peter debates his opponent, Simon Magus, he attacks ideas that are often similar to Paul's views—for instance, that one can become an apostle on the basis of a vision of Jesus.

The most striking thing about the Jewish Christian version of Jesus in comparison with gentile beliefs about Jesus is his attitude toward the law. Jesus was a prophet wanting to *increase* the strictness of the Jewish law, in contrast with Paul, who insists that allegiance to the law is now unnecessary or perhaps even harmful. For the Jewish Christians, it was not enough to help the poor; they had to become poor. It was not enough to abstain from murder; they had to abstain from killing even in wartime, from killing animals, and from anger. It should also be clear, incidentally, that they have almost nothing in common with the modern "Jews for Jesus," who are essentially Jewish converts to *gentile* Christian doctrine. The "Jews for Jesus" and "Messianic Jews" accept the trinity, the virgin birth, the literal truth of the Old Testament, and so forth—all of which were rejected by the Ebionites.

It is generally understood that Paul's message broadened Jesus' audience, spreading the message to the gentiles. The common view is that Paul's "conservative" Jewish Christian opponents wanted the message restricted to Jews and insisted that those accepting the message of Jesus also be born or converted Jews. The Jewish Christians, however, may have seen the issue very differently. They probably thought that Paul broadened the appeal of Christianity by watering down Jesus' message— by diluting the radical lifestyle that Jesus called his followers to in the Sermon on the Mount. The Jewish Christians were "Jewish" because they took Jewish theology for granted, assuming that God had revealed an eternal, indestructible law to the people of Israel through Moses. Upon examining this law, however, they reached radical conclusions.

Other Jewish Christian Groups

The Ebionites are not the only Jewish Christian group in the first centuries of Christianity, but were the most important. The Ebionites are mentioned by more of the church fathers than any other such group; they are also mentioned in the earliest material and are mentioned more often. Up to the fourth century, there are almost twice as many mentions of the Ebionites as there are of all the other Jewish Christian sects combined.[2] The earliest, best, and most voluminous information we have on Jewish Christianity is that concerning the Ebionites.

There are other groups usually classified as "Jewish Christian"— namely the Elchasaites, the Nazoraeans, and the Ossaeans. The evidence concerning these groups is fragmentary and complex and will be considered in more detail later; but, to summarize, all these groups were similar to the Ebionites on at least these three points: they adhered to the Jewish law, they were vegetarian, and they rejected animal sacrifice. Epiphanius goes to some lengths to describe the cozy relationship between the Ebionites and the Elchasaites, Nazoraeans, and Ossaeans; he also explicitly states that the Ebionites, Elchasaites, and Ossaeans were vegetarian and rejected animal sacrifices.

What about the Nazoraeans? Based on statements by Jerome and Theodoret, the Ebionites and the Nazoraeans are actually the same group—using two different names. The story of the name "Nazoraean" is interesting because of its relationship to the term "Nazarene" (as in "Jesus the Nazarene") and the existence of another similarly named Jewish group, the Nasaraeans, who are also very similar to the Ebionites: vegetarian, rejecting animal sacrifices, and rejecting false texts in the scriptures. However, for now we can simply say that what we know about these other Jewish Christian groups reinforces what we know about the Ebionites and our conclusion that the Ebionites are the best and most important representatives of early Jewish Christianity.

Earlier and Later Jewish Christians

What is the relationship between these later Jewish Christians—who were around in the second, third, and fourth centuries—and the very first Jewish followers of Jesus, namely Jesus himself and his disciples? Why should we believe the later Jewish Christian version of Jesus, rather than the later orthodox, gnostic, or any other versions of Jesus?

While many people will readily admit that Jesus and his immediate followers were Jewish, they will hotly deny there was any significant relationship between these early Jewish Christians (Jesus and his first disciples) and the later Jewish Christians (the Ebionites). It's purely a coincidence, in their view, that they shared the same religion.

No one has a problem with identifying Jesus and his followers as Jews in the first century; but, by the fourth century, those Ebionites and other Jewish Christians who *still* claim allegiance to the Jewish law, in however Christianized a form, find themselves condemned as heretics by the church and condemned to oblivion by scholars. Both Christians and scholars see a tremendous difficulty in getting from Jewish followers of Jesus in the *first* century to Jewish followers of Jesus in the *fourth* century.

This difficulty is essentially a prejudice. This is not to say there are no valid questions to be raised or that the case cannot be argued both pro and con. However, the difficulty that both scholars and ordinary Christians see in getting from early Jewish Christianity to later, fourth-century Jewish Christian Ebionites far exceeds the evidence. Curiously, no one sees problems in getting from the first century Jewish followers of Jesus to the fourth century *gentile* followers of Jesus. This is seen as something inevitable, a natural outgrowth of Jesus' teachings. In this way, the Jewishness of Jesus, universally acknowledged, is in the telling of Christian history then implicitly denied.

The reason this denial of the Jewishness of Jesus seems natural is because this is the version of Christianity that has been taught for 1900 years. The prevailing myth that Christianity has perpetuated is that Judaism rejected Jesus at the very outset. "His blood be on us and on our children" (Matthew 27:25), cries an angry Jewish mob, demanding Jesus' crucifixion. This myth, repeated and elaborated and embedded in Christian scripture for nearly two millennia, is also the basis for all Christian anti-Semitism: "the Jews" killed Jesus, the son of God, and therefore persecution or even (in the extreme case) a blood vendetta against Jews is justified.

Such a line of thinking of course does not exculpate the Nazis for the Holocaust by any means, as if the entire blame for the Holocaust can be put on Christian theology. But the point is, that what seems to us moderns like an easy or natural separation between Judaism and Christianity was not so easy or natural at all. This separation only occurred after "the Jews" had been demonized. The Nazis did not have to invent anti-Semitism; they found a tool ready at hand to use in oppressing and killing Jews. The separation between Judaism and Christianity is of utmost importance, not only for the understanding of the historical Jesus, but for understanding what precisely it means to be a follower of Jesus in the first place. This separation between Christianity and Judaism often seems natural to Jews as well as Christians. The very term "Jewish Christianity," even when used in a historical context, sometimes meets with resistance from Jews. "Either you are a Jew or you are not," is the natural response of some Jews; there is no such thing as "Jewish Christianity." For these Jews the term is (and always was) an oxymoron.

Not only was this separation problematic in early Christianity; at the very beginning, it was unthinkable. Most scholars, when they think about the subject at all, hold some version of the view that later Ebionite Jewish Christianity was fundamentally different from "early" Jewish Christianity (when Jewish Christianity consisted of the Jewish Jesus and a few of his Jewish followers). Jesus and the apostles were Jews because, well, in those days everyone in the Jesus movement was Jewish. But then the Jews rejected Jesus and the movement he founded, while the message was successfully preached to the gentiles. Followers of Jesus, therefore, had no choice but to separate themselves from Judaism. Unfortunately, by the fourth century some of the later followers of Jesus (the Ebionites) still hadn't gotten this message, and retreated into a reactionary form of Christianity that still held to the Jewish law.

Anyone who thinks about this for a moment can see that there are a number of problems with this view. First of all, it is apparent that Jesus in the gospels *did* hold to the Jewish law himself, in a manner quite different from that of Paul. Paul eliminated the necessity to follow the Jewish law at all, saying that "the law was our custodian until Christ came" (Galatians 3:24), and that Jesus was "abolishing in his flesh the law of commandments and ordinances" (Ephesians 2:15). In contrast, Jesus declares, "think not that I have come to abolish the law," and condemns those who deviate from even the least of the law's demands (Matthew 5:17–19). We do not have to decide whether Jesus actually made these sweeping statements to see that there is a significant problem here; Jesus in the gospels frequently invokes the authority of the law to support his own positions.

Secondly, the views presented by the fourth-century Jewish Christian Ebionites do not at all conform to the idea of a reactionary group clinging to Jewish legalism while still trying to embrace Jesus. The Ebionites unequivocally condemned one of the central aspects of Judaism, namely the practice of animal sacrifice; and they kept this grievance against animal sacrifice alive in their traditions long after the practice of animal sacrifice had ended when the temple in Jerusalem, the site of the sacrifices, was destroyed by the Romans in the year 70. They also condemned some of the Jewish scriptures as being false texts—not part of the law of God but the creation of human scribes. These are hardly the actions of a group whose defining characteristic was Jewish legalism. Loyalty to the law of Moses did not mean blindness to everything being broadcast as part of the Jewish tradition in the first century.

I argue in this book that Jewish Christianity in the first century (Jesus and his first followers) was the direct spiritual ancestor of Jewish Christianity in the fourth century (the Ebionites). Jewish Christianity cannot be divided into a "good" phase (when it was Jesus and his followers in the first century) and a "bad" phase (when it was the supposedly conservative Ebionites in the fourth century). Jewish Christianity is a *single* continuous entity, defined by two characteristics: loyalty to the Jewish law and acceptance of Jesus as the prophet of this law. Perhaps the Jewish Christians distorted or elaborated on the tradition in some ways; but in the end it was the Jewish Christian Ebionites, and not the gentile Christians, who most faithfully preserved the traditions handed down to them by Jesus.

Conclusions

Christianity was highly fragmented in the first centuries of its existence. A central issue among the various factions was disagreement over the relationship between the followers of Jesus and Judaism. We know what the beliefs of the later Jewish Christian Ebionites were with some degree of accuracy. They believed in simple living, nonviolence, were loyal to the Jewish law once the scriptures were purged of falsifications made by those coming after Moses, and thought of Jesus as the "true prophet" predicted by Moses. Their focus was on the *content* of the law, not on rewriting Jewish theology to include Jesus as part of the trinity. Their view that the sacrificial system did not originate with Moses and was falsely attributed to Moses was unorthodox but, it should be noted, hardly without justification—many modern scholars believe the same thing.[3]

The Ebionite explanation of Jesus makes the most sense in the context of history. It explains numerous things that virtually everyone agrees are part of the historical Jesus: his Jewishness, his baptism, his opposition to violence and materialism, and his death. It also explains the subsequent development of Christianity: the development of schisms in the early church, the opposition between Paul and the Jewish Christians, the impact of the Jewish revolts on Jewish Christianity, the development of gnosticism, the successes of Marcion, and the broad diversity among New Testament texts.

Jewish Christianity continued to exist for over 400 years, but was eventually condemned by other Jews and other Christians and ceased to exist. This much is a historical fact. The view of the Christian churches, that Jesus was understood better by his gentile followers than by those who actually shared his religion, is highly questionable. A new but devastatingly simple hypothesis—that Jesus was a Jew and that the Jewish followers of Jesus were his spiritual heirs—now commands our attention.

Part II
THE MESSAGE OF THE TRUE PROPHET

3

A VOICE IN THE WILDERNESS

JOHN THE BAPTIST AND THE JEWISH CHRISTIAN MESSAGE

THE WILDERNESS EXERTS A ROMANTIC APPEAL FOR US today and probably had a similar appeal in the first century. The children of Israel were in the wilderness when they were between Egypt and the promised land; the wilderness was also a place where one could free oneself from the contaminations of the world and perhaps get closer to God. Jesus in the gospels is said to have fasted for forty days in the wilderness before he began his ministry.

There are two groups from the "wilderness" that may have exerted a decisive influence on Jesus: the Essenes and John the Baptist and his followers. Both existed on the fringes of the social order; both testify to the surprisingly turbulent and diverse nature of first-century Judaism; and both had elements which were picked up by Jewish Christianity but dropped by gentile Christianity.

The Essenes

The Essenes are a popular topic in discussions of early Christianity. The Essenes exert this fascination because they resembled the early Christians in a number of interesting ways. Like some early Christians, the Essenes lived communally; like some early Christians, they scorned wealth; like some early Christians, the Essenes did not swear oaths; like some early Christians, they were pacifists.

The Essenes are mentioned by several ancient writers, including Josephus, Philo, Pliny, and Porphyry. Philo mentions another group, the Therapeutae, who seem to be very similar to the Essenes. The basic ideas of the Essenes in this literature, while sometimes described in contradictory ways, are generally fairly clear. Philo states that the Essenes rejected animal sacrifices, despised wealth and lived communally, did not make oaths, and rejected slavery (*Every Good Man is Free* 12), saying "there is not a single slave among them." Josephus agrees on all of these points (*Antiquities* 18.1.5, *Wars* 2.8.3, 2.8.6). Porphyry and Jerome go further and say that the Essenes were vegetarian (*De Abstinentia* 4.3, *Against Jovinianus* 2.14). Philo describes the Essene opposition to war in simple and moving terms: the Essenes refused to attend to "any employment whatever connected with war."

Many scholars try to go considerably beyond the "classical" sources at this point and tie the Essenes to the Dead Sea Scrolls. The Dead Sea Scrolls, constituting a number of ancient manuscripts discovered in the mid-twentieth century near Qumran on the Dead Sea, are a very important archeological find, but almost certainly have very little to do with the Essenes as described by Josephus, Pliny, Philo, and Porphyry. The beliefs of the Dead Sea Scrolls stand in stark contrast to those of the Essenes of Josephus and Philo on these and other points.[1]

The Dead Sea Scroll community clearly supports animal sacrifice, as the most significant scroll (the "Temple Scroll") attests repeatedly, in passages that parallel the instructions on animal sacrifice in Deuteronomy (*Temple Scroll* 52.13–18). The Dead Sea Scroll community is not pacifist at all and hopes to achieve its aims through violence and warfare (*Temple Scroll* 52:5–11). The Dead Sea Scroll community accepts and indeed seems to encourage slavery (*Damascus Rule* 11.12, 12.10). The Dead Sea Scroll community accepts the making and keeping of oaths (*Temple Scroll* 53:14–16). The Essenes were not only pacifist but generally celibate, though evidently one group of Essenes did marry (Josephus, *Wars* 2.8); the *Temple Scroll* allows a warrior to take for a wife a beautiful woman who is a captive—a text denying celibacy and affirming war and slavery in a single breath (*Temple Scroll* 53:10–15, roughly paralleling Deuteronomy 21:10–13).

Indeed, the Dead Sea Scrolls are ambiguous even on the question of communalism, the one significant similarity between the Essenes and the writers of the Dead Sea Scrolls. The Essenes had no private property at all. But some of the Dead Sea scrolls imply that only the earnings of two days of the month need be given to the community (*Damascus Rule* 14); other scrolls state that if community members cause property damage through negligence, they must reimburse the community out of their own pocket—implying that individuals must have financial resources from which to reimburse the community (*Community Rule* 7).

Instead of this search for the Essenes in the Dead Sea Scrolls, we should look at the Pythagoreans. While the similarities between the Essenes and the Dead Sea Scrolls community seem to be nebulous and tenuous at best, the similarities between the Essenes and the Pythagoreans are obvious and striking. The followers of Pythagoras, a Greek philosopher of the 6th century BCE, are an easy choice for comparison with the Essenes for two reasons: first, they had so much in common with the Essenes and the Therapeutae that it would be correct to speak of these latter groups as Jewish Pythagoreans; and secondly, because Josephus states flatly that the Essene lifestyle and the Pythagorean lifestyle were the same (*Antiquities* 15.10.4).

We don't have to look far to find similarities between the Pythagoras described by Iamblichus and the Essenes described by Josephus, Pliny, Porphyry, and Philo—as well with the Jewish Christians. The neo-Pythagorean Iamblichus in his book *On the Pythagorean Way of Life* states that: Pythagoras was an opponent of slavery (33); he taught his disciples to avoid oaths, "that their language should be such as to render them worthy of belief even without oaths" (47, 144, 150); he was an opponent of the materialism or the pursuit of wealth and luxury (56–57, 69, 171); he counseled against seeking revenge or doing harm to one's enemies (155); he also did not wear wool, wearing a white robe of linen instead (149). Most importantly, he was a vegetarian and condemned animal sacrifices (54, 108, 150); he ordered his closest disciples to abstain from all animal food (168, 187, 225) and from wine (69, 188). This sounds enough like both the Essenes and the Jewish Christians that it is hard to resist the conclusion that there is an ideological or organizational connection somewhere between these groups. The Qumran group resembles the Essenes (as known from the "classical" sources) at most only on the question of communalism; the Pythagoreans resemble the Essenes on numerous points.

The problem for us is that (barring some startling new archeological discovery) there is no *direct* evidence linking the Essenes to any Christian group. There is no mention of the Essenes by name in the New Testament; and no ancient writer makes any explicit connection of the Essenes to other groups, *unless* one interprets the reference to the "Ossaeans" by Epiphanius (*Panarion* 19) to be in fact a reference to the Essenes—in which case the Essenes actually merged with Jewish Christianity.

The indirect evidence, however, is substantial. The Jewish Christians did not drink wine, did not eat meat, despised wealth, were pacifists, and opposed animal sacrifices. The Jewish Christians probably did not make oaths; there is no specific evidence on this, but this prohibition is in the Sermon on the Mount. It is significant, also, that Eusebius quotes Philo's description of the Therapeutae, a group similar to the Essenes which lived communally and abstained from meat and wine, and assumes that this is a Christian group (*Ecclesiastical History* 2.16–17)! While Eusebius may be incorrect, it is significant that he would make this assumption without batting an eyelash.

There are two differences that should be pointed out, though. The Essenes, according to Philo, chose to interpret scripture allegorically when it came to confronting difficult passages; the Jewish Christians chose to deny the passages altogether. The Essenes chose to remain apart from society, in isolated communities; the Jewish Christians set out to spread their message far and wide. Jewish Christianity may not be a *direct* offspring of the Essenes—in the sense that Jesus was an Essene, or that the Essenes commissioned Jesus or other Jewish Christians to go and spread their beliefs—but Jesus or the Jewish Christians may have been heavily influenced by their ideas.

The Mission of John the Baptist

We lack any direct testimony linking the Essenes to Jesus. For John the Baptist, however, the connection to Jesus is direct and concrete: John the Baptist stands at the beginning of Jesus' public ministry. Jesus began his work only after John baptized him, and thus—at least at first—Jesus was one of John's followers.

John's baptism of Jesus sets the stage on which Jesus preached, and John also resembles the Jewish Christian ideal; but John also differs from the sages who were to be later immortalized in the Talmud. These similarities and differences were a matter of style as well as substance. He did not calmly instruct the people based on his years of study of the law; rather, he exhorted them to repentance with apocalyptic images and a simple and blunt morality. He did not come from the great centers of learning or study with respected teachers; rather, he was an isolated voice that called from the outside of society, "the voice of one crying in the wilderness" (Matthew 3:3).

"Rabbinic Judaism"—a Judaism based not only on the Jewish scriptures (the "Old Testament") but also on the sayings of the sages who had received the "oral law"—was still not dominant at this time. This form of Judaism, the ancestor of the major forms of modern Judaism, would not fully crystallize until several centuries after Jesus. When John baptized Jesus, the path that Judaism would ultimately take was still uncertain. Jewish Christianity, while an improbable option, was not yet an impossible option for Judaism to choose.

Josephus, the Jewish Christians, and the New Testament all paint a picture of John that is remarkably similar: John lived exceedingly simply, John lived in "the wilderness" away from the cities, John's initiation of Jesus was a baptism, and John's baptism was the starting point of Jesus' life work. In these basic facts we see several themes that were prominent in Jewish Christianity.

John puts forward a slogan that Jesus also adopts: "Repent, for the kingdom of heaven is at hand" (Matthew 3:2, 4:17). John's images are moralistic and apocalyptic. He calls the Pharisees and Sadducees a "brood of vipers," and uses the celebrated image of separating the wheat from the chaff to dramatize the importance of purifying the corruption of society (Matthew 3:7–12). Both the New Testament and Josephus give a similar account of John's death: Herod had him killed after John objected repeatedly and forthrightly to Herod's sexual immorality. John the Baptist, we can safely say, did not stand on ceremony.

The Jewish Christians saw John the Baptist in much the same way. The Jewish Christian gospels have disappeared from history, but that arch-nemesis of Jewish Christianity, Epiphanius, quoted from the Jewish Christian Ebionites in order to refute them. From Epiphanius we have quotations from the Ebionite gospel account of John the Baptist that are remarkably similar to that in the New Testament (*Panarion* 30.13.4, paralleling Matthew 3:4–6). However, Epiphanius notes (with considerable indignation) that the Ebionites changed the part about John eating "locusts and wild honey" to "wild honey . . . as a cake made with oil." The Ebionites did not think that John ate insects! The Ebionites were vegetarians and, therefore, denied that John the Baptist, a favorite Christian hero, ate locusts.

Who is right about John eating locusts—Epiphanius or the Ebionites? Before trying to answer this question, we should note a significant point of agreement between Epiphanius and the Jewish Christians: John may have eaten insects, but he did not eat any *other* animal flesh, or any alcoholic beverages: "John did not partake of flesh and wine, but partook only of locusts and honey, and certainly also of water" (*Panarion* 30.19.3). It is significant, also, that both Epiphanius and the Ebionites agree with Luke (1:15) that John did not drink alcoholic beverages; the Ebionites disapproved of alcohol.

The statement in the gospels that John the Baptist ate insects has puzzled many, and some think that something may have gotten lost in the translation process at an early stage. It has been suggested, for example, that the term translated as "locusts" should be translated as "locust beans," i. e. carob. Also, the Greek word for tree fruits (*akrodrua*) is very close to the word for locusts (*akrides*), suggesting the possibility of an accidental or malicious scribal error. The tradition of the Greek church was that John did *not* in fact eat insects, the text of the gospel being said to refer to the "shoots" of certain plants.[2]

There is another testimony that John the Baptist was a vegetarian, and this comes from Josephus. The standard text of Josephus contains no reference to John the Baptist's diet; but one of the non-standard texts, called the "Slavonic Josephus," has quite a bit to say. In the "Slavonic" edition of Josephus' book *The Wars of the Jews*, Josephus describes a "wild man," a man "savage" in appearance, with a message that almost exactly matches that of the John the Baptist we become acquainted with in the New Testament. Josephus does not specifically name the person he is describing as "John the Baptist," but in context it is hard not to reach the conclusion that this is who in fact it is. Josephus describes this person (in his Slavonic edition of *The Wars of the Jews*) as follows:

- He has animals' hair as his clothing, and his countenance was like a savage.
- He baptizes those who come to him in the Jordan, warning them to renounce their evil deeds.
- He is the only one to denounce Herod for marrying his brothers' wife, and is killed by Herod.
- He does not eat bread, even the unleavened bread at Passover; nor does he drink wine, or eat any animal food.
- When brought before Archelaus, he describes his diet as "bulrushes, roots, and wood-shavings"—a strict, though rather unappetizing, vegetarian diet.[3]

These details of the "wild man" match the description of John the Baptist in Mark and in the accepted text of Josephus almost exactly. Both Mark and the standard text of Josephus explicitly name John the Baptist and describe how John denounces Herod Antipas, who retaliates by having John executed after an initial period of tolerance (*Antiquities* 18.5.2, Mark 6:17–29). The "wild man" in the Slavonic Josephus has to be none other than John the Baptist; and the Slavonic Josephus, who does not appear to have an axe to grind one way or the other, does not think that John ate insects, but ate a strict (and rather dull) vegetarian diet.

Everyone agrees that John's lifestyle even apart from diet is quite simple. Josephus speaks of him as like a "fleshless spirit," so unconnected is he to the world of material things. Jesus alludes to the roughness of John's clothing when asking the crowd why they came to see John the Baptist:

> Why then did you go out? To see a man clothed in soft raiment? Behold, those who wear soft raiment are in kings' houses. (Matthew 11:8)

In all of this we see a precursor of both Jesus' own admonitions against wealth, and the Ebionites' own manner of designating themselves as "the poor." Those who have left behind meat, wine, fancy clothes, and king's houses, are probably not living a life of conspicuous consumption.

Baptism as a Ritual

Most modern Christians associate baptism with joining the Christian community, so the real significance of Jesus' baptism can easily be lost. For John the Baptist, *baptism was an alternative to animal sacrifice.* Both the New Testament and Josephus present baptism in this way, rather than as a rite of initiation into a community. In Mark, John preaches "a baptism of repentance for the forgiveness of sins" (Mark 1:4). Josephus puts it slightly differently, saying of John the Baptist that he baptized not simply for the forgiveness of sins, but for purification following sin (*Antiquities* 18.5.2). Baptism, therefore, had a function similar to some of the animal sacrifices described in the Old Testament (Leviticus 4:2, 6:6, etc.). It *may* have also had social significance as a sign of joining the community of John the Baptist; but the texts nowhere suggest this, and in fact seem to imply that many admirers *outside* John's community came to be baptized ("there went out to him all the country of Judea, and all the people of Jerusalem," Mark 1:5). However, the only immediate religious significance described in Josephus or the New Testament had nothing to do with that, but rather with the purification for forgiveness of sins—one of the functions of animal sacrifice.

The Jewish Christians were acutely aware of this function of baptism, and made explicit that baptism was a substitute for animal sacrifice. According to Jewish Christianity, when God decided to do away with animal sacrifices, he instituted baptism to replace it (*Recognitions* 1.39).

The Jewish Christians persisted in believing it was *baptism* that symbolized or conferred forgiveness of sins. It became a ritual to be practiced daily (*Panarion* 30.15.3), rather than a once-only sign of identification with the Christian community. While the *Recognitions* and *Homilies* contain no specific reference to daily baptism, it is interesting that there are frequent references to Peter bathing (e. g. *Recognitions* 4.3, 8.1; *Homilies* 8.2, 11.1). This contrasts with the later church's doctrine of the atonement, in which it is Jesus' *death* that achieves forgiveness of sins, much as animal sacrifices were supposed to do in the Old Testament. Later in the New Testament, the shedding of Jesus' blood atones for sin as a replacement for animal sacrifice: "In him [Jesus] we have redemption through his blood," says Ephesians 1:7.

Yet if we accept the accounts of Jesus' baptism, then there was already in place an alternative method for purification from or forgiveness of sin *before* Jesus even approached his death on the cross. The rejection of animal sacrifice, or at the very least an alternative to animal sacrifice, *must* have existed before Jesus' death, rendering the whole concept of the atonement superfluous. What Jesus' death is supposed to have replaced, was *already* replaced when John baptized Jesus.

John's Baptism of Jesus

In all of the synoptic gospels, as well as the Ebionite gospel, John baptizes Jesus before Jesus begins preaching. This baptism is also the occasion on which the divine inspiration for Jesus' ministry begins, as is evident both from the accounts of the baptism itself and from the depiction of the spirit of God descending upon Jesus.

Epiphanius provides us with the Jewish Christian account of this event when he quotes the *Gospel of the Hebrews* to show the Jewish Christian idea of how Jesus became God's son. The *Gospel of the Hebrews* differs in a single but crucial respect from the other New Testament accounts: "And a voice from heaven said, 'You are my beloved son; I am pleased with you,' and again; '*This day I have begotten you*' " (Panarion 30.13.7; emphasis added).

This account is close to Matthew 3:13–17 and its parallels in Mark and Luke, with one key difference—the addition of the phrase, "This day I have begotten you." The Ebionites chose the moment of Jesus' baptism by John as the key moment in which Jesus became God's son, rather than the moment of Jesus' birth. Jesus became God's son by being "adopted" by him (a "spiritual birth," so to speak) rather than by being literally fathered by God and born of a virgin. This idea is called *adoptionism*.

Was this critical phrase part of the original story? There are two strong reasons for thinking so. First of all, this phrase is a direct quote from Psalm 2:7 ("You are my son, today I have begotten you"). Matthew is fond of quoting the Old Testament and it is quite believable that the original version of the story in Matthew had precisely this citation from the Old Testament. Justin Martyr, in the second century, twice gives an account of Jesus' baptism that *also* directly quotes Psalm 2:7 and thus agrees with the Ebionite version (*Dialogues With Trypho* 88.8, 103.6).

But secondly, the whole thrust of the story of the baptism by John— the image of the spirit descending from above—is an adoptionist metaphor that completely contradicts the virgin birth story. The spirit descends upon Jesus in the form of a dove, one of the most celebrated of all Christian images, in both the canonical account and the Ebionite account. If Jesus were *already* the son of God since the beginning of the world, and *already* fully divine, this image would be completely superfluous.

The most obvious explanation of the image of the spirit descending on Jesus is that, at this moment, the holy spirit entered Jesus, even though this contradicts the orthodox idea that Jesus was fully God even prior to his birth. The original Ebionites rejected the idea of the virgin birth and thought that Jesus was the human offspring of Joseph and Mary (*Panarion* 30.3.1). It is more than conceivable that some editor of Matthew eliminated the phrase "This day I have begotten you" in order to attempt to preserve the orthodox idea of divine incarnation through the virgin birth—not discerning that the story of the spirit descending upon Jesus, which was left intact, has a straightforwardly adoptionist intent.

This text also shows how different the concept of being "God's son" was for Jewish Christianity and modern Christianity. The saying in the Psalms, "You are my son, today I have begotten you" was originally addressed to David; but it hardly indicates that David was God incarnate, but rather that David had some special relationship to God as his messenger or agent. The Jewish Christian gospel is making a parallel claim for Jesus. For Jewish Christianity, Jesus never claimed to be God (*Homilies* 16.15, *Panarion* 30.20.5), and the same oil that anoints Jesus is poured out for all believers (*Recognitions* 1.45). This is precisely what is affirmed in the "Lord's Prayer" (Matthew 6:9–13), in which Jesus urges us to pray to "*our* Father in heaven"—that *all* believers are in some sense God's children.

Conclusions

Even if we disregard the suggestive evidence relating the Essenes to Christianity, Jesus' beginnings already indicate a strong affinity with the later development of Jewish Christianity. John the Baptist is a vegetarian who lives with very few possessions. He substitutes the water of baptism for the fire of animal sacrifice. At the moment of Jesus' baptism, the spirit of God descends on Jesus and God declares Jesus to be his son. All of this resonates very closely with a Jesus who was, according to the Ebionites, a very human prophet who preached simplicity and nonviolence. From the accounts of his life and the company in which he traveled, we can conclude that John the Baptist was much more in harmony with the Jewish Christian teachings than the later orthodox Christian churches for which he is thought to have cleared a straight path.

4 FOLLOW ME

THE GOSPEL OF SIMPLE LIVING

I N THE GOSPELS, JESUS' INVITATION TO "FOLLOW ME" IS THE central focus of the primitive Christian message. The kingdom of heaven is not just something piously to be hoped for or believed in; it is something that has *arrived*: "Repent, for the kingdom of heaven is at hand" (Matthew 4:17). One's response to the call, therefore, has to be correspondingly concrete; one must put the kingdom first—before property, before family, before everything else in this system of things.

In the gospels, Jesus advises us not merely to donate ten percent of our after-tax earnings to a good cause, but to give up *everything* (Luke 14:33). On the other hand, Jesus also counsels against anxiety concerning material things like food and clothing. "Be not anxious," Jesus says repeatedly, God knows that you need food and clothing; put God's domain first, and these things will be yours as well (Matthew 6:32–33). To respond to the call to "follow me" meant abandoning one's possessions in the hope of a simple but secure lifestyle in which one's basic needs are provided for.

The gospels and the Jewish Christian position on this matter are practically identical. The main Jewish Christian group was called the "Ebionites"—a name derived, as we have already seen, from the Hebrew *ebionim* meaning "the poor." The Jewish Christians who thought of themselves as followers of the true prophet (Jesus), therefore, did not conceive of themselves as merely giving to the poor, being nice to the poor, or defending the poor: they *were* the poor.

The Poor

The Hebrew *ebionim* refers to those who are very poor, in a wretched state, or who are begging. Epiphanius, that bitter critic of Ebionism, relates how these Jewish Christians explained their poverty: they traced it back to the time when the primitive Christian community, just after Jesus' departure, lived communally (*Panarion* 30.17.1–2). Epiphanius' sneering denunciation of the Ebionites points outs several pertinent facts about the Ebionites: they were called "the poor," and they actually were poor as well—it was not an empty title, even in the fourth century. It also shows that the Ebionites claimed their spiritual descent from the time when the primitive church really *was* sharing everything in common, from that pivotal event when the followers of Jesus "were of one heart and soul." The followers of Jesus laid everything they owned at the feet of the apostles, and everyone received according to their need (Acts 2:44–45, 4:32–35).

It is precisely this event—the sharing of all their possessions in the primitive church—that in the minds of the Ebionites gave them the name of "the poor." This was simple living, but it was not destitution, as they were supported in a simple and secure spiritual household: "There was not a needy person among them" (Acts 4:34). The simplicity of their lifestyle was evidently one of the defining ideals of the Ebionites. In the *Recognitions* Peter is depicted as living an extraordinarily simple lifestyle, living on a strict vegetarian diet and wearing simple clothes (*Recognitions* 7.6).

Jesus in the gospels never gives a specific command that *all* Christians should live communally and share all their worldly goods, but we do see strong suggestions to this effect. Jesus does give *some* people the advice to join such a Christian community; his most celebrated advice to his immediate disciples is to "follow me." When he is approached by a rich young man who says he is already keeping the commandments and asks him what more he should do, Jesus advises him to sell everything he has, give it to the poor, and "follow me" (Luke 18:22, Matthew 19:21, Mark 10:21).

What does Jesus mean when he asks his disciples and others to "follow me"? On the face of it, it would seem to mean literally abandoning everything else and joining the community of which Jesus was the leader. It seems to have involved at least an abandonment of home and family (Luke 18:28–29), and most likely all possessions as well (Luke 14:33, 18:22).

Modern Christians become somewhat uncomfortable and start to rationalize when they read these verses. For those wishing to evade this radical rejection of materialism, some counter-arguments are possible. First, Jesus addresses his advice to a specific people (the disciples, the rich young man); perhaps he did not intend this advice for everyone. Secondly, in the passage about the rich young man in Matthew, Jesus presents this advice with the preface that giving everything away is not necessary in order to enter eternal life (simply obeying the commandments would suffice for that) but is only necessary if the young man would be perfect. However, at best this only slightly ameliorates the message. We are still left with the original, radical advice to "follow me"; and evidently Jesus' invitation to his disciples to "follow me" involved precisely such a commitment to abandon one's possessions.

The *Gospel According to the Hebrews* (a Jewish Christian gospel) repeats the story about the rich man invited to follow Jesus, but has Jesus draw the important conclusion that sharing all one's worldly goods really follows from the law of Moses! When the rich young man hesitates to follow Jesus, Jesus responds:

> Is it not written in the Law: Love your neighbor as yourself? And see, many of your brothers, sons of Abraham, are covered with dung, dying from hunger, and your house is filled with many good things, and absolutely nothing goes out of it to them.[1]

This version has the ring of authenticity; it establishes a Jewish underpinning for a Christian ideal. Jesus plainly states that the "golden rule" is part of the law ("You shall love your neighbor as yourself,"

Leviticus 19:18). If we take this concept seriously, Jesus is saying, love of neighbor implies sharing *everything* with them. We want these good things; therefore we share them *all* with others. We do not even need to expand the concept of "neighbor" to include those outside our community (as Jesus does elsewhere in the case of the parable of the Good Samaritan) to see that the rich man has an obligation to share, because even those of his own faith and nation are hungry and covered with excrement.

"You cannot serve two masters," Jesus insists: we must choose between God and money (Matthew 6:24). The obvious question is, if we surrender everything, how are we going to stay alive? This is a question that Jesus spent some time explaining in one of the most celebrated sections of the Sermon on the Mount (Matthew 6:24–33). "Do not be anxious," Jesus advises us; God feeds and clothes the birds of the air and the lilies of the field, so he will do the same for you.

This is an appeal to nature: the care of God for those who put the kingdom first is something that is *natural*. Moreover, this is not an ascetic renunciation of the world in the expectation of future rewards in heaven. The kingdom is on earth as well as in heaven; that is why "seeking first the kingdom" is tied to the question "what shall we eat?" and not merely to the question of finding eternal life.

A similar appeal to nature is found several times in the Jewish Christian *Homilies*. The eternal law of God is nowhere concealed, and can be "read" by all (*Homilies* 8.10). This "reading" of the law cannot be the literal reading of a written text—since most people in ancient times were illiterate—but is rather the contemplation of the world created by God. Even more striking, when Simon Magus (Peter's antagonist) asks Peter how we can tell the true scriptures from the false texts, Peter responds—

> Whatever sayings of the Scriptures are in harmony with the creation that was made by Him [God] are true, but whatever are contrary to it are false. (*Homilies* 3.42)

Nature, as part of God's creation, actually has a *priority* over any written texts—one might say that *nature* is the word of God. The practical answer to the question "what shall we eat?" provided by Jesus and the first Christians described in Acts is to seek the kingdom of heaven *first*, giving up all our possessions, and to be confident that we will receive from God's kingdom what we truly need, something as natural as the birds of the air or the lilies of the field. Other Christian writers such as Arnobius (c. 300 CE) echoed this sentiment, saying that if animals, trees, or even stones could speak, they would follow nature and declare that God is Lord of all (*Against the Heathen* 1.33).

"Voluntary poverty" is often associated with asceticism. Later Christian monks and nuns often took vows of poverty to deny themselves the pleasures of the world, in order to draw themselves closer to God—turning inward, removing the seeker from the temptations of the world. The motivation behind this primitive Christian poverty, however, is *not* ascetic. It is outward-looking, emphasizing the rewards and satisfactions of righteousness and positive involvement with the world. Jesus advised his followers not to be anxious about food or clothing, because these would be provided. The early community presented itself as one big happy family (Acts 4:32, Matthew 12:46–50), so one was actually gaining a new spiritual family by following Jesus. Jesus stated that we would gain eternal life through our allegiance to righteousness, but would receive manifold blessings in this life as well (Luke 18:29–30). God's kingdom was to come on *earth* as well as in heaven (Matthew 6:10). Everywhere we see evidence both in the synoptic gospels and in the Jewish Christian texts that the motivation behind this voluntary simplicity is not a renunciation of the world, but a positive involvement in the world.

The value of non-attachment to material possessions is one of the clearest of Jesus' teachings in the gospels. Jesus declares that the Spirit has "anointed me to preach good news to the poor" (Luke 4:18) and that the poor are blessed and that they possess the kingdom of God (Luke 6:20). He says that those who give a banquet should invite the poor, rather than their friends, to obtain eternal life (Luke 14:12–14). And

finally, there is the celebrated Last Judgement passage, in which the Son
of Man judges both the righteous and the wicked by the same standard—
when the Son of Man was hungry, thirsty, a stranger, naked, sick, or in
prison, did they give him food, drink, clothing, and companionship? To
both he says the same thing:

> As you did it to one of the least of these my brethren, you did it
> to me. (Matthew 25:40)

Call No Man Master

Did Jesus' teachings about the obliteration of economic distinctions also
mean an obliteration of social distinctions?

Christianity has been invoked on all sides of issues relating to
women and slaves, the two most prominent social issues present in Jesus'
time. Slavery continued to exist throughout much of the Christian-
dominated world until just the last few hundred years; the oppression of
women remains commonplace today. However, the synoptic gospels
present a very different story, and suggest strong egalitarian preferences
at several points. First of all, there are the sayings, "the last shall be first,"
"call no man master," and the beatitudes, which seem to bless precisely
those at the lower end of the social order. Secondly, there is the rejection
of family relationships as less important than one's relationship to the
word of God. Third, there is the relatively high position Jesus accords
women.

Jewish Christian texts do not say much on this subject, but are
broadly in accordance with the synoptic gospels. The *Recognitions* and
Homilies—like many other ancient texts—are largely about males
debating other males, with some female characters emerging from time
to time; so Jewish Christianity hardly completely liberated itself from
patriarchy. However, Jewish Christianity does accept the concept of the
divine feminine; Jesus refers to the holy spirit as his *mother* in the *Gospel
According to the Hebrews*, a gospel used by both the Ebionites and by the
Nazoraeans.[2] The *Homilies* speak of the "Wisdom" or "Sophia" of God as
if it were part of God's feminine aspect (16.12). The Elchasaites, another

Jewish Christian group, believed that the Holy Spirit was female and was either the equal of Christ or his sister (*Panarion* 30.17.6, 53.1.9). All of this makes sense because it is in accordance with Hebrew, which spoke of the holy spirit or divine presence, the *shekinah*, as feminine. It is significant that the Elchasaites also had two women leaders in the fourth century who according to Epiphanius were "worshiped as goddesses" (*Panarion* 53.1.2). Not only does the divine presence incorporate feminine aspects, but women in at least one Jewish Christian sect were able to take leadership roles as late as the fourth century.

The canonical gospel of Matthew—of which the *Gospel According to the Hebrews* was a version (*Panarion* 30.3.7)—provides some additional indirect evidence about Jewish Christianity. Matthew is often thought of as the most "Jewish" of the gospels, albeit with some strident anti-Jewish material thrown in as well. Interestingly, however, in Matthew women tend to be depicted more positively than in the other gospels. Kathleen Corley points out that only in Matthew are women allowed an equal place at the meal table; only in Matthew do women join the miraculous feedings of the multitude; and in Matthew the women who follow Jesus are held up as examples of true faith.[3]

In the synoptic gospels, the most direct reference to the obliteration of social distinctions is in Matthew:

> But you are not to be called rabbi, for you have one teacher, and you are all brethren. And call no man your father on earth, for you have one Father, who is in heaven. Neither be called masters, for you have one master, the Christ. He who is greatest among you shall be your servant; whoever exalts himself will be humbled, and whoever humbles himself will be exalted. (Matthew 23:9–12)

This does not merely downplay any hierarchical arrangement: it calls for the complete obliteration of hierarchical arrangements. The saying "the last shall be first, and the first last" appears at several other places in the synoptic gospels, sometimes in the form of promising rewards to those who have left their families (Matthew 19:30, 20:16; Mark 10:29-

–31; Luke 13:30). Jesus is not an advocate of traditional family values; he goes out of his way to reward those who have put service to God ahead of service to family.

The position of women in Jesus' ministry appears to be significant. Women, as well as men, are healed by Jesus (e. g., Matthew 8:14–15, 9:18–26). Women are among Jesus' first followers (Luke 8:1–3). Women are present at the crucifixion, after some of the prominent male disciples (such as Peter) have run away (Matthew 27:55–56). In Matthew, Mark, and John, Jesus appears after his resurrection first to a woman—Mary Magdalene (Matthew 28:1–10, Mark 16:9–11, John 20:1–18). Many in the early church accorded Mary Magdalene the role of an apostle; Hippolytus of Rome was only the first to refer to her as "the apostle to the apostles."[4]

The one depiction of women that is *not* prominent in the gospels, interestingly enough, is that of women as submissive wives and mothers. In fact, at three points such roles for women are specifically rejected. In one case, as Jesus is preaching, Jesus brushes aside a tribute to his own mother, implying that it is not in bearing children but by bearing the word of God that women are blessed (Luke 11:27–28).

The unimportance of biological relationships is stressed again when news is sent to Jesus that his mother and brothers want to speak to him. Jesus stretches out his hands toward the disciples, saying: "Here are my mother and my brothers!" (Matthew 12:49). Not only does this episode denigrate the importance of family relationships, but it also makes clear that among Jesus' disciples at this public or semi-public gathering were both men and women followers, or he would have referred to them only as "brothers," rather than "brother, and sister, and mother" (Matthew 12:50).

The Mary and Martha story gently but favorably contrasts a woman who talks with Jesus to a woman who does housework. Martha is distracted by "much serving," and asks Jesus to tell Mary (who is listening at Jesus' feet) to help her. Instead of sending Mary into the kitchen to help out, Jesus replies that Mary has chosen the better path

(Luke 10:38–42). True, this is a choice between one submissive role (helping in the kitchen) and another (listening at Jesus' feet). However, it certainly does not affirm the traditional role of women as taking care of the household first; sitting at the feet of the master was generally the prerogative of *male* disciples, a prerogative here conspicuously extended by Jesus to include women. What is striking in all of this is precisely the lack of wife-and-mother role models in the gospels. With the possible exception of the accounts of Jesus' birth and the incidental passing remark about Peter's mother-in-law, *at no time is the "traditional role" of woman affirmed; at several times it is explicitly rejected.*

While there is no clear, unequivocal declaration that women are equal to men, or that slaves should be freed, the whole thrust of the injunction that the last shall be first and the first last strongly suggests that we not lay a heavy emphasis on displays of authority over other human beings, regardless of whether that authority is based on money, gender, or social position. Both Jewish Christianity and the synoptic gospels welcome the elimination of family and social distinctions as well as economic distinctions. This view contrasts sharply with the ambivalence of Paul, who wanted both to recognize equality (Galatians 3:28) and still preserve the traditional, subservient role of women and slaves (I Corinthians 11:3–16, 14:34–35, Ephesians 5:22, 6:5, Colossians 3:18–22).

Communalism, Sharing, Voluntary Simplicity

The emphasis on simple living is one aspect of primitive Christianity that not only occurs in the New Testament, but continued to be an ideal throughout early Christianity, whether Jewish or gentile, and is acknowledged at least as an ideal by most modern-day Christians. The Ebionite identification with the poor is well grounded in the synoptic gospels, where those who wish to follow Jesus are urged to give up possessions, status, and family. What is less clear, however, is how the possessions that one gives up should be given out, and we get different answers at different points. Are they simply to be given to the poor or to those in need, as Jesus advises the rich young man and as the Good Samaritan does in Jesus' parable? Or are we supposed to surrender them to the Christian community, as the first Christians do in Acts? Or can we actually retain a few of our possessions, providing that we live very simple lives, as Peter does in the *Recognitions*?

Communalism is the most "practical" advice given. In the first chapters of Acts (4:32–35) the followers of Jesus share everything and hold everything in common. God both demands everything and at the same time gives us everything we truly need. Part of God's work is to support us, because when we give everything to God we are absolutely destitute—thus the words of Acts, "there was not a needy person among them" (4:34), despite the fact they had abandoned their possessions. Jesus expected his followers to adopt a simple lifestyle and encouraged them to trust that God would provide enough to eat, drink, and wear.

Communal living has an undeniable romance and attraction to it; but communal living also presents problems, even for modern groups of people who are well-educated and relatively well-off. It is hard to imagine that illiterate first-century peasants would not have encountered some of the same problems. The discipline might be excessively strict, and one might fear expulsion from the community for perceived or actual wrongdoing after having given away all one's possessions. At the other extreme, discipline might be too slack and lazy people might join the community to get free meals and a "free ride." In addition, the community might be prone to factionalism, or collapse just through inefficient management.

This sort of anxiety is found in the story of Ananias and Sapphira (Acts 5:1–12) who hold back part of their possessions when joining the community and then lie about what they have done. Other Christian texts show concern about others taking advantage of one's Christian hospitality. One text recommends that an "apostle" that comes to you should be sheltered for one or two days, but "if he remain for three days, he is a false prophet" (*The Teachings of the Twelve Apostles* 11). The pastoral epistles recommend that younger widows not be supported by the community, because they become idlers and gossipers (I Timothy 5:11–13). The letters of Paul are full of information on factionalism in the early church, as we shall see in later chapters.

Questions about how to run a sharing community are not rhetorical. Outside of the New Testament itself, there is no mention of early Christians living communally. The monastic orders are the first real communities after Acts of which we have definite knowledge, but they only developed hundreds of years later. No one in the early church deals with the practicalities of communalism—e. g. receiving property from converts, penalties for false accounting, or the method of allotment of necessities, indicating that communalism must have collapsed as a practical alternative for most Christians at a fairly early stage.[5]

Other early Christians struggled with this problem and came up with different solutions. Clement of Alexandria wrote a lengthy essay in which he tried to answer the question, "How can the rich man be saved?" Clement suggests that it is not necessary to give away all one's possessions, but that one should abandon one's *attachment* to possessions (see *Who is the Rich Man Who Shall Be Saved*, sections 11, 13, and 26). A simple moderate life is required, with any surplus wealth above one's simple needs given to the poor, the disciples, and those in need. The rich man who is saved remains the *custodian* of his wealth without actually consuming more than he needs for a very simple lifestyle. Indeed, the rich man should be prudent with his possessions; if he dissipates them indiscriminately, the poor would not benefit from receiving them.

Not everyone availed themselves of this solution; others literally *did* give everything they had to the poor. Antony, the hermit-saint who was one of the original Desert Fathers, was one of these. Six months after the death of his parents, when Antony had inherited a considerable amount of land, he was walking to church and thinking about Jesus' advice to sell everything and the communalism of the first Christian community described in Acts. As it turned out, the text that day was precisely the text in the gospel where Jesus advises the rich man to sell everything he possesses and give it to the poor. When Antony left the church, he immediately went out and gave to the townspeople all his possessions, after seeing to it that his sister was provided for (Athanasius, *Life of Antony* 2). St. Basil the Great was another early church leader who took

Jesus' instructions more or less literally. However, though he did give away all his wealth, Basil did follow Clement's advice in distributing it over a number of years.

Given this strong anti-materialistic bias, it is *very* surprising to find out that Christianity in the Roman Empire had most of its initial support from the upper classes. This is a paradox that, as the sociologist Rodney Stark explains in his book *The Rise of Christianity*,[6] is due to the fact that new religions typically do spread in the upper classes before they take root in the rest of society. A "sect" (i. e., a branch of an *existing* religion), on the other hand, typically appeals to the lower classes. It is this fact that, more than any other, explains why Christianity largely abandoned a principle that is so firmly embedded not only in its sacred texts but also in the other writings of the early church. However, this only applies to the gentile Christianity that took over the Roman Empire; it does not apply at all to the Jewish Christianity that rejected Paul. The Jewish Christians really *did* consider themselves Jews, and therefore were in sociological terms a "sect"—a splinter group of an existing religion— rather than a new religion. The picture that then emerges is a movement that when it was predominantly a Jewish sect *did* indeed appeal to the lower classes, but lost its "sect" character in the missionary efforts of Paul and others to the Gentiles.

The fact that all these texts favoring the poor survived even in a church spreading among the upper classes is further proof of their authenticity. One has only to read Clement of Alexandria's essay in the context of Stark's argument to see that there were a number of "rich" who were attracted to Christianity and were disturbed by Christian texts that were much too obvious to be denied. These texts, which were quite "inconvenient" from the point of view of a gentile Christianity spreading among the upper classes, would not have been invented along the way; they must come from the very earliest traditions.

Conclusions

The evidence from Jewish Christianity, the gospels, and the history of early Christianity all points in the same direction. For a follower of Jesus, it would appear that the kingdom of God demands everything: the only lack of clarity is in the disposition of our possessions. There are countless Christian denominations, although today there are only a few practicing communalism in any form; the Hutterites, the Shakers, and the monastic orders are the most prominent modern exceptions to this rule. For the time being, anyone taking Jesus' anti-materialistic message seriously is forced back to Clement of Alexandria's solution: we are custodians of our possessions, which we should use as sparingly as possible, giving the balance to the service of those in need. The kingdom of God must have priority over everything—over family, possessions, and concerns about safety and well-being: we must seek *first* the kingdom of God. It is a natural thing to live a simple life, and not be anxious about food, drink, and clothing, but to rely on God.

The Jewish Christian followers of the true prophet emphasized voluntary simplicity to the maximum extent possible, and taught that this was the true law. On this point the teaching of the Ebionite Jesus and the Jesus of the synoptics is practically identical. The goal is not to dominate, but to serve. When we have put this principle first, ahead of everything else—only then are we ready to follow Jesus:

> So therefore, whoever of you does not renounce all that he has cannot be my disciple. (Luke 14:33)

5 THE LAW AND THE PROPHETS

JESUS PREACHES THE ETERNAL LAW OF GOD

D ID JESUS BRING SOMETHING OLD OR SOMETHING NEW to first-century Judaism? It is widely assumed by both Jews and Christians that Jesus brought something new—new principles, a new understanding, a new law, a new faith. Somehow, somewhere, there was a break between the law of Moses and the new principles brought by Jesus. Otherwise, why did Jesus come in the first place—why couldn't all questions be referred to the law of Moses?

Yet the New Testament is not at all clear on this point. We find a wide variety of attitudes towards the law, ranging from the affirmation "not an iota, not a dot will pass from the law until all is accomplished" (Matthew 5:18) in the Sermon on the Mount, to the statement in Ephesians that Jesus had "abolished in his flesh the law of commandments and ordinances" (2:15). Where does the truth lie?

The Jewish Christian view was not that Jesus brought something new; Jesus was a prophet who sought to *restore* the original law. The Jewish Christians did not perceive their principles as a new doctrine, but rather an old doctrine—the original law of God, forgotten and ignored by the tradition.

In the New Testament, the gospel is announced in Jewish terms. Jesus declares that he has not come to abolish, but to fulfill the law; that the law and the prophets are summarized in the two commandments to love God and to love your neighbor; and that following the commandments is the path to eternal life (Matthew 5:17–20, 19:17, 22:37–40). Wouldn't we expect the followers of a great teacher to follow the same religion as the teacher? Doesn't this validate in an important way the Jewish Christians' claim to be the true heirs of Jesus' teachings?

Jewish Thinking in the Jesus of the Synoptics

For Jewish Christianity, the law of God was given to Moses (*Recognitions* 1.35); indeed, the law is eternal and was present at the creation:

> The only good God having made all things well . . . appointed a
> perpetual law to all, which neither can be abrogated by enemies,
> nor is vitiated by an impious one, nor is concealed in any place,
> but which can be read by all. (*Homilies* 8.10)

Not only is the law affirmed, but it applies to everyone equally, Jews and gentiles alike. This has clear parallels in the synoptic gospels. Jesus constantly reminds his listeners that they are to obey the revealed law of God, and responds to questions by referring to the law. He may sometimes be critical of the tradition, but never of the law. In the Sermon on the Mount, Jesus says "Think not that I have come to abolish the law and the prophets; I have come not to abolish them but to fulfill them" (Matthew 5:17). This celebrated passage, the subject of so much controversy and exegesis, is a simple affirmation of the law and the value of keeping the commandments of God. Modern Christian scholars twist and turn to avoid the necessary and obvious conclusion: Jesus believed that the entire law should be kept. Jesus in fact announces the "golden rule" in exactly these terms, as a principle that is the building block of the Jewish law:

> So whatever you wish that men would do to you, do so to them;
> for this is the law and the prophets. (Matthew 7:12)

This "golden rule" is in fact a different expression of Leviticus 19:18: "You shall love your neighbor as yourself." A famous story from the Talmud relates that a gentile approached the sage Shammai, requesting that he be accepted as a proselyte on condition that he could be taught the whole of the Torah while standing on one foot. Shammai threw him out. When he made the same request of Hillel, however, Hillel accepted him, on his acceptance of the teaching "What is hateful to you, do not do to your fellow." Hillel then added that this is the Torah, and the rest is commentary (B. Shabbath 31a). There seems to be no difference between Jesus and Hillel on this point.

When Jesus is asked what the greatest commandment is, he answers with two commandments, to love God with all your heart, soul, and mind, and to love your neighbor as yourself—adding that on these two commandments depend the law and the prophets (Matthew 22:37–40). In the parallel passage in Luke, it is Jesus who asks the question, to a lawyer wanting to know how to obtain eternal life. The lawyer responds with the same two commandments, whereupon Jesus responds: "You have answered right; do this, and you will live" (Luke 10:28). And to the rich young man, Jesus says: "If you would enter life, keep the commandments" (Matthew 19:17).

It is very clear that in Matthew, Mark, and Luke, Jesus on numerous occasions teaches from the law, quotes from the law, and without a trace of embarrassment advocates conformity to the law. He explicitly denies that he seeks to abolish the law; he sets forth commandments from the law as the highest ethical ideal; he denounces others for not obeying the law; and he states that those who follow the two greatest commandments in the law will have eternal life. This is certainly not something that gentile Christianity would have added later; it must have been present in primitive Christianity and have represented Jesus' original intent: *a reform of Judaism based on a radical interpretation of the law of Moses.*

Moreover, not only does Jesus defend and explicate the law, he does so in a way characteristic of the Jewish rabbis. There are numerous occasions on which Jesus uses the *a fortiori* method of argumentation: an argument from the lesser to the greater, which goes from a statement that is accepted to conclude that it is all the more true in another case. If you know how to give good gifts to your children, how much more will God know (Matthew 7:11); if sparrows are not forgotten before God, how much more will you not be forgotten (Luke 12:6–7). This form of argumentation, referred to as *qal wechomer*, was common among the rabbis.[1]

Indeed, so close is Jesus' identification of his teaching with the law in the synoptic gospels, that we need to ask in what ways he was *different* from other Jews of his day. Why did Jesus not simply become one of many Jewish moral teachers—an early rabbi? There are some today who think that is precisely what Jesus was.[2] At one time there were Jewish scholars who spoke of "reclaiming" Jesus for Judaism—that is, of presenting Jesus as basically an orthodox Jewish thinker with a flair for public relations that got out of hand.

There is a substantial element of truth in this view. Jesus *did* affirm the law. Jesus was a part of the life situation of first-century Judaism; and his thought had to reflect this general background. We now need to examine the differences between Jewish Christianity, the Jesus of the synoptics, and first-century Judaism, concerning the question of what the law commanded. These differences affect two types of tenets: moral principles and ritual observance.

Morality and the Law

On moral matters, the Jesus of the Ebionites certainly seems to go beyond what was commonly believed to be the law's requirements. The traditional first-century interpretation of the law did not require us to renounce wealth and live communally; it did not require us to become pacifists or vegetarians. Yet for the Ebionites, all of this was part of what *their* Messiah had taught.

The synoptic gospels present a view of Jesus that is parallel to that of the Ebionites. Like the Ebionite Jesus, the Jesus of the synoptic gospels also wants to make the law *stricter* than did other Jews of his day. This is exactly the opposite of what most modern Christians, or anyone who has read the letters of Paul, would expect; but it is quite clear from a number of well-known passages. The standards of moral conduct put forward "intensify" the standard interpretation.

The Sermon on the Mount depicts Jesus as quoting the law in order to extend its traditional application even further. In a string of celebrated passages, Jesus first quotes a teaching with the preface, "you have heard it said"; then he adds his own interpretation with the words, "but I say unto you." In quick succession he comments on killing, divorce, compensation for injustice, and love—in each case making the command *more stringent*. It is not enough simply not to kill, we must not even be angry with our brother (Matthew 5:21–22); it is not enough to love one's friends, we should love our enemies as well (5:43–44); it is not enough to give a woman a certificate of divorce, men should not divorce their wives at all (5:31–32); we should not ask for equal compensation ("an eye for an eye"), but should not resist one who is evil at all (5:38–39). This certainly sets a more stringent moral standard, and explains why Jesus prefaces his remarks with the comment, "unless your righteousness exceeds that of the scribes and Pharisees, you will never enter the kingdom of heaven" (5:20).

How does Jesus argue for his "intensification" of the law in the synoptic gospels? Is this perhaps a "new" command not previously given to the Jews? Jesus takes care in all these cases to draw attention to the original revealed intention of God. In some cases, Jesus' position straightforwardly follows from the law. Not even being angry with your brother (Matthew 5:22) seems to follow from Leviticus 19:17, "you shall not hate your brother in your heart." Jesus even indirectly argues that loving one's enemies follows from the law (Luke 10:25–37). Jesus states that there are two primary commandments: to love God and one's neighbor. When he is asked who one's neighbor is, he responds with the parable of the Good Samaritan: it is the hated foreigner who befriends the man in need of assistance who is the man's true neighbor. The implication is that even hated foreigners are (or should be) our neighbors; thus everyone—even an enemy—is ultimately our neighbor.

In the case of divorce, Jesus gives a slightly different argument—an argument from a God-created order as being, in fact, the original law of God. When the Pharisees, citing Moses, object to Jesus' prohibition of divorce, Jesus replies:

"For your hardness of heart he [Moses] wrote you this commandment. But from the beginning of creation, 'God made them male and female.' " (Mark 10:5–6)

Jesus accepts the commandment of Moses that allows divorce, but explains that it is a concession to human weakness. He then refers to the statements in Genesis that humans were created male and female, and that a husband and wife become one flesh (Genesis 1:27, 2:24). The point appears to be that the creation of humans by God as sexual beings implies that wives are not to be "put away" by their husbands. The argument is not completely clear, but it implicitly refers to a natural order at the beginning of time, created by God, that is not to be put aside by human fiat; thus the command of Moses is a later, secondary command, made as a concession to human weakness.

Similarly, when Jesus argues for simplicity of lifestyle, saying, "Do not lay up for yourselves treasures on earth" and "no one can serve two masters," he advances a similar argument that God will provide based on a God-created order:

Look at the birds of the air: they neither sow nor reap nor gather into barns, and yet your heavenly Father feeds them. . . . Consider the lilies of the field, how they grow; they neither toil nor spin; yet I tell you, even Solomon in all his glory was not arrayed like one of these. But if God so clothes the grass of the field, which today is alive and tomorrow is thrown into the oven, will he not much more clothe you, O men of little faith? (Matthew 6:26, 28–30)

This may not totally convince all hearers that they should cease accumulating treasures on earth, but the appeal is *not* to a new moral principle: it is to a God-created order in which the grass of the field, the birds of the field, and humans (even those with inadequate faith!) are all provided for. Because of this God-created order, we should reject the anxiety that comes with pursuing money. Jesus does not announce a new moral law, but refers to an *original* directive already implicit in God's creation. *God has made it plain* how we should live; the listeners are invited to inspect God's creation and draw their own conclusions.

Many Christians think that Jesus objected to burdensome and puritanical legalism or that the Jews went too far in their allegiance to the law. The position of Jewish Christianity, in striking agreement with the Sermon on the Mount, is that when Jesus disagrees with the religious authorities in *moral* matters it was because they *did not go far enough* in their allegiance to the law.

Ritual Observance in the Jesus of the Synoptic Gospels

It would be nice if all issues relating to the historical Jesus were very straightforward. Unfortunately, this is not so when we turn to the question of the importance of religious rituals—those customs and practices such as observing the Sabbath, going to church, and taking communion that are part of religion but that do not bear directly on moral behavior. Both Jewish Christianity and the Jesus of the synoptics take a distinctly muddy approach toward the ritual aspects of the law—sometimes they seem to approve of Jewish rituals, sometimes they disapprove. There is no clear or consistent pattern.

It is almost an article of faith among some Christians, and even many liberal scholars, that Jesus in the synoptic gospels chose to *attack* the superficial attitudes toward religious custom held by many Jews of his day. This view is not completely without support in the synoptic gospels: Jesus performs healings on the Sabbath (Mark 3:1–5, Luke 6:7–11, etc.), the disciples pick heads of grain on the Sabbath (Matthew 12:1–8); Jesus condemns those who observe ritual matters but neglect the more important commands (Matthew 23:23–26, 15:18–20); Jesus even declares all foods clean (Mark 7:19). However, by choosing different scriptures, you can also make the case that Jesus *supported* ritual observance: Jesus observes the Passover (Matthew 26:17–29); he commands a leper to make an offering in the temple (Mark 1:44, Matthew 8:4, Luke 5:14); and he says that even the least of the commands (presumably those concerning rituals) should be followed (Matthew 5:19). Where does the truth lie?

There is an important point here that casts serious doubt on all these stories: Galilee simply was not a hotbed of ritual observance in the first place. *All* the gospel discussions of ritual observance—both pro and con—are therefore suspect. It is most doubtful that Jesus—or any other prophet working in first-century Galilee—either criticized *or* defended ritual observance per se, simply because in Galilee this wasn't much of an issue. Most likely, it did not become an issue until after the death of Jesus, when the Jesus movement migrated into areas outside Galilee.

Galilee in the north was separated from Jerusalem in the south by a considerable distance. In between the two was Samaria, the residents of which had initially been Jews, but then refused to accept the Jerusalem temple and instead established their own temple on Mount Gerizim sometime after the conquests of Alexander the Great. The most obvious difference between those who lived in Galilee and those from the Jerusalem area was their distinctive accent. In itself this would not seem that this would make the Galileans' religion any different; but the Talmud comments on the "inexactness" of the Galileans' speech and connects it with lack of knowledge (B. Erubin 53a). The accent of the Galileans is ridiculed (53b): because of their sloppy way of speaking, Galileans cannot be understood. In the New Testament, Peter's accent stands out when he is accused of being a follower of the Galilean after Jesus' trial: "certainly you are also one of them, for your accent betrays you" (Matthew 26:73).

This inexact manner of speaking is connected with the general feeling that Galilee is inexact in following the Jewish law.[3] Thus, the Mishnah discusses at some length the question of when and whether oaths should be considered valid, with one of the general presuppositions being that sometimes an oath cannot be binding on the person uttering it—for example, one made in ignorance by a young child. It is said that if anyone makes an oath relating to the temple offering in Judea it is binding, but it is not in Galilee, because Galileans are unfamiliar with temple offerings (B. Nedarim 18b). A Galilean, like a little child who doesn't know any better, may make a vow with respect to a temple offering, but the oath can't be binding on him because it is spoken in ignorance. The ignorance of Galileans is presupposed as general knowledge.

Galilee is accused of "hating" the Torah by Johanan ben Zakkai, who lived in Galilee in the first century during the same period of time that Jesus lived (P. Shabbat 16.8). There were probably a few Pharisees in Galilee—though based on Johanan ben Zakkai's comment just cited it's unlikely they were numerous.[4] While the picture of Galilee in the Talmud is not entirely unfavorable, the Talmudic view of Galilee is of a rather remote rural area that is generally ignorant of certain aspects of the law. This "resistance" to religious ritual persisted into the second and third centuries.[5]

Therefore, we have to question the stories in the gospels that feature Jesus debating the Pharisees (or anyone else) over questions of ritual. Jesus may have objected when ritual observance conflicted with a *moral* principle (as in the case of animal sacrifice), but it is unlikely that Jesus objected to ritual observance as such. Most likely, few in Galilee cared one way or the other. What we would expect on the basis of looking at John the Baptist, as well as other Galilean figures roughly around the time of Jesus—such as Honi the Circle-Drawer (Josephus, *Antiquities* 14.2.1), Hanina Ben Dosa, and Abba Hilkia[6]—is a more "rough and ready" sort of Judaism; a Judaism that was moral, surely, but not based on either great learning or great attention to religious ritual. None of these other famous Galileans were particularly noted for their great learning or precision in arguing matters of law; they were revered as persons who acted *ethically*.

Jesus, in all likelihood, was a similar figure. He doubtless had a great deal to say on *moral* issues; but he probably did not attach much importance to ritual observance, simply because no one else in Galilee did either. We can conclude that the celebrated statements from Jesus—both for and against ritual observance—almost certainly come from a later period, when ritual observance *had* become an issue, and then "retrofitted" into the New Testament to show that Jesus had explicitly held these views all along.

Ritual Observance in Jewish Christianity

One of the biggest myths about ancient Jewish Christianity is that the belief in Jewish ritual observances such as circumcision, keeping the Sabbath, making temple sacrifices, and keeping the kosher laws, is what caused the split between Jewish Christianity and gentile Christianity. The foundation of this view comes from a few fragmentary references in Acts: the "Christian Pharisees" argue that you must be circumcised in order to be saved (15:1); a reluctant Peter has a vision in which he is given the command to "kill and eat" various unclean animals (10:9–16); and James instructs Paul to appease those Christians who are "zealous for the law" by making an animal sacrifice in the temple (21:20–25). The Jewish Christians are depicted as keeping the kosher laws, desiring temple sacrifices, and wanting circumcision of males mandated a part of Christianity.

This view is fraught with difficulties and falls apart on serious examination. Acts is somewhat suspect as a source of historical information to begin with; it is regarded by many as a later writing, and contains many questionable passages in it which contradict things we know to be true from other sources (such as the letters of Paul).[7] Moreover, there is at least one Jewish ritual observance, the practice of animal sacrifice, that the Jewish Christian Ebionites vehemently rejected. Epiphanius, the *Recognitions*, and the *Homilies*—specifically contradicting Acts—are unanimous in describing the absolute rejection of animal sacrifice by Jewish Christians. The idea of a Jewish Christianity slavishly observing Jewish tradition falls apart at the outset.

According to Epiphanius, the Ebionites did observe both the Sabbath and circumcision (*Panarion* 30.2.2). Gentile Christians kept Sunday as the holy day instead of Saturday, but there is no indication that either gentile or Jewish Christians considered this essential to salvation. Likewise with male circumcision; just because the Jewish Christians circumcised their males, does not imply they thought it essential for salvation. Many modern Protestant Christian males, as well as males in the ancient pagan Arab world, were routinely circumcised without any thought about "salvation." Moreover, the idea that circumcision is essential to salvation was held only by a minority of first-century orthodox Jews. Even Paul at his angriest in Galatians says that circumcision was not the real issue in his dispute with James, John, and Peter.

Circumcision is nowhere mentioned in the *Homilies*; it is briefly mentioned a few times in the *Recognitions*, where at one point it is said that one can obey God's law without being circumcised (5.34). Indeed, except for baptism and prayer—rituals shared with gentile Christianity—ritual matters receive almost no attention in the *Homilies* and *Recognitions*, nor is there any suggestion they are essential or important for salvation. Epiphanius *never* suggests that the Jewish Christians thought circumcision was necessary for salvation, and such a detail would surely not have been overlooked by such a bitter opponent of Ebionism.

In fact, it is fairly easy to identify where the picture of "Jewish Christianity" in Acts comes from. The portrayal of Jewish Christianity in Acts is based on gentile Christianity's reaction to *orthodox Judaism*. The "Jewishness" of Peter and James in Acts conforms perfectly to objections that orthodox Jews probably raised with gentile Christians; it does not correspond at all with anything we know of Jewish Christianity from Paul or other sources. Orthodox Jews probably asked questions like "aren't you circumcised?", "didn't your followers offer temple sacrifices?", and "don't you follow the rules regarding clean and unclean foods?" From this, the writer of Acts concludes that since Jesus was a Jew, the first Christians must have required male circumcision, offered temple sacrifices, and followed the rules regarding clean and unclean foods. What we see in Acts is a later reaction—and not against Jewish Christianity, but against orthodox Judaism.

In a confused way, this attempt to "retrofit" orthodox Judaism sometimes reaches back to Jesus himself in the synoptic gospels, making Jesus into an ultra-orthodox Jew. In one case, Jesus heals a leper and then commands him to make the offering commanded to Moses, namely various animal sacrifices. Such an incident is completely out of place in first-century Galilee, where, as I have argued, neither Jesus nor anyone else particularly paid attention to ritual. And it is completely out of character for Jesus to advise someone to make a ritual observance to priests in a temple several days' journey away and then later be executed after disrupting this highest shrine of ritual observance and enraging the priests in charge there. This incident is almost certainly a later insertion by someone who concluded that, since the Old Testament required a sacrifice at this point, Jesus as a Jew must have then commanded the man to offer the required sacrifice. It sounds, in fact, like an anti-Marcionite insertion; Marcion said that the God of the Jews was not the God of Jesus at all, and a passage showing exact obedience to the God of the Jews would tend to refute this view.

The synoptic gospels are inconsistent; they not only try to make Jesus into an ultra-orthodox Jew, they also sometimes do the exact opposite, insisting that Jesus was a rebel who *broke* with orthodox Judaism over the question of ritual. For example, Jesus declares all foods clean (since "whatever goes into a man from outside cannot defile him"), thus allowing the eating of pork or any other kinds of animals (Mark 7:19).

But this is transparently a later insertion to accommodate the gentiles who were converting to Christianity: Jesus himself allowed us to eat anything, you don't have to keep the kosher laws. This becomes clear when looking at Peter's vision in Acts 10:9–16, when Peter (after Jesus' departure from earth) has a vision of a giant sheet filled with animals descending from heaven, and the voice from heaven saying, "Rise, Peter, kill and eat!" If Jesus really did declare all foods clean, then Peter's vision makes no sense. Peter's response to his vision should have then been to *recall* the words of Jesus. But this is all coming to Peter as a *new revelation*; this suggests that during Jesus' lifetime and for sometime afterwards nothing was said about eating unclean animals.

Jesus doubtless had many things to say about the moral aspects of the Jewish law. But on the question of religious ritual, these labored attempts to make Jesus into an orthodox Jew, or alternatively to make Jesus a *rebel* against the rituals of orthodox Judaism, have very little to do with the teachings of Jesus or with Jewish Christianity. They are a reaction (one way or the other) to orthodox Judaism on the part of gentile Christians, reflecting the struggles of a much later period. The historical Jesus and the Jewish Christians were most likely in quite close agreement on the question of the observance of religious rituals. They most likely approved of baptism and prayer and disapproved of animal sacrifice, but beyond that, had very little to say one way or the other about religious ritual.

Conclusions

Jesus affirmed the Jewish law. Jesus probably had very little to say about many of the religious rituals of orthodox Judaism, since in Galilee these weren't much of an issue. What Jesus *did* have to say about the law had to do with morality—a morality that does not deny the Jewish law, but relies on and indeed intensifies that law. If Jesus really intended to replace the Jewish law with something else, then the question has to be why the references to the law in the synoptic gospels so uniformly indicate otherwise. In the synoptic gospels, Jesus seems to move in a completely Jewish environment, never questioning the law itself but rather questioning the *use* of the law and pointing out the radical nature of the law. The synoptic gospels and the Ebionite gospel are, therefore, in striking agreement on this point. Jesus did not bring something new, he brought something old to those to whom he preached.

6 THE LYING PEN OF THE SCRIBES

THE FALSIFICATION OF THE SCRIPTURES

I F JESUS WAS JUST ANOTHER JEWISH TEACHER, THEN HOW did he become controversial and why was he killed? Where, precisely, did he deviate from the tradition?

We would expect the Ebionites, being "Jewish," to have a reverence for the Jewish scriptures. However, the truth is both surprising and disturbing. The Ebionites condemned many of the texts in the Jewish scriptures as false texts: they believed they were not inspired by God but were false and shouldn't be part of the scripture at all. If the Ebionites had respect for the law and constantly emphasized Jesus as a prophet of the law, then how could the Ebionites turn around and reject the Jewish scriptures? This seems completely contradictory.

The answer to this puzzle is that the Ebionites distinguished between the law and the scriptures. The driving force behind this distinction was a number of questions that the Ebionites' opponents must have asked repeatedly: if the Ebionites believed that sacrifice or warfare was wrong, how do we explain the existence of commands in the Jewish scriptures to offer animal sacrifices and commands to engage in bloody warfare? Commands to make animal sacrifices are found throughout Leviticus, and accounts of wars sanctioned by God are found throughout Joshua.

The problem of dealing with troubling passages in scripture is an old one. One answer, taken by both the Jewish philosopher Philo and the

Christian writer Origen, is to call troubling passages allegorical. Thus, Origen (who was a pacifist) interprets much of the violence in the Old Testament wars of Joshua as allegories, so that the "extermination" of our enemies means destroying wrath, lust, melancholy, and other vices (*Homilies on Joshua* 15.3); elsewhere Origen describes other Old Testament passages which he believes could not be literally true and which must be considered allegorically (*De Principiis* 4.1.8).

The Ebionites were not alone in feeling uncomfortable about these texts. However, they did not take this allegorical path. Confident that they followed the law of God, they concluded that if scripture did not measure up to this law, it was not a problem with the law—it was a problem with the scripture.

The Ebionite Theory of the Corruption of Scripture

A question must first be clarified here: what is the law, anyway? Is it the written text of the Old Testament ("Tanakh"), or is it just the first five books of Moses, known as the Pentateuch or the Torah? Does it also include an oral tradition, handed down from the time of Moses, and eventually written down as the Talmud? Jesus in the synoptic gospels never appears to criticize the law, though he *does* criticize the tradition. But isn't the tradition to a certain extent the law as well?

The Jewish Christians could not accept the standard interpretation of the Old Testament text given by orthodox Jews. They most obviously would oppose the lengthy and detailed commands to sacrifice animals in Leviticus, but would also be concerned with other passages in the Pentateuch and throughout the Old Testament. Jewish Christianity affirmed the law given to Moses, but denied that the written books of Moses (the Pentateuch) were the same as this law. The written tradition (the Jewish scriptures) had been corrupted with false texts:

> For the Scriptures have had joined to them many falsehoods against God on this account. (*Homilies* 2.38)

Since the *Homilies* speak of false texts being inserted, but never of true texts being removed, it appears that a document acceptable to

Jewish Christianity could conceivably be entirely contained within the Old Testament text. This Jewish Christian "Bible" would be an edited-down version of the Old Testament, deleting just the false insertions. This is astounding at first glance because in this one respect, Jewish Christianity is *less* "Jewish" than orthodox Christianity, which accepted the entire Hebrew Bible as (part of) its scriptures.

Why this Ebionite rejection of parts of the written scripture? To many readers, God appears in the first books of the Bible, and in Joshua and Judges, as a vengeful and partisan deity who delights in bloodshed and violence. Not pleased with how his creation is turning out, he sends a flood that destroys most life on earth. Of course, not everyone in ancient times was upset by such views; many doubtless wanted to worship such a deity. Origen says that the orthodox Jews understood Joshua in a way that condoned their own participation in violent warfare (*Homilies on Joshua* 14.1).

Besides making an unwelcome text an allegory, there were other ways to evade the literal meaning of the Old Testament. A second method of dealing with problematic texts was to rank the commandments in importance (putting the unwelcome commands lower in priority), or explain unpleasant commandments as divine concessions to human weakness. In the synoptic gospels, Jesus takes this path when he says that Moses allowed men to put away their wives because of the men's hardness of hearts (Mark 10:5–6). A third method is simply to denounce the text as not being from God at all—it is a false text, not properly part of the scripture at all.

Interestingly, the *Recognitions* and the *Homilies* are not consistent on this point. At times the *Homilies* denounces an unpleasant text as a false text which never came from God; but the *Recognitions* takes a different approach, admitting that the text was really from God but explaining that it was not God's highest will but a concession to human weakness. For example, when faced with the commands about sacrifice, it would seem to be the perfect opportunity to denounce these as false insertions (as indeed the *Homilies* does). Instead, we get the "concession to human weakness" theory:

Moses, that faithful and wise steward, perceived that the vice of sacrificing to idols had been deeply ingrained into the people from their association with the Egyptians, and that the root of this evil could not be extracted from them, he allowed them indeed to sacrifice, but permitted it to be done only to God, that by any means he might cut off one half of the deeply ingrained evil, leaving the other half to be corrected by another, and at a future time [i. e., Jesus]. (*Recognitions* 1.36)

The *Homilies*, however, chooses the solution that, in its view, is most consonant with the "omnipotent nature of the Almighty Creator of the Universe" (*Homilies* 2.44), and that means that parts of the Old Testament are just wrong. In the *Homilies*, we find Peter saying:

. . . with good reason said our Master [Jesus], "Be ye good moneychangers", inasmuch as in the Scriptures there are some true sayings and some spurious. And to those who err by reason of the false scriptures He fitly showed the cause of their [the Sadducees'] error, saying, "Ye do therefore err, not knowing the *true* things of the Scriptures, for this reason ye are ignorant also of the power of God." (*Homilies* 2.51; emphasis added)

Peter here quotes a slightly different version of Matthew 22:29, which omits the word "true." Thus for the Ebionites it is not just the scriptures that the Sadducees do not know, but the "*true* things" of the scriptures—implying that there are false things in the scriptures as well. In fact, Peter continues by listing some specific false statements in the Old Testament: that Adam was a sinner, that Noah was drunken, that Abraham had three wives, that Jacob associated with four women, that Moses was a murderer (*Homilies* 2.52). In this passage, Peter attacks several well-known Old Testament passages head on, concentrating on the sexual behavior of the Patriarchs. But Peter's denunciation becomes even more sweeping:

For the Scriptures have had joined to them many falsehoods against God on this account. The prophet Moses having by the order of God delivered the law, with the explanations, to certain chosen men, some seventy in number, in order that they also might instruct such of the people as they chose. After a little the written law had added to it certain falsehoods contrary to the law of God, who made the heaven and the earth, and all things in them. . . . Everything that is spoken or written against God is false. (*Homilies* 2.38, 2.40)

And how, according to the *Homilies*, do we know which are the false texts? We simply need to analyze them to determine if they "diminish the omnipotent nature of the Almighty Creator of the Universe." We cannot believe that God lies, is unjust, loves war, and makes evil things:

For if He lies, then who speaks truth? Or that He makes experiments as in ignorance; for then who foreknows? If He is unjust, who is just?. . . If He loves war, who then wishes peace? If He makes evil things, who makes good things? (*Homilies* 2.43, 44)

It is not always clear which Old Testament passages Peter is referring to in each of these cases, though there are certainly many passages that would arguably fit the bill in each case. Many passages leave the impression that God supports war and even the killing of prisoners (Numbers 10:9, Deuteronomy 20:1, Deuteronomy 20:10–14). Many arbitrary laws and killing of humans for seemingly trivial reasons leave the impression that God does evil and unjust things: Numbers 15:32–36 shows God imposing the death penalty for a man gathering sticks on the Sabbath, and Isaiah 45:5–7 has God declaring that he creates suffering. The first chapters of Genesis often suggest that there is more than one God ("let *us* make man in *our* image," Genesis 1:26); and God, far from being omniscient, appears genuinely surprised at how badly his creation is turning out when he sends the flood.

Peter's "historical criticism" has an interesting counterpart in modern analysis of the Old Testament. Many modern scholars of the Old Testament today tell us that the writings we know as the Old Testament grew by accretion, as different authors or editors added their contributions over hundreds of years, and that parts of the first five "books of Moses" (the Pentateuch) were written long after Moses was dead. Indeed, the writings in Leviticus pertaining to the sacrificial cult— the "Priestly" writings—were probably some of the last to be added.[1] Did the Ebionites retain some memory that these writings were not originally part of the Jewish religion? It is startling that *Homilies* 3.47 presents something very reminiscent of this modern theory, stating that Moses did not write the "books of Moses."

Hans-Joachim Schoeps argues that the Ebionite rejection of false texts was not an Ebionite creation but was based on ancient recollections that the Pentateuch was not what was given to Moses on Mt. Sinai.[2] The blunt words of Jeremiah likewise support the Ebionite position on the textual corruption of the Old Testament:

> How can you say, "We are wise, we have the law of the Lord," when scribes with their lying pens have falsified it? (Jeremiah 8:8)

The New Testament and the Jewish Christian Critique

What does the New Testament say about the conflict between Jesus and the Jewish tradition? Unfortunately, history is often not as clear cut as we would like it. Sometimes the New Testament supports, and at other times it opposes, the three most interesting Jewish Christian claims regarding this conflict:

- **The law is "eternal" and thus predated Moses.** This is flatly contradicted by Paul, even though it seems to agree with the traditional Jewish understanding.
- **Jesus ranked some of the commandments as being more or less important than other commandments.** This is directly supported by the synoptic gospels.

- **Jesus condemned some Old Testament verses as "false texts."**
  The synoptic gospels hint at this, but nowhere spell it out.

Jewish Christianity saw the law as eternal and present from the beginning of time. But Paul directly contradicts this idea. Paul stated that the law came 430 years after Abraham (Galatians 3:17), making the point that the giving of the law to Moses *followed* the promise made to Abraham. Since Jewish Christianity maintained that the law was eternal, it must have *preceded* the text given to Moses as well as the instructions to Abraham. So the conflict between Paul and Jewish Christianity is not just a conflict over the significance of the law, with Jewish Christianity applauding and Paul denigrating the importance of the law; it is also a conflict over the *nature* of the law. The Jewish Christian idea of the law as eternal, while not endorsed by the New Testament, is closer to the subsequent orthodox Jewish development than is Paul's understanding:

> When we review the rabbinic doctrines about the nature of the Torah, we can see most clearly how the rabbis and Paul take antithetical stands. From the rabbis' standpoint *the Torah was eternal, extant even before Moses*, so that the patriarchs observed it in advance of Sinai. (Samuel Sandmel, *The Genius of Paul*, p. 47; emphasis added.)

For both Jewish Christianity and orthodox Judaism, the patriarchs *did* observe the law, even without the written text. This law was "the original saving worship which was committed to humanity" (*Homilies* 9.19) and revealed to Adam. It is on this eternal law that the Jewish Christians based their faith. The Jewish Christian idea of the law, at least on this point, is closer to that of orthodox Judaism than is Paul's concept of the law.

How does Jesus in the synoptic gospels deviate from the tradition? Two methods suggested by the *Recognitions* and *Homilies* are (1) to rank the commandments, or (2) to denounce an offensive passage as a false text. The first method is definitely found in the synoptic gospels; the second is hinted at but never made explicit.

Jewish Christianity clearly felt that some commands were not the highest will of God (most especially, the commands concerning animal sacrifice). In the synoptic gospels, Jesus either explicitly or implicitly ranks the commandments at several points. In one passage, he is asked what the greatest commandment is; he responds by citing two commandments, to love God and love one's neighbor (Matthew 22:36–40). On another occasion, he disapproves of divorce because the law of Moses allowing divorce is secondary to Genesis 1:27 and 2:24, "God created them male and female," and husband and wife become "one flesh" (Matthew 19:3–9).

On a third occasion, Jesus criticizes the Pharisees because "for the sake of your tradition, you have made void the law of God" (Matthew 15:6). The view of the particular Pharisees in question is that anything promised to God ("Corban") need not be given to one's parents, despite the command "honor your father and your mother." The dilemma which the Pharisees and Jesus are addressing is the problem that it may not always be possible to keep all the commandments. Numbers 30:2 specifically says that we should keep all our oaths; yet Exodus 20:12 says we should honor our parents. But what happens if someone swears an oath to give anything that might benefit one's parents to God? One either has to dishonor one's parents or break the oath. Jesus' answer is that one should break the oath rather than dishonor one's parents—thus, the commandment to honor one's parents is greater than the commandment to keep our oaths.

When the disciples ask Jesus if he knows that the Pharisees are offended by this, he replies: "Every plant which my heavenly Father has not planted will be rooted up" (Matthew 15:13). This particular passage is also quoted with some relish in *Homilies* 3.52, indicating that the Jewish Christians used this verse to refer to the principle of false texts. Jesus was, in their view, talking about all the false texts in the Old Testament that needed to be "rooted up."

It is debatable whether Jesus' response to the Pharisees actually requires that we reject a text as a "false text," or rather merely that we reject the Pharisees' *interpretation* as false. Most Christians, after thinking about this problem, would probably not fault the Old Testament text itself but merely the Pharasaic interpretation. On the other hand, Jesus *does* denounce oaths elsewhere, urging his followers "not to swear at all" (Matthew 5:33–37), so it's certainly possible Jesus thought that Numbers 30:2 (which enjoins us to keep our oaths) was an outright fabrication of the scribes. Regardless of how we sort this out, though, the Jewish Christian insistence that a scriptural command might not be God's highest will (*Recognitions* 1.36–37) is directly supported by the synoptic gospels. *The word of God, that is, does not reside in any text*; at the very least, we must have an *interpretation* of the law to make sense of it, there is no such thing as the "literal meaning."

Do the synoptic gospels support the more daring Jewish Christian argument that some of the texts in the scripture were outright fabrications? At no point in the synoptics does Jesus quote an Old Testament passage and then clearly denounce it as a false insertion, though at times he comes pretty close (as in Matthew 5:34). On the other hand, however, at no point does Jesus make any declaration that "all scripture is inspired by God" (II Timothy 3:16); and there are some hints that Jesus did not think that highly of everything in the Old Testament texts. Three celebrated agricultural parables occur in quick succession: the parable of the sower, the parable of the weeds in the field, and the parable of the mustard seed (Matthew 13:3–32, Mark 4:1–20, 26–32; cf. Luke 8:4–15, 13:18–21). In one of these parables, a man sows seed in his field, but an enemy sows weeds. The man directs his servants to let them both grow, but sort out which is which at the harvest. If we assume the same general interpretation for this parable as for the other agricultural parables, then it would appear that the good seed and the bad seed stand for the word of God and the word of the devil, that have *both* found their way into the tradition.[3]

The saying about the Father pulling up weeds that he has not planted (Matthew 15:13) further suggests corruption or mixing together of good and bad elements. This mixing together of good and bad elements is also reflected in the celebrated image of John the Baptist, when the Baptist talks about separating the wheat from the chaff (Matthew 3:12, Luke 3:17). The three metaphors of the wheat and chaff, the parable of the weeds in the field, and the Father pulling up weeds he did not sow, all suggest that a mixing together of good and bad elements in the tradition has occurred—exactly what the Ebionites wanted to convey. The *Homilies* make clear that the objection is to both spoken and written sayings (everything "spoken *or* written against God is false," *Homilies* 2.40). The saying "Be skilled moneychangers"—a saying of Jesus not in the Bible but quoted by both the *Homilies* (at 2.51, 3.50, and 18.20) and orthodox writers such as Clement of Alexandria (*Stromata* 1.28)—implies that just as there are true and false coins, there are also true and false scriptures. Thus, we have no definite support for the Ebionite idea of false texts in the synoptic gospels, though we do have some fairly substantial hints. Jesus simply rejects the "tradition," leaving it ambiguous as to precisely what this rejected tradition consisted of.

Later Christian theologians said that Jesus only rejected the oral law or the Pharisaic interpretations of the Hebrew Bible.[4] That Jesus intended to launch a precise theology that would draw a fine line between the oral and written law or between interpretation and text is highly debatable; most likely, he simply intended to attack the tradition, letting the theological assumptions fall where they might. In the synoptic gospels, Jesus often denounces the scribes—who were precisely that class of people who wrote things down—as "hypocrites" just like the Pharisees. Since Jesus distrusted those who were wealthier and better educated, why wouldn't he also distrust what they wrote down?

Conclusions

During the lifetime of Jesus, and for some time afterwards, Jewish Christianity was one possible approach to Jewish history; and the eventual rejection of Jewish Christianity by the orthodox Jews was not the only possible outcome. Judaism was fragmented and much different from what it would be only a few generations later. The consensus that could have excluded Jesus' views as heretical did not exist at the time he lived and taught; and it is possible, though unlikely, that Judaism could have been remade in accordance with the ideas of early Jewish Christianity rather than those of rabbinic Judaism.

If Jesus did accept the Old Testament, then did he believe that it was all right to annihilate men, women, children in warfare—or that it was ever right? Does Jesus teach that God requires the blood of innocents in order to atone for wrongdoing—or that God ever did? Does God love war and reward sexual lust—or did he ever love and reward these things? Above all, does God change his mind? If God had a message for humanity, why did he not reveal it at the beginning instead of telling God's people one thing from Mt. Sinai and then sending his Son later to give them a different message? These are hard questions. If we accept the Ebionite explanation, then Jesus' answers to the above questions are that God *did* reveal his word at the beginning, but humans forgot it and falsified it.

7 CHILDREN OF PEACE

THE GOSPEL DEMANDS NONVIOLENCE

T HE PEACEFUL NATURE OF CHRISTIANITY IS ONE OF THE most established parts of Christian doctrine. It is part of the gospels. It is part of the early history of the church. It is often more obvious to non-Christians than it is to Christians, because many Christians disregard it. Gandhi noted that "the only people on earth who do not see Christ and His teachings as nonviolent are Christians."[1]

Early Christians, by contrast, took Jesus' advice seriously, and often paid for it with their lives. There are many examples of early Christians being martyred because of their pacifist beliefs. If Christianity, which had no refuge in a world completely dominated by Rome and was much smaller than it is today, was unhesitatingly pacifist, then why isn't Christianity pacifist today?

Pacifism in the New Testament

Pacifism was a common practice in early Christianity, and the support for pacifism was taken directly from the words of Jesus:

> Blessed are the peacemakers, for they shall be called sons of God. (Matthew 5:9)

> You have heard that it was said, 'An eye for an eye and a tooth for a tooth.' But I say to you, Do not resist one who is evil. (Matthew 5:38–39)

You have heard that it was said, 'You shall love your neighbor and hate your enemy.' But I say to you, Love your enemies and pray for those who persecute you. (Matthew 5:43–44)

Those supporting war sometimes refer to such passages as "Render unto Caesar the things that are Caesar's, and to God the things that are God's" (Matthew 22:21) and "I bring not peace, but a sword" (Matthew 10:34). These passages, however, are not in any way a rejection of pacifism. The passage on Caesar has nothing to do with serving in the armed forces; it has to do with paying taxes, that is, giving to Caesar certain material possessions (which, as we have seen, the early Christians despised anyway). Certainly, it would be a distortion of the passage to say that rendering to Caesar the things that are Caesar's involved obeying Caesar's orders to kill when these orders violated the laws of God (e. g., "You shall not kill"). If Caesar ever thought he could make Christians violate the law of God, the martyrs show how wrong he was.

Similarly the passage in which Jesus says "I have not come to bring peace, but a sword," occurs in a context related to divisiveness and controversy rather than violence: father is pitted against son, daughter against mother, and daughter-in-law against mother-in-law. Interestingly, the parallel passage in Luke uses a different term, "division" rather than "a sword" (12:51–53). The implications of this division are certainly not that Jesus' followers are going to kill their relatives; on the contrary, the implication is that "the sword" that Jesus' message provokes is to be used *against* his own followers:

You will be delivered up even by parents and brothers and kinsmen and friends, and some of you they will put to death; you will be hated by all for my name's sake. (Luke 21:16–17)

Non-resistance is certainly the example that early Christian martyrs set and which Jesus himself sets, by specifically renouncing armed struggle when he is arrested. In Matthew, one of Jesus' followers actually cuts off the ear of the slave of the high priest—whereupon Jesus admonishes him: "Put your sword back into its place; for all who take the sword will perish by the sword" (Matthew 26:52).

Mark gives a similar account. In Mark, Jesus does not admonish the one who uses his sword, but submits to arrest, noting that the priests could have arrested him at any time when he was in the temple teaching (14: 47–50). In Luke, Jesus' response to this attempt at violence is met with the exclamation, "no more of this!" Jesus also heals the person who was struck (22:50–51). John says that it was Peter himself who used his sword (18:10–11).

This famous incident, related in slightly different forms in all four gospels, makes the response of Jesus consistent with his own teachings: nonresistance to evil, abuse, and persecution. Evidently this was a controversial stance, since some of the followers were sufficiently outraged to betray the teachings Jesus had previously given. Yet Jesus remains steadfastly opposed to violence.

Jewish Christianity and Pacifism

Even by the time at which many of the New Testament books had crystallized (end of the second century CE), pacifism was still part of Christian testimony; so all the main pacifist texts in the Sermon on the Mount are still in the New Testament. The Jewish Christians emphasized pacifism as much or more than other Christians. In the *Recognitions*, this occurs in a celebrated passage describing a speech by James, the brother of Jesus, delivered in the temple seven years after Jesus' death. James denounces animal sacrifices and predicts the destruction of the temple. At this time James is on the point of converting the people when a "certain enemy" (Paul before his conversion) starts attacking them:

> Much blood is shed; there is a confused flight, in the midst of which that enemy attacked James, and threw him headlong from the top of the steps; and supposing him to be dead, he cared not to inflict further violence upon him. But our friends lifted him up, for they were both more numerous and more powerful than the others; but, from their fear of God, *they rather suffered*

themselves to be killed by an inferior force, than they would kill others. (Recognitions 1.70–71; emphasis added)

Peter, in the *Recognitions*, draws the necessary conclusions from the teachings of Jesus:

Why are you afraid of hearing frequently of peace? Or do you not know that peace is the perfection of law? For wars and disputes spring from sins; and where there is no sin, there is peace of soul; but where there is peace, truth is found in disputations, righteousness in works. (Recognitions 2.36)

Under the hope of future good things, I will not suffer men to take up arms and fight against one another, plunder and subvert everything, and attempt whatsoever lust may dictate. And what will be the condition of that life which you would introduce, that men will attack and be attacked, be enraged and disturbed, and live always in fear? For those who do evil to others must expect like evil to themselves. (Recognitions 3.42)

Pacifism is presented as not just an opportunistic strategy adopted when one is opposed by a vastly superior force, but a matter of principle. Pacifism was clearly part of Jewish Christianity. We can see in these passages the clear imprint of pacifism on other Jewish Christian themes—one pacifist passage occurs when James has just made a speech denouncing the animal sacrifices, while a second says that "peace is the perfection of law."

Some have argued that Jesus was actually a Zealot and a militarist, and that pacifism was a later (gentile) development, a reaction to the disastrous Jewish rebellions against Rome.[2] The problem with this point of view is not just that it contradicts Christian belief, but that such a complete and total reversal of Jesus' teachings would surely have left a trace somewhere in the history of the early church. Since the Zealots were a Jewish revolutionary sect, Jewish Christianity is just where we would have expected any "Zealot" tendencies in Jesus' followers to have survived, had Jesus been a Zealot. There is much evidence from the church fathers of all kinds of other heresies, but there is no trace at all of any dissident militaristic Christians who wanted to violently oppose Roman rule.

The idea of passive resistance was not foreign to the Jewish mind of the first century. In Josephus there are two striking examples of Jewish passive resistance. The first is under Pilate. Pilate tries to bring the Roman standards, on which Caesar was portrayed, into Jerusalem at nighttime. This of course greatly offends the Jews because of the prohibition of any graven images, much less an image of Caesar. When the Jews come to Caesarea to petition Pilate to remove the images, Pilate surrounds them with soldiers and threatens them with death unless they return home. The response of the Jews is striking: they throw themselves on the ground, declaring that they would rather meet death than break their laws. Pilate gives in and removes the images from Jerusalem to Caesarea (*Antiquities* 18.3.1).

A second example occurs later, when Caligula is emperor, about the year 40. In the course of a dispute between the Jews and the Greeks in Alexandria, the accusation is made before Caligula that the Jews despise Caesar because they refuse to erect a statue of Caesar in their holy city— again, the same issue Pilate confronted. In this case, Caligula's angry reaction is to order Petronius, one of his generals, to invade Judea with as many troops as necessary and to erect his statue in the Temple, using force if necessary.

Of course, the presence of Caesar's image (or anyone else's) in Jerusalem, and especially in the temple, was outrageous to the Jews. The effect of this demand, when it was learned by the Jewish population, was immediate. Petronius and his troops were met by tens of thousands of Jews who petitioned him not to force them to violate the laws of their forefathers by putting Caesar's statue in the Temple. The Jews begged Petronius to kill them before putting Caligula's statue in Jerusalem. Finally, Petronius asked them if they planned to make war on Caesar, to which the Jews responded:

"We will not by any means make war with him; but still we will die before we will see our laws transgressed." So they threw themselves down upon their faces, and stretched out their throats, and said they were ready to be slain; and this they did for forty days together, and in the meantime left off the tilling of the ground, and that while the season of the year required them to sow it. Thus they continued firm in their resolution, and proposed to themselves to die willingly, rather than to see the dedication of the statue. (*Antiquities* 18.8.3.)

Petronius did not cause a war. The story ended happily both for Petronius and the Jews. He wrote a letter to Caligula urging Caligula to relent. Caligula angrily ordered Petronius to kill himself; but Caligula shortly thereafter died, and news of Caligula's death reached Petronius before his order to Petronius to kill himself. Nonviolent resistance as a strategy was not something foreign to first-century Palestine.

Pacifism in the Early Church

How did the early Christians interpret Jesus' teachings about war and violence?

Most of the early church writers were pacifist as a matter of course. Opposition to war is clear from reading what the church fathers said about war. Origen, Ireneaus, Tertullian, Hippolytus of Rome, Cyprianus, Arnobius, and Lactantius all express opposition to participation in war in any form. Ireneaus, Justin, and Origen quote the celebrated pacifist passages in the Old Testament (about turning swords into plowshares) to support Christian doctrine. Irenaeus used the Old Testament pacifist passages to "prove" that Jesus' coming was predicted by the Old Testament:

... from the Lord's advent, the new covenant which brings back peace, and the law which gives life, has gone forth over the whole earth, as the prophets said: "For out of Zion shall go forth the law, and the word of the Lord from Jerusalem; and He shall rebuke many people; *and they shall break down their swords into*

plowshares, and their spears into pruning-hooks, and they shall no
longer learn to fight" [Isaiah 2:3–4; Micah 4:2–3] . . . but if the
law of liberty, that is, the word of God, preached by the apostles
(who went forth from Jerusalem) throughout the earth, caused
such a change in the state of things . . . then the prophets have
not spoken these things of any other person, but of Him who
effected them. This person is our Lord. (Irenaeus, *Against*
Heresies 4.34.4; emphasis added.)

Justin also invokes the Old Testament pacifists to show that there is
a continuity of Jesus with the Old Testament (*Dialogue With Trypho* 109).
In both cases the pacifist ideal of opposition to war is clearly and
unequivocally invoked. Origen quotes the same passages, saying that we
no longer take up "sword against nation" or "learn war any more" for the
sake of Jesus (*Against Celsus* 5.33). Indeed, Origen quotes Celsus
complaining about Christian pacifism—something that shows the
widespread perception among both the supporters and opponents of
Christianity at that time that Christians opposed war (*Against Celsus*
8.68–71).

Hippolytus (170–236 CE), in recounting the *Apostolic Tradition*,
discusses which professions are acceptable for Christians:

A soldier of the civil authority must be taught not to kill men and
to refuse to do so if he is commanded, and to refuse to take an
oath; if he is unwilling to comply, he must be rejected [from
membership in the Christian community]. A military
commander or civic magistrate that wears the purple must resign
or be rejected. If a catechumen or a believer seeks to become a
soldier, they must be rejected, for they have despised God.[3]

From this, it would appear that it was possible, strictly speaking, for
a Christian to be in the army. If he was not already a soldier, he must not
become one; but if a nonbeliever was "surprised by faith" while serving
in the army and became a Christian, he need not immediately risk
martyrdom by desertion. As long as he did not receive a command to kill,

there was nothing in principle wrong with a Christian remaining in the army. Being a soldier would be a highly dangerous occupation for a conscientious Christian, since he might have to disobey the order to kill at any time and incur martyrdom; but it would not be an absolutely impossible profession.

Arnobius speaks of pacifism at the beginning of the fourth century, just a few decades before the Council of Nicaea, as if it had always been official Christian policy.

> . . . we, a numerous band of men as we are, have learned from His teaching and His laws that evil ought not to be requited with evil, that it is better to suffer wrong than to inflict it, that we should rather shed our own blood than stain our hands and our conscience with that of another . . . . (*Against the Heathen* 1.6)

Minucius Felix says that it is not even permitted for Christians to voluntarily *look* at bloodshed (that is, in the arena), and that for this reason Christians avoid the blood of animals used for food (*Octavius* 29.6). Here, the connection between the abstinence from all blood, whether human or animal, is emphasized. Lactantius, writing at about the same time, castigates the pagans for their use of war as an instrument of national policy (*Divine Institutes* 6.6). He states unequivocally that Christians should not kill even if the state commands it, whether this is warfare or capital punishment—"with regard to this precept of God, there ought to be no exception at all; but that it is always unlawful to put to death a man" (*Divine Institutes* 6.20).

Tertullian, writing over a century before the Council of Nicaea, frequently denounces military service, saying:

> Has the Creator, withal, provided these things [iron, poison, magical enchantments] for man's destruction? Nay, He puts His interdict on every sort of man-killing by that one summary precept, "Thou shalt not kill." (*De Spectaculis* 2)

... I think we must first inquire whether warfare is proper at all for Christians. What sense is there in discussing the merely accidental, when that on which it rests is to be condemned? ... Shall it be held lawful to make an occupation of the sword, when the Lord proclaims that he who uses the sword shall perish by the sword? And shall the son of peace take part in the battle when it does not become him even to sue at law? ... Then how many other offenses there are involved in the performances of camp offices, which we must hold to involve a transgression of God's law, you may see by a slight survey. (*De Corona* 11)

There is no problem in finding abundant condemnation of war as such in the writings of the early church; in fact, before this time it is impossible to find any statement allowing Christians to fight in wars at all:

No church writer before Athanasius ventured to say that it was not only permissible, but praiseworthy, to kill enemies in war, without the qualification—expressed or implied—that he was speaking of pagans only.[4]

This was more than an intellectual position; stories were told of martyrs who refused to fight or who refused to join the army almost up until the time of Constantine. In 295 CE Maximilianus, a young African Christian, just over 21 years old, was martyred for refusing to serve in the Roman army. He was brought before the Roman proconsul who tried repeatedly to talk him out of his refusal. The proconsul even pointed out that there were some Christians already serving in the army, but this did not deter Maximilianus.

It is fairly clear from the martyr's own words that his objection was largely, if not solely, to the business of fighting. The question of sacrificing to idols or to the Emperor is not mentioned by either party. "I cannot serve as a soldier," said Maximilianus; "I cannot do evil; I am a Christian."[5]

The proconsul failed in his efforts to dissuade Maximilianus, and he was sentenced to death and killed. His body was taken to Carthage and buried next to that of Cyprianus. His father, who had not tried to talk Maximilianus out of martyrdom, approved of his son's actions; and his words and deeds were recorded and Maximilianus became one of the saints of the Catholic church.[6] This all happened less than two decades before Constantine took power, demonstrating that pacifism was alive and well in the church over two centuries after Jesus' death.

The End of Christian Pacifism

Christianity abandoned pacifism at its very moment of victory. Suddenly, in the fourth century, the church switched to a pro-war position. Not only Athanasius (who defended the orthodox position at Nicaea in 325) but later Ambrose and Augustine also embraced the pro-war stance, which now became the "official" stance of virtually all Christianity outside of a few pacifist sects. How did this happen?

Undoubtedly there were a variety of factors; but they had nothing to do with Jesus' acceptance of war or the presence of any "just war" theorists among the apostles or anyone in the early church. War wasn't a big issue in the early church, because by and large conscription did not exist.[7] No one was being *forced* to fight, so the war issue never became a grievance: Constantine, Augustine, and Ambrose (three who defended war as an acceptable occupation for Christians) did not require Christians to fight, but allowed them to fight under certain circumstances.

The main explanation for this switch was the emergence of Constantine as a stabilizing force in the Roman Empire, following on the heels of the most brutal and effective of all the persecutions that Christianity had to endure. In the year 312 CE Constantine had a vision and told his soldiers to put a Christian symbol on their shields before the battle at Milvian Bridge. After his victory, Constantine unilaterally supported and subsidized the church, and many of his soldiers embraced the new religion. Suddenly soldiers become a part—indeed, an important part—of Christianity. The previous resistance to war was interpreted (in retrospect) as resistance not to war as such or to bloodshed, but resistance to fighting for paganism. The heart of Christianity suddenly shifted from the objection to bloodshed to the objection to bloodshed on behalf of the wrong cause. Killing for Christ, or for a Christian emperor became acceptable.

In the absence of a draft, the shift in doctrine did not affect most individual Christians. There was nothing for Christian pacifists to resist, since they were not being commanded to kill, just being allowed to kill should they decide to take up the profession of a soldier. This pro-war stand is totally without support in anything we know of in the history of early Christianity. When war is discussed in early Christianity—and indeed in almost all the orthodox and heretical variations of Christianity that existed before the Council of Nicaea—pacifism is commanded by God and required of Christians. It carried over from the early Jewish Christian community to the gentile Christians, was inscribed in the gospels as coming from Jesus himself, and had the support of the orthodox, the Ebionites, and most other "heretics" as well. Most likely, the pressure of the intense persecution initiated by Diocletian at the end of the third century (probably the most severe the church had ever known to that point), followed with the sudden support of Constantine, led to this shift.

Conclusions

The history of early Christianity demonstrates that there is at least one instance in which pacifism as a strategy worked quite well. The early Christians had no weapons and the Romans had a mighty empire and the best army in the world. But the practical problem in advocating pacifism is whether enough people are willing to risk their lives for the kingdom of heaven on earth. This is, to say the least, very frightening. Yet, the early Christians did risk their lives in exactly this way, and as long as this principle was not abandoned, Christianity crossed many barriers. After the principle was abandoned, Christianity still spread, but primarily as a phenomenon of the spread of Western culture. Those who accepted the rule of the Roman emperor, or the successors of the Roman Empire in the Western, European, and American spheres, may have accepted Christianity, but they were primarily following the religion of the Empire rather than the teachings of Jesus.

Even though in the minority at the present time, those who view the peace testimony as a vital and important part of Christianity are still to be found around the world and throughout history. There is a tradition of pacifism that stretches from the modern Quakers, Anabaptists, Mennonites, Hutterites, and some individuals in the "mainline" Protestant and Catholic churches, back to the early martyrs who refused to serve in the Roman army, and indeed back to Jesus himself, who declared the peacemakers to be the children of God.

8 THE BLOOD
OF THE LAMB

*THE ORIGINS OF
THE HOSTILITY
TO THE TEMPLE*

TO UNDERSTAND A MOVEMENT, WE MUST FIRST understand its origins; and the distinctive origin of Jewish Christianity lies to a large degree in its opposition to animal sacrifice. Jewish Christianity saw Jesus as a vegetarian for ethical reasons. Therefore, they first and foremost opposed the animal sacrifices in the temple.

The idea that Jesus would have opposed the temple practice is disconcerting at first, and to attribute such opposition to Jewish Christians even more so. Wasn't the temple the center of Jewish religious observance in the first century? Wouldn't Jesus and his family and followers, as good Jews, have gone to the temple to make offerings? How could the Ebionites, claiming to be "Jewish," possibly have been opposed to temple practice? Isn't this something we might expect from gentile Christianity, but not from Jesus or any of his Jewish followers?

In point of fact, the temple was a more controversial institution within ancient Judaism than is generally recognized. Opposition to the temple, while a minority viewpoint, was very much present in ancient Judaism. The Old Testament prophetic books have abundant material denouncing the practice of animal sacrifice. Galilee, the region from which Jesus came, was notorious for its ignorance and frequent non-observance of temple practice. Before we consider the actions of Jesus and the early church against the temple, we need to consider the origins of the Jewish Christian hostility to the temple.

Why Animal Sacrifice?

Animal sacrifice was a controversial issue in ancient Judaism, but ceased being a concern over 1900 years ago, and it is not a divisive issue today in either Judaism or Christianity. The temple where the sacrifices were offered was destroyed in 70 CE after the Romans captured Jerusalem during the Jewish revolt against Rome. Since in the eyes of first-century Jews the temple was the *only* place where sacrifices could legitimately be offered to God, with the destruction of the temple, the practice of making sacrifices stopped. A very small minority of modern-day Jews hope for the eventual rebuilding of the temple and the resumption of animal sacrifices; but aside from this, animal sacrifice has disappeared as a subject for more than historical discussion within Judaism.

Animal sacrifice is more of a living image in Christianity than it is in Judaism. To most modern Jews, the period of animal sacrifices is a historical episode. For Christians, however, the image of animal sacrifice is all-pervasive in the blood of Christ. The "blood of the lamb" is a well-known Christian allusion to the blood of Jesus, said to have been shed for the forgiveness of sins just as animals were sacrificed for forgiveness of sins in the Old Testament. God expected blood sacrifices, and Jesus provided it in some final sense, so that animal sacrifices (while once legitimate) were no longer necessary. In the Eucharist or communion sacrament, the communicants are fed either the literal or symbolic flesh and blood of Jesus, thus making the image of sacrifice one with which Christians are constantly confronted. (In Catholic doctrine, through "transubstantiation" the bread and wine literally become the body and blood of Christ.)

For Jews who offered animal sacrifices, the motivation to sacrifice was simple: animal sacrifice was perceived as a way to improve one's relationship with God. Atonement for sin was certainly one prominent motive, but peace offerings and offerings of thanksgiving were also possible. It was also possible to make offerings other than animals (for example, of grains). Jews were hardly the only ancient people to utilize this practice; pagans sacrificed animals to their gods as well, and it has been suggested that the Jews picked up the practice of animal sacrifice from their pagan neighbors.

There was another practical aspect of animal sacrifice—the final disposition of the meat of the sacrificed animal. Some sacrifices were "whole offerings"—that is, the meat of the dead animal was completely consumed by the fire when the offering was made. But many sacrifices resulted in some or all of the meat of the killed animal going to the priests. Animal sacrifice was thus a way of supporting the priests in the temple economically, with all Jews required to tithe ten percent of their herds "for the Lord" (Leviticus 27:32).

There was only one temple in first-century Judaism. This created awkwardness and logistical problems, first because it was difficult for the many Jews who lived hundreds of miles from Jerusalem to bring sacrifices to the temple, and second because of the sheer number of Jews all focused on one place of worship. Because of the distance, some Jews probably disregarded their obligations to visit the temple altogether: there were actually more Jews *outside* Palestine than in Palestine in the first century.[1]

Most importantly, though, the temple in Jerusalem was different from our modern churches or synagogues in one key respect: the temple resembled a butcher shop more than any modern place of worship. There were large areas around the temple where cattle, sheep, pigeons, and other animals involved in the sacrifice could be held and sold to worshippers arriving from out of town. We don't have precise statistics on how frequent or often sacrifices were offered, but references to animal sacrifice in Josephus and the Old Testament suggest that it was quite frequent and may have gone on almost continually.

Was animal sacrifice a necessity or an obligation for a good Jew in these times? There were a lot of Jews, including the priests, who thought so. But there were others who disagreed and felt it was one way—but not the only way—to atone for sin. We can see the evidence for both points of view in the Old Testament.

The History of Animal Sacrifice

In the Bible, animal sacrifice has an ancient provenance. Abel makes an animal sacrifice which meets with God's approval; Abraham is prepared to offer his son but substitutes a ram instead; Moses is given instructions about sacrifice in the desert. This would appear to take the practice back to very ancient times. However, the picture is made considerably more complicated when we discover that the institution of animal sacrifice was one of the last elements to be added to the Hebrew Bible. Many scholars think that most of the book of Leviticus, which contains the instructions about animal sacrifice, was incorporated into the Bible sometime around the 6th century BCE, many centuries after the time of Moses or David.

Whatever the actual practice of animal sacrifice before Solomon, it achieved an institutional legitimacy when Solomon built the first temple in Jerusalem around 950 BCE. The account given in the Bible says that it took seven years to build and the finished project was evidently very impressive. At the dedication of the temple, there were so many sheep and oxen sacrificed that "they could not be counted or numbered" (I Kings 8:5). This temple endured for over 350 years, until Jerusalem was captured by the Babylonians at the beginning of the sixth century BCE. After the return of the Jews from captivity about sixty-five years later, the returning exiles very soon began the task of rebuilding the temple, and animal sacrifices resumed. In the centuries that followed there were many struggles against foreign domination, and Judea came under Roman rule; but temple worship continued and indeed, under Herod the temple was expanded. However, dissatisfaction with Roman rule spread, and revolutionary movements sprang up. Ultimately, these revolutionary movements gained the upper hand, leading to a series of Jewish revolts against Rome. The largest revolt was the first, which lasted from 66 to 74 CE. After the capture of Jerusalem by the Romans in 70, the temple was destroyed and has never been rebuilt.

The temple thus lasted about 1000 years, with a single interruption during the Babylonian captivity. The site of the ancient temple, incidentally, is now also the site of two of Islam's holiest shrines in the

Moslem quarter of the old city of Jerusalem. Even in the very unlikely event that sentiment among the Jews in the modern state of Israel were to favor rebuilding the temple on its ancient site, it would be virtually impossible for political and religious reasons to do so.

Was animal sacrifice an expression of the original law received by Moses or was it the result of a later adaptation of the Jewish religion to the pagan custom of animal sacrifice? To give a complete answer to this question would perhaps require another book, or several books. For our purposes, however, it is enough simply to note that there were different points of view on this question even in ancient times.

Opposition to Animal Sacrifice: Isaiah

Isaiah is prominent among those who have negative things to say about the sacrificial cult:

> Your countless sacrifices, what are they to me? says the Lord.
> I am sated with whole offerings of rams and the fat of buffaloes;
> I have no desire for the blood of bulls, of sheep and of he goats.
> Whenever you come to enter my presence—who asked you for this?
> No more shall you trample my courts. The offer of your gifts is useless, the reek of sacrifice is abhorrent to me. . . .
> There is blood on your hands; Wash yourselves and be clean. . .
> (Isaiah 1:11–13, 15–16; New English Bible)

Those wishing to defend both Isaiah's words and the practice of sacrifice in ancient Israel might say that Isaiah's objection is not to the practice of animal sacrifice itself but to the sins of the Israelites, and that because of these sins, the sacrifice was still rejected by God. However, such an interpretation is clearly contrary to this text. "I have no desire for the blood of bulls" is stated without qualification; God (quoted by Isaiah) does not say "Because your sins are so great, or because you still have a hard heart, I have no desire for the blood of *these* bulls you are offering me," but simply, "I have no desire for the blood of bulls."

No qualification is offered, either, for the statement "The reek of sacrifice is abhorrent to me." It is not "Your sins are abhorrent to me," or "Your hypocrisy is abhorrent to me"; the objection is to the *stench of slaughter itself*. Further, the question that is asked, "Whenever you come to enter my presence—who asked you for this?" does not make sense unless it is the *sacrificial cult itself* that is in question. If one accepts that Leviticus demands animal sacrifice, the answer to the question "who asked you for this?" is that it is precisely God himself who asked for the bloody sacrifices. In this case, the question becomes meaningless or we have to suppose that God is suffering from some sort of memory lapse. That God is asking this question clearly implies that (for Isaiah) God never asked for these sacrifices. "This" in the question "who asked you for this?" is precisely the behavior cited in the previous verse—namely, the multitude of sacrifices, which God through Isaiah views as "trampling [his] courts." The temple is God's court, and it is thus not the sinful behavior of the people generally that is being objected to (though there is probably enough of that as well), but rather some *specific* sinful behavior performed in the temple—namely, the animal sacrifices.

Vegetarianism is not explicitly endorsed in these passages, though Isaiah is more forthright later:

He who slaughters an ox is like him who kills a man. (Isaiah 66:3)

Jews and Christians who are troubled by the apparent inconsistency of these verses with the sacrificial legislation in Leviticus—where God *does* command animal sacrifice and appears to delight in sacrifices—can, of course, offer other interpretations. They may insist that, in fact, God's objection in Isaiah is only against empty sacrifices, or sacrifices without repentance, or hypocritical sacrifices. The driving force behind all such interpretations is the dogmatic assumption that "God's word" cannot be contradictory. Such interpretations fly in the face of the text, however, which is clearly a bitter denunciation of sacrificial practices themselves, not just the context in which the sacrifices were offered.

Opposition to Animal Sacrifice: Amos

Amos likewise indicates a contempt for the sacrificial ceremonies:

> Even though you offer me your burnt offerings and cereal offerings, I will not accept them, and the peace offerings of your fatted beasts I will not look upon. Take away from me the noise of your song; to the melody of your harps I will not listen. But let justice roll down like waters, and righteousness like an ever-flowing stream. (Amos 5:21–24)

Once again, one has to distort the text if one makes the assumption that Amos is only objecting to some sacrifices, to the way the sacrifices are performed, or to the moral condition of those offering the sacrifice. Amos is fond of comparing complete opposites; in the previous verses, Amos (speaking for God) has just said things such as "Seek good, and not evil . . . hate evil, and love good . . . Why would you have the day of the Lord? It is darkness, and not light" (Amos 5:14, 15, 18).

Evil and good; darkness and light; these are all contrasts of complete opposites. Following this pattern, we have burnt offerings and sacrifice contrasted with justice and righteousness—again, in the vision of Amos, complete opposites. Sacrifices are compared to idolatry:

> Did you bring to me sacrifices and offerings the forty years in the wilderness, O house of Israel? You shall take up Sakkuth your king, and Kaiwan your star-god, your images, which you made for yourselves; therefore I will take you into exile beyond Damascus. (Amos 5:25–27)

Were sacrifices and offerings made to God in the wilderness? The context suggests that the answer to this rhetorical question must be "no!" Otherwise, the denunciation of sacrifice makes no sense, since Israel was supposed to be in an especially holy and pure state in the wilderness (Jeremiah 2:2–3). Immediately following the question, we have a declaration that Israel will take up idolatry and be driven into exile. There is evidently an association between sacrifice and idolatry that is quite striking. This same passage is quoted in the New Testament—in the speech that Stephen gives in Acts just before he is killed (Acts 7:42–43). Stephen follows this passage with a denunciation of the temple. The followers of Jesus, therefore, were doubtless aware of the moral ambiguity of the status of animal sacrifice within Judaism.

Opposition to Animal Sacrifice in Other Prophets

The prophetic passages that condemn animal sacrifices or the killing of animals can be multiplied further. Ezekiel is brief and stark about sacrifice. In this book, God admits that he ordered sacrifice, but expresses profound regret about the matter: "I gave them statutes that were not good and ordinances by which they could not have life, and I defiled them through their very gifts in making them offer by fire all their first-born, that I might horrify them" (Ezekiel 20:25–26). The first-born are evidently the first-born animals of the herd (Exodus 22: 29–30, Numbers 18:15). This is hardly an endorsement of animal sacrifice: quite the opposite, it is the most grudging acceptance of the divine source of animal sacrifice possible. Yes, God commanded sacrifices; but obeying these commands won't do you any good, and their intention is to horrify you.

Micah rejects animal sacrifices as unnecessary and urges his listeners to substitute a moral life in its place (6:6–8); he does not absolutely reject animal sacrifices, but does regard them as unnecessary. Jeremiah, though, goes further, clearly denying that God gave any sacrificial commandments:

> Add whole-offerings to sacrifices and eat the flesh if you will. But when I brought your forefathers out of Egypt, *I gave no commands about whole-offering and sacrifice*; I said not a word about them. (Jeremiah 7:21–22, New English Bible;[2] emphasis added)

Hosea likewise objects that God does not want sacrifices (a passage cited twice by Jesus at Matthew 9:13 and 12:7):

Loyalty is my desire, not sacrifice; not whole offerings but the knowledge of God. (Hosea 6:6, New English Bible)

Hosea also accuses the priests of murder, says that the Lord has no delight in sacrifice, and looks for a day when God will make a covenant between Israel and the animals so that violence and war will be abolished (6:9, 8:11–13, 2:18).

The objections in the Old Testament to the sacrificial cult are quite striking, as it seems that parts of the Old Testament scriptures contradict one another. Apologists for the sacrificial cult can, of course, argue that sacrifices are only being repudiated by the prophets in a context of other sinful behavior. However, the texts do not support this interpretation; the problem these prophets have with sacrifice is with the cult itself.

Original Ideal and Ultimate Hope

For Jewish Christianity, opposition to animal sacrifice was closely connected with pacifism and vegetarianism. In this short chapter we cannot fully explore the history of Biblical traditions about violence and nonviolence. However, we will point out that traditions supporting vegetarianism and pacifism, and related to animal sacrifice, can easily be found in Genesis and the prophets.

In Genesis, the original diet of humans is vegetarian, and indeed the animals are also completely vegetarian:

And God said, "Behold, I have given you every plant yielding seed which is upon the face of all the earth, and every tree with seed in its fruit; you shall have them for food. And to every beast of the earth, and to every bird of the air, and to everything that creeps on the earth, everything that has the breath of life, I have given every green plant for food." (Genesis 1:29–30)

All creatures are vegetarian, and the creation is "very good." While permission is later given to eat meat after the flood (Genesis 9:2–4), the original diet of humanity was strictly vegetarian. According to the

Talmud, meat-eating was not allowed to Adam, but after the flood, meat-eating was permitted (B. Sanhedrin 59b).

There is also the message that God desires us to be compassionate toward animals. God cares and wants us to care for animals (Psalms 145:9, Proverbs 12:10). We have an obligation to relieve the suffering of animals, whether the animal belongs to our neighbor or even to our enemy (Deuteronomy 22:4, Exodus 23:5)—passages cited by some Talmudic commentators as evidence that kindness to animals is a Biblical law (B. Babia Mezi'a 32b). It is irrelevant whether it is your friend's animal or you enemy's animal: your obligation is *toward the animal*, not towards the human being who owns it. Other passages suggest that animals are similar to (or actually superior to) humans in many ways (Ecclesiastes 3:19, Proverbs 6:6–8, 30:24–28; Isaiah 1:2–3; Exodus 21:28–32; Deuteronomy 32:10–12).

Some of the same prophets who denounced the sacrificial cult, also predicted a future world of peace in which not only humans would not kill each other, but we would not kill animals, nor would animals kill other animals—a return to the Garden of Eden in which neither humans nor animals killed each other. Hosea ties in the pacifist vision with the vegetarian one—this day will be when Israel is again induced to go into the wilderness, where it is thought that Israel will (again) be holy and pure, and where animals and humans will live in peace (Hosea 2:18): there will be no more war and no more killing. Isaiah's celebrated "peaceful kingdom" also envisions such a world, when the wolf, the lamb, lion, little child, and cow will all live together in peace, and:

They shall not hurt or destroy in all my holy mountain;
for as the waters fill the sea,
so shall the land be filled with the knowledge of the Lord. (Isaiah 11:9)

Both Isaiah and Micah use very similar words to spell out the celebrated pacifist image of swords being beaten into plowshares, when nation shall not lift up sword against nation, nor learn war any more (Micah 4:3–4, Isaiah 2:4). Those early Christians wishing to find pacifist and vegetarian sentiments did not have to look far in some of the Old Testament prophets—some of the same prophets who had problems with the animal sacrifice cult.

Conclusions

The opposition of Jewish Christianity to animal sacrifice, an opposition seemingly so un-Jewish, is both understandable and plausible for Jesus. The early Christians were quite aware of the Old Testament remarks on animal sacrifice, since the New Testament cites both Jesus and Stephen as having quoted them (Matthew 9:13, 12:7; Acts 7:42–43).

It is into this context that we should attempt to determine what Jesus' attitudes toward the temple were. The crucible of Jesus' ministry, for Jewish Christianity, was the opposition to animal sacrifice and Jesus' confrontation in the temple. To kill animals in the name of God was an abomination, and the permission given to sacrifice animals was at best a temporary concession to human weakness—a concession whose time was at an end. This opposition to animal sacrifice culminated in the angry disruption of temple practice by Jesus sometime during Passover week, an event that led directly to Jesus' death.

9 CONFRONTATION IN THE TEMPLE

THE CRUCIBLE OF THE GOSPEL IN JESUS' FINAL CONFLICT

I F WE HAVE ANY SECURE HISTORICAL KNOWLEDGE ABOUT Jesus at all, it is that he was crucified. The synoptic gospels all depict his arrest and crucifixion immediately following one of the key events in the final week of Jesus' life—an angry confrontation in the temple. Since this incident is the event that likely precipitated Jesus' death, it is clearly of the greatest importance in understanding his life and mission. But what was at issue in this confrontation?

Traditional Sunday School thinking leaves us with the impression that Jesus simply wanted to rid the temple of some dishonest moneychangers. Others have suggested that Jesus was making a symbolic demonstration. The problem with these and similar interpretations is that they do not explain the depth of the conflict between Jesus and the temple hierarchy. They have the curious effect of saying that what Jesus was attacking actually had nothing to do with the temple. What Jesus was *really* doing was attacking hypocrisy or making a symbolic gesture.

The Jewish Christian texts present something much more striking: Jesus was attacking the practice of animal sacrifice. "I came to abolish sacrifices," says the Ebionite Jesus, "and unless you cease sacrificing, my anger will not cease from you" (*Panarion* 30.16.5). Now *there* is a pronouncement explosive enough to cause the temple hierarchy to want Jesus crucified!

This alternative explanation has several virtues in relation to the others; mostly, it establishes a motive for both sides of this dispute. If Jesus was attempting to abolish animal sacrifices, of course the priests would be angry; they derived much of their support from the meat on the altar (see I Corinthians 9:13). This explanation also provides a motive for Jesus to make the attempt anyway: Why would he have risked his life over an issue not essential to his message? Finally, it makes sense of history, as it explains the continuing hostility between the Jesus movement and the priests: the persecution of the early church in Acts and the judicial murder of James the brother of Jesus by the high priest many decades later.

Which explanation is more likely in the light of history?

The Jewish Christian Rejection of Animal Sacrifice

How did the Jewish Christians perceive the conflict between Jesus and the temple leadership? The *Recognitions* and *Homilies* have abundant references to their hostility to the sacrificial cult.

In the *Recognitions*, Peter states that Moses himself understood God's desire to bring an end to animal sacrifice; he allowed it to be continued, but eliminated its idolatrous aspects, and specifically predicted a future prophet who would correct the rest of the error (*Recognitions* 1.36). At the appropriate time,

> . . . they should learn by means of the Prophet that God desires mercy and not sacrifice [Matthew 9:13, 12:7]. . . and that on the other hand they might hear that this place [the temple] . . . was at last to be wholly destroyed. (Recognitions 1.37)

Here, the theme of "mercy, not sacrifice" (Hosea 6:6, Matthew 9:13, and Matthew 12:7) is tied in with the prediction that the temple will be destroyed (Matthew 24:2, Luke 19:44). Later, Peter states that the destruction of the temple is a direct consequence of the failure to heed the message of the true prophet that the time of sacrifices has ended (*Recognitions* 1.64). There are numerous other texts that also attack animal sacrifices.[1] Many scholars believe that the "predictions" of the temple's destruction (in the synoptic gospels and elsewhere) were actually written after the fact, with the gospel writers and others concluding that Jesus must have prophesied the temple's destruction; but regardless of when they were written, they all underline the hostility of the early followers of Jesus towards the temple.

Neither the *Recognitions, Homilies,* nor Epiphanius' description of the Ebionites supply any substantial account of the last week of Jesus' life. However, the saying of Jesus that Epiphanius quotes from the Ebionite gospel is the key to understanding the Ebionite view of the cause of Jesus' death: "I came to abolish sacrifices" (*Panarion* 30.16.5; compare *Recognitions* 1.54). Epiphanius doesn't tell us the context of this quotation. However, it is clearly addressed to someone who is sacrificing or supports the sacrifices, and the most logical time for Jesus to have said it is precisely during the last week of his life in Jerusalem. This could have been either during the incident in the temple or at his trial.

There is an interesting feature of this saying that distinguishes it from other, similar anti-temple statements from Jesus: it contains a prediction, but it does *not* predict the destruction of the temple. Even in the *Recognitions,* the temptation is irresistible to put the prediction of the destruction of the temple into the mouth of Jesus. Instead, the Ebionite Jesus makes a different, more vague statement—that the failure to stop the sacrifices would result in "my anger" coming down upon them. This saying, we can surmise, most likely comes from *before* the year 70 CE. An Ebionite scribe, writing down a gospel *after* this date, would have been unlikely to have resisted the temptation to change this statement into an exact prediction of the destruction of the temple.

A second interesting feature of this text is that it supplies what is curiously absent in the gospels: *a forthright answer by Jesus to the charges against him.* For Jesus to be crucified by the Romans, it had to be alleged that *he was a threat to public order,* not just that he uttered blasphemy. The Romans, as the chief blasphemers, would hardly have been interested in fighting blasphemy.

Perhaps Jesus claimed to be the Messiah, and this was the focus of the charges? But in the gospels Jesus is reluctant to admit being the

Messiah. Jesus is accused during his last week of claiming to be able to destroy the temple and of being the Messiah, but at several points Jesus says equivocally, "You say that I am" or is silent (Luke 22:70; cf. Luke 23:3, Mark 15:2, Matthew 26:64). Indeed, the gospel accounts state that on another occasion—when Peter declares that Jesus is the Messiah—Jesus quickly admonishes his followers to keep this a secret (Matthew 16:13–20, Mark 8:27–30, Luke 9:18–21). Since any such claim from Jesus would likely be prominently featured in any gospel, we can only understand this reticence as a consequence of it being well-known that Jesus did *not* claim to be the Messiah.

But we may imagine that Jesus at his trial—rather than remaining silent or noncommittal on the charges against him—said instead "I came to abolish sacrifices and unless you cease sacrificing, my anger will not cease from you." Then the High Priest might well ask, "Why do we still need witnesses?" (Matthew 26:65)—a statement that is puzzling since, in the orthodox account, Jesus does not seem to supply the "ammunition" the high priest needs to go to Pilate.

Whether a literal account of events, or a subsequent explanation of what Jesus' followers imagined "must have" happened, the descriptions of Jesus' trial are an important testimony to the understanding that the primitive church had about the conflict that led to Jesus' death. The outburst, "I came to abolish sacrifices," provides an explanation of precisely what it was that Jesus was trying to do, and *also* explains why he was perceived as a threat to public order—something conspicuously absent both from the gospel accounts and from the accounts of most modern scholars.

Jesus' Attack on the Temple

What happened in this incident in the temple, and what were Jesus' motivations? The confrontation in the temple is one of only a few of the events in Jesus' life that is described in all four gospels. John's account describes how Jesus made a "whip of cords" and drove both the cattle and sheep, as well as their owners, out of the temple (John 2:14–16).

Matthew, Mark, and Luke have Jesus quoting the Old Testament as he justifies his behavior toward those in the temple:

> And Jesus entered the temple of God and drove out all who sold and bought in the temple, and he overturned the tables of the moneychangers and the seats of those who sold pigeons. He said to them, "It is written, 'My house shall be called a house of prayer,' but you make it a den of robbers." (Matthew 21:12–13; parallels in Mark 11:15–17, Luke 19:45–46)

There are several points to be made about these accounts. First of all, there are several groups that Jesus directs his anger against, and the moneychangers are nowhere at the top of the list (in Luke they are not even mentioned). Rather, it is the "dealers in cattle, sheep, and pigeons," "those who sold," or "all who sold and bought" who are his primary target. Secondly, those he speaks to are not primarily the money changers; in fact, in John, he speaks *only* to the dealers in pigeons, and in Luke, he speaks *only* to "those who sold."

The primary practical effect of this so-called "cleansing of the temple" was (in John) to empty the temple of the animals that were to be sacrificed, or (the synoptics) to drive out those who were taking them to be killed or were selling them to be killed. We must remember that the temple was more like a butcher shop than like any modern-day church or synagogue. "Cleansing the temple" was an act of animal liberation.

The conventional interpretation of Jesus' motivation is that the moneychangers and dealers in animals were overcharging those Jews who had come to the temple to make a sacrifice and were not employed in animal agriculture. This has crept into popular imagination and Sunday School lessons everywhere—"Jesus chases the dishonest moneychangers out of the temple."

Nowhere else in the New Testament is there any suggestion that profiteering by animal dealers was a problem in the temple precincts. The only evidence that Jesus intended his action to be a response to this relatively modest charge, in fact, is Jesus' description of the temple as a "den of robbers." However, a quick glance at the Old Testament passages from which Jesus quotes shows that his charge is much more significant than that the animal dealers were making a profit. Jeremiah 7:11, to which Jesus alludes, describes the temple as a "den of robbers"; but this passage follows only after Jeremiah describes murder, adultery, and blatant idolatry (7:9), and ends by denying that God ever required sacrifices, anyway (7:22). Once we look at the whole passage in Jeremiah, Jesus' quotation becomes much more suggestive and concrete than our Sunday School lessons would imagine; the whole sacrifice business was a fraud anyway, God never having required sacrifices. Now *here* is something almost worth being crucified over!

If, of course, the animal sacrifice cult *was* a fraud—as the Ebionites believed—then the extortion of animals from the populace on religious pretenses was indeed *literal* robbery and a matter considerably more serious than the figurative "robbery" involved in overcharging. It is implausible that the motivation behind Jesus' attack on the temple was a concern for dishonest moneychangers. We could well imagine a Jew from outside Palestine who is coming to present a sacrificial animal and is acquainted with the real rates of exchange becoming outraged because he was overcharged and himself indignantly overturning one of the tables of the moneychangers. Would this have led to his being crucified? If he had been crucified, would this have provided the impetus for a new religious movement?

The extreme reaction to Jesus' demonstration betrays a concern that the *heart* of temple practice is being attacked. Mark and Luke say that the "chief priests and scribes" sought a way to destroy him (Mark 11:18, Luke 19:47). In Matthew, it is said that the "chief priests and the scribes" were "indignant" (21:15); the next day, the "chief priests and elders of the people" return and demand to know "by what authority are you doing these things, and who gave you this authority?" (21:23) Jesus silences them by asking them about John the Baptist; they try to arrest him (21:46), but fail. Finally, a crowd of people with swords and clubs, sent from "the chief priests and elders of the people" succeed in arresting him (26:47–57).

At every juncture, it is the *priests* who are seeking to have Jesus killed. It is not the Romans (yet), nor the "multitude" who are after Jesus; indeed, Jesus seems to be protected by the "multitude." The hostility of the priests toward the followers of Jesus continues even after his death: in Acts, it is the priests and the Sadducees who arrest Peter and John (Acts 4:1–3); it is the high priest who demands of Stephen an answer to the charges that lead to Stephen's martyrdom (Acts 7:1); and it is the high priest who gives Saul (not yet converted) his commission to go to Damascus to persecute Christians there (Acts 9:1–2), while other Jews, such as Gamaliel the Pharisee, are urging tolerance (Acts 5:34–39).

Everyone—both the Jesus movement and the priests—acts as if Jesus did something that struck at the core of temple practice. The priests want Jesus killed, and even after Jesus is dead, they want to destroy his followers. Is all this effort simply to safeguard some dishonest moneychangers? It is much more plausible that Jesus objected to the practice of animal sacrifice itself, and that his actions during the volatile Passover week were the immediate and most important cause of his death. *It was this act, and its interpretation as a threat to public order, that led immediately to his crucifixion.*

Destroy This Temple

Jesus' hostility to the temple is a theme that appears throughout the gospels. Besides the incident in the temple just discussed, there is more evidence that Jesus did not look with favor on the current operations of the temple: this evidence consists of the accusations that the priests brought against him to have him crucified. In Matthew, the accusation is brought that Jesus said that he was able to destroy the temple and rebuild it in three days (Matthew 26:59–63). In Mark, one of the charges is roughly similar (Mark 14:58); and while Jesus is on the cross, he is ridiculed by onlookers who repeat the charge of threatening to destroy the temple (Mark 15:29–30). Luke and John do not have the priests making this accusation.

However, according to the gospels, Jesus *does* in fact say things that could easily be understood as a threat to the temple. Pointing at the temple, Jesus says that "there will not be left here one stone upon another, that will not be thrown down" (Mark 13:2, Matthew 24:2). In the Gospel of Thomas, Jesus undoubtedly refers to the temple when he says,

> I will destroy [this] house and no one will be able to build it.
> (Gospel of Thomas 71)

In John, Jesus during the confrontation in the temple does not explicitly say he will destroy the temple, but he does emphasize its unimportance: "Destroy this temple, and in three days I will raise it up" (2:19). The gospel writer adds parenthetically, "he spoke of the temple of his body," but it is possible that Jesus meant exactly and literally what he said when stating that if the temple was destroyed, he could rebuild it in three days, rather than (as John presents it) making a figurative reference to his own future bodily resurrection. Perhaps Jesus was thinking of replacing the temple built by Solomon with a portable tabernacle like that originally built by Moses, and carried from place to place by the Israelites in the wilderness—something that indeed could have easily been accomplished in three days. Stephen, the first Christian martyr after Jesus, depicts this portable tabernacle favorably compared to the temple built by Solomon (Acts 7:44–50).

There is other support for the Jewish Christian opposition to animal sacrifice in the synoptic gospels. The most important of these is at Matthew 9:13, where Jesus refers to the Old Testament text at Hosea 6:6 in saying "I require mercy, not sacrifice." This is repeated at Matthew 12:6–7, where Jesus elaborates:

> I tell you, there is something greater than the temple here. If you had known what that text means, 'I require mercy, not sacrifice,' you would not have condemned the innocent. (New English Bible)

The Jewish Christians cited this text with approval (*Recognitions* 1.37, *Homilies* 3.56). In context, Jesus is urging his listeners to *show mercy to the animals, rather than sacrificing them on the altar*. Jesus says that because they did not understand this saying, they have *condemned the innocent*, namely, the innocent animals. Who else could Jesus have been speaking of as being condemned? His disciples, perhaps? This makes no sense, as Jesus specifically says that it is the Pharisees' lack of understanding of Hosea 6:6 that has caused them to condemn the innocent, and Hosea 6:6 has nothing to do with plucking corn (the objection the Pharisees are raising in the previous verses) and everything to do with sacrifice of animals.

Eusebius, the orthodox fourth-century church historian, expressly states that Jesus was hostile toward animal sacrifice:

> He [Jesus] left no command that God should be honored with sacrifices of bulls or the slaughter of unreasoning animals, with flood, fire, or the incense of earthly things. *He thought these mean and lowly*, and in no way worthy of the immortal nature of God. (*Proof of the Gospel* 3.3; emphasis added)

Eusebius then proceeds to quote approvingly from Porphyry's *On Abstinence from Animal Food* and from the *Theology* of Apollonius of Tyana, two books by well-known ancient pagan authors, who also objected to animal sacrifice (and were vegetarian). Eusebius points out their opposition to animal sacrifice and their vegetarianism, and then rhetorically asks:

> If there is agreement on these things among the outstanding philosophers and theologians of the Greeks, how could Christ be a deceiver? (*Proof of the Gospel* 3.3)

By favorably quoting pagan authors who oppose animal sacrifice and are vegetarian, Eusebius is asking: Can this view be absurd, since Porphyry and Apollonius also hold it? Eusebius implies not only that Jesus did not support animal sacrifice, but that he was vegetarian as well—since he prefaces his question with the phrase "if there is agreement on these things." In all this, we see reflected the Ebionite hostility toward the temple and the sacrificial cult.

Not a Sparrow Shall Fall

What is the motivating factor behind the opposition to animal sacrifice in Jewish Christianity? It is clearly related to the Jewish Christians' vegetarianism and opposition to killing animals. The text "I require mercy, not sacrifice," cited both in the Jewish Christian writings and in Matthew, suggests both the problem (sacrifice of animals) and the remedy (compassion for animals). God never desired the killing of animals and, therefore, he did not ordain sacrifices (*Homilies* 3.45).

While it is not a prominent theme, there is evidence of compassion for animals in a vegetarian context both in early Christian writings and in the gospels. Arnobius (c. 300 CE) attacks the practice of *pagan* animal sacrifices by appealing to our sympathies for animals:

> Lastly, what pleasure is it to take delight in the slaughter of harmless creatures, to have the ears ringing often with their piteous bellowings, to see rivers of blood, the life fleeing away with the blood . . . we ourselves accuse and condemn ourselves when the thing is seen and looked into thoroughly, because, *neglecting the law which is binding on men, we have broken through the bonds which naturally united us at the beginning.* (*Against the Heathen* 7.4; emphasis added)

Compassion for animals is a motive for not killing animals in pagan sacrifice. Arnobius depicts meat-eating as savagery that cannot be looked at objectively without having pity for animals, and *a violation of the laws uniting us with animals in the beginning* (evidently a reference to Genesis 1:29, where both humans and animals are given a vegetarian diet).

There is also evidence of compassion for animals in the gospels. We have the birth stories in which animals appear. In Luke, Jesus is born in a stable—a home for animals. Shepherds who are watching their flocks come and visit the newborn child. Luke does not specifically place animals around the birth scene, but it is a natural assumption, reflected in virtually every depiction of the Christmas scene in popular art and crèches. At the beginning of his life, as well as at the end in the confrontation in the temple where he drives out the animals to be sacrificed, Jesus is presented as being in harmony with the animal kingdom.

There are several references to animals in the teachings of Jesus. Jesus admonishes us not to be anxious about our material state of being; "the birds of the air neither sow nor reap nor gather into barns, and yet your heavenly Father feeds them" (Matthew 6:26). Here we have an argument from the lesser case to the greater: God feeds the birds, so surely he will feed you as well. This may disappoint any animal rights advocate wanting to put the birds of the air on an equal footing with humans: humans are, after all, worth more than birds. Nevertheless, *God feeds them anyway*, and so does care for animals. Then again:

> Are not five sparrows sold for two pennies? And not one of them is forgotten before God. . . . Fear not, you are of more value than many sparrows. (Luke 12:6–7)

Though animals do not count for as much as humans, they still count for something—and God does not forget them. Sheep and oxen also fall within our care:

> He said to them, "What man of you, if he has one sheep and it falls into a pit on the sabbath, will not lay hold of it and lift it out? Of how much more value is a man than a sheep!" (Matthew 12:10–12)

Luke gives a similar parable, mentioning "a son or an ox" instead of a sheep (14:5). What is more natural than to rescue a sheep or an ox fallen into the pit? Helping animals, as well as healing humans, is allowed on the sabbath, because it is allowed to do good on the sabbath. Again we have the argument from the lesser to the greater: if we, or God, does something even for animals and it is counted for good, how much more if it is done for humans.

    The cynical might object that this is just the prudent businessman's approach to his property. But other texts belie this interpretation. In John, Jesus goes so far as to state, "The good shepherd lays down his life for the sheep" (John 10:11). This indicates a concern for animals that goes considerably beyond that of the prudent businessman. Even if intended symbolically, the symbolism of caring for animals reflects a positive image of animals as beings whom we should care for.

    Even more striking is another case of Sabbath healing. When the ruler of the synagogue objects to Jesus' healing the woman who was bent over, Jesus replies:

> You hypocrites! Does not each of you on the sabbath untie his ox or his ass from the manger, and lead it away to water it? And ought not this woman, a daughter of Abraham whom Satan bound for eighteen years, be loosed from this bond on the sabbath day? (Luke 13:15–16)

    The obligation to untie animals on the sabbath is part of the Jewish principle concerning compassion for animals. Rashi, in his commentary on the sabbath laws, concludes that to allow animals to go out in the field and graze on the sabbath is not only permitted, but is actually required[2]—otherwise, animals could not rest on the sabbath, and the sabbath includes animals. Jesus makes the same point that Rashi would defend a thousand years later; of course we will untie animals on the sabbath. Jesus is again arguing from the validity of the lesser case to the validity of the greater. Animals must be released on the sabbath, therefore this woman held by the bond of disease can also be released on the sabbath.

    Jesus is in all these cases again arguing from the lesser case to the greater; and Jesus' argument thus assumes the validity of the lesser case, which in these instances involves an animal. The principle of compassion for animals is, therefore, a *presupposition* of all of Jesus' references to animals cited above. Jesus in the gospels does not, therefore, *argue* the question of whether we should be compassionate to animals; rather, he *assumes* it from the outset.

The Later Distortion of Jesus' Position

The Ebionite picture of a vegetarian Jesus who opposed animal sacrifices is *seriously* contested at several points in the gospels. We now need to mention and to some extent evaluate these competing traditions. The most important of these are the Last Supper—supposedly a Passover meal—and the cases of Jesus distributing or eating fish. It may be that Jesus ate fish after the resurrection, distributed fish to the multitude, ate the Passover meat, and actually supported the temple cult. We need to ask ourselves, therefore: Are *these* the original traditions and are the Ebionites the ones who have distorted history?

When faced with contradictory texts—in this case, the New Testament and Ebionite texts that oppose animal sacrifice and those New Testament texts that seemingly favor it—the temptation is strong either to try to harmonize the texts or just to throw up one's hand and say that we just can't know where the truth lies. But here it is not a case of one text colliding with another; it is a case of opposing *traditions* colliding with each other: the Ebionite tradition and the various orthodox and gnostic traditions. As long as the texts are considered abstractly, outside of the historical context, we can spin out equally plausible but opposing interpretations as to which texts are authentic. What we *cannot* do, is to set these text traditions into equally plausible historical contexts.

The Last Supper presents a problem for this view of Jesus as a vegetarian who opposes the sacrificial cult: Doesn't this mean that Jesus celebrated the Passover meal with his disciples in which he drank alcoholic wine and ate the paschal lamb, just killed in a sacrificial rite? Epiphanius raises this objection himself in discussing the Ebionites (*Panarion* 30.22.1). However, while the Last Supper is recorded in the synoptic gospels as a Passover meal (a Seder), the only items consumed at this event are bread and a drink. A dip is also mentioned in Matthew and Mark, in the passages describing Judas' betrayal (but there is no mention of Jesus eating from it, and it was most likely vegetarian anyway, probably the "bitter herbs"). In John, the Last Supper is not a Seder at all. The Jewish Christians had their own version of the Last Supper in which Jesus specifically rejects the Passover meat (*Panarion* 30.22.4).

It is the bread and a drink (grape juice or wine) that ancient and modern Christians take when imitating and remembering Jesus. However, "bread and a drink" sounds more like a *kiddush* ceremony with which the sabbath is celebrated, than a Passover Seder. The *kiddush*, pronounced over a cup of wine, was a prayer sometimes followed by distribution of bread. A number of scholars have argued convincingly that the last supper was a kiddush ceremony.[3] Skeptical readers are urged to attend a sabbath celebration and judge for themselves—the resemblance between this celebration and modern Christian communion services is striking. None of the accounts of the Last Supper mention lamb—which, if it was the Passover meal, would surely have been mentioned. In addition, if we assume that early Christians imitated the last supper, there are *no* accounts of any early Christians *ever* celebrating the Eucharist using lamb (which an imitation of the Last Supper would require, if lamb was really eaten). If this is a Passover, then it is a vegetarian Passover; and if a vegetarian Passover, this striking deviation from Jewish custom argues strongly *for* a vegetarian Jesus rather than against.

What about the depiction in the canonical gospels of Jesus serving and in one instance (after the resurrection) eating fish? The most well known instance of his serving fish to others is the feeding of the multitudes with loaves and fishes (Matthew 14:13–21, 15:32–38 and parallels). However, several references to the feeding of the five thousand outside the Bible eliminate fish from the menu. Irenaeus, in his book written in the second century, twice states that Jesus fed the multitude with bread alone (*Against Heresies* 2.22.3, 2.24.4). Arnobius refers to the miracle of the feeding of the 5000 in this way, without mentioning fish (*Against the Heathen* 1.46). Eusebius also refers to this miracle without mentioning fish (*Proof of the Gospel* 3.4). Thus three ancient authors, in four different places, refer to the feeding of the multitude by referring to bread only and conspicuously omitting fish. Indeed, even in the gospels,

Jesus refers back to this incident only by mentioning the bread, not fish: "Do you not remember the five loaves of the five thousand . . . or the seven loaves of the four thousand?" (Matthew 16:9–10, Mark 8:18–20).

The repeated mention of this story by several diverse church fathers (and even by Jesus himself) *without* fish strongly suggests that the original tradition did not include fish as recorded in our canonical gospels. The bread is everywhere remembered, but the fish is omitted on numerous occasions. Most likely, later redactors added fish to the story when only bread was recorded in the original tradition, but forgot to also insert fish in the passages where Jesus refers back to the miraculous feeding of the multitudes.

The incident in which Jesus is said to have eaten fish or fed fish to his disciples after his resurrection is recorded in Luke and John. In neither case is it *unambiguously* stated that Jesus actually *ate* fish. In both cases, these incidents betray obvious evidence of an original text being tampered with—overlaid with "fish stories." In John, Jesus instructs the disciples to cast their nets to starboard, and they do so, to find that they have caught so many fish they cannot haul the catch on board. Jesus then distributes bread and fish to the disciples—though he does not actually eat the fish himself (John 21:4–13).

Luke seems to state outright that Jesus ate fish after his resurrection: Luke 24:42–43 states that the disciples offer Jesus a piece of fish, which he ate before their eyes. The translation of this passage is, however, disputed. The King James version of these verses mentions a honeycomb as well as fish:

> And they gave him [Jesus] a piece of broiled fish, *and of an honeycomb*. And he took *it* and did eat before them. (Luke 24:42–43; emphasis added)

In this case, the King James version actually represents the *majority* of ancient Greek texts, which include the reference to the honeycomb. In translating this passage, most modern translations omit the reference to the honeycomb, arguing that its appearance in the Greek texts is most likely an insertion, relying on a minority of other texts to represent the original Luke.[4] The modern translators may be right: the "honeycomb" reference may in fact be deliberately inserted, and possibly just to deflect the criticism that Jesus actually ate fish. But if this is the case, then we have to ask: What caused a majority of ancient texts to have this text inserted? Isn't it likely that this insertion—if it is an insertion—is evidence of a significant belief that rejected the notion that Jesus ate fish? And, of course, if it is not an insertion, where does this leave the account of our story? Either way, doubt exists about the validity of the account that Jesus ate fish. This verse is sometimes cited to bolster fundamentalist disbelief that Jesus was a vegetarian, but clearly a fundamentalist who accepts the King James version of the Bible can consistently say that Jesus *was* a vegetarian.

From a historical point of view, it is hard to take these stories seriously as evidence about Jesus' diet. All the resurrection stories are latecomers in the overall narrative and the most subject to later elaboration. Why should not such a central event in the Christian narrative suffer this kind of fate? The earliest accounts, by general agreement certain versions of Mark, end the Easter story with the shock of the discovery of an empty tomb, at Mark 16:8, omitting verses 9–20. There is no appearance to Mary Magdalene, no conversation with the disciples, much less any leisurely philosophical dialogue by the lake.

Moreover, these verses in Luke serve an obvious polemical purpose when viewed in the light of early Christianity, besides that of combating the heresy of vegetarianism. Most likely, it was penned or edited specifically to refute the idea of the "docetic Christ"—the idea, held by certain gnostics such as Marcion, that Jesus had no real body, being merely a spirit or a ghost. Much of Luke 24 is spent combating precisely these doctrines. Jesus challenges the disciples to touch him; when they still do not believe, *only then* does he consume the fish (or the honeycomb). The eating of food, that is, is a specific demonstration by Jesus that he is not a ghost: "No ghost has flesh and bones as you can see that I have" (Luke 24:39). This sounds like a story very much directed towards the concerns of an era nearly a century after Jesus. Marcion in fact used a version of Luke as his own gospel, and the insertion of this story may have been the "remembering" of an event that may have not appeared in Luke until after the mid-second century.

There is a final consideration. The Greek word for fish, "Ichthus," was an acronym whose initials (in Greek) stood for "Jesus Christ, Son of God, Savior." Because of this, fish became one of the favorite mystical symbols among the Greek-speaking gentile Christians. A bishop of the early church wrote of fish symbolically in writing his own epitaph: "Faith has provided as my food a fish of exceeding great size, and perfect, which a holy virgin drew with her own hands from a fountain."[5] Similarly Tertullian says: "We little fish, after the image of our Ichthus (fish) Jesus Christ, are born in the water" (*On Baptism* 1). "Fish" is a symbolic term for Jesus, a symbol that would only make sense in the Greek world.

In this context, it is easy to imagine someone saying that faith has provided us with "fish" as a holy food, as the early bishop did in his own epitaph, and such statements could easily lead to others that Jesus provided fish or even ate it himself. It is possible that the "fish" stories in the New Testament were never intended to be literal descriptions of the truth, but symbolic descriptions from the beginning; or that they were derived from symbolic stories and then misinterpreted in a literal way. But this whole literary excursion would not make sense in Aramaic or Hebrew or to any of the first followers of Jesus.

I believe that these stories were later additions to the gospel accounts, and not present in the original tradition. I find both motive (the desire to refute vegetarianism and Marcionite gnosticism at the same time) and opportunity (the widespread use of "fish" in gentile Christianity as a symbolic term) for this addition; we have the historical lateness of all the accounts including fish as an item Jesus served or ate; and we have the absence of fish in early accounts of the same events.

There are other scattered references to Jesus approving of sacrifices, approving of meat-eating, or telling parables involving meat.

- There are several descriptions of Jesus or his family either offering or suggesting animal sacrifice. We may seriously doubt that Jesus' family offered two young pigeons at the Temple as purification after his birth (Luke 2:22), or that Jesus commanded a leper he had healed to make an animal sacrifice that Moses commanded (Mark 1:44). As I have argued, no one in Galilee was that much concerned with ritual purity, and it is highly unlikely that Jesus or an orthodox Galilean family would be preoccupied with such matters.

- Similarly, the passage that urges one not to offer one's gift at the altar before becoming reconciled with one's brother (Matthew 5:23–24) may or may not be a later insertion referring to a Christian altar (rather than the Jewish temple altar), but in any case does not recommend the sacrifice of animals.

- There are several parables in which meat-eating or killing animals play an incidental role: for example, the parable of the prodigal son, in which the fatted calf is killed (mentioned only at Luke 15:11–32), Jesus sending demons into some pigs, who rush into the sea and drown (Matthew 8:28–33), and the parable of the wedding feast in which oxen and fat calves are killed (Matthew 22:1–14). The wedding feast has two versions; the version in Luke (at 14:16–24) conspicuously omits the oxen and the fat calves from the banquet description. In any event, the wedding feast appears to portray the invitation of non-Jews to join the Jesus movement, and thus be a response to a situation that historically only became an issue years after Jesus had left the earth—and thus not from the historical Jesus.

- Epiphanius, in arguing against the Ebionites, cites the passage "the Son of Man came eating and drinking," in contrast to John the Baptist, who did neither (Luke 7:33–34, Matthew 11:18–19), as signifying that Jesus ate meat. However, this is evidently not a dispute over meat-eating, but rather over fasting—as all the synoptics relate a dispute between the disciples of Jesus and the disciples of John over fasting (Matthew 9:14, Mark 2:18, Luke 5:33).

None of these competing traditions offer a significant rebuttal to the argument that the Ebionites best understood Jesus. Of course, there were competing traditions; that's why early Christian history is so messy. But they all reflect later patterns and events. In one case—the Last Supper—a close reading of the text actually argues in favor of a vegetarian Jesus, since why else would Jesus have failed to eat lamb at Passover?

Vegetarianism and Compassion for Animals in Early Christianity

In Jewish scriptures such as Exodus 23:5, Deuteronomy 22:4, and others, there is clear reason to be compassionate to animals. One might assume that the position of animals within modern Christianity could not be worse than in Judaism, since modern Christianity incorporates these texts into their scripture. Instead, the position of animals actually deteriorates. In the first place, vegetarianism for ethical reasons becomes quite difficult, since most of the orthodox writers believe that Jesus ate meat and invited others to eat meat.[6] To say that it is wrong to eat meat, therefore, condemns Jesus himself (in this orthodox viewpoint). Worse still, throughout most of its history (beginning with Augustine), the Christian church has held the position that we have no obligations to animals *whatsoever*. This is the teaching of Augustine in the fifth century and Aquinas in the thirteenth. This is a radical alteration of the position of rabbinic Judaism. Even the typical meat-eating Jew believes that animals are entitled to *some* consideration: they must be rested on the sabbath, oxen must not be muzzled while treading the corn, and one must take steps to relieve their suffering.

This is a critical issue for vegetarians and Christians. If Christianity is tied to the views of Augustine and Aquinas, and maintains the picture of a meat-eating Jesus, then it is much more difficult to find a place for ethical vegetarianism within Christianity. A Christian could become a vegetarian for health reasons; but it would be much more problematic to practice or advocate ethical vegetarianism based on our obligations not to kill or cause suffering to animals, because this would seemingly condemn a meat-eating Jesus. Likewise, many ethical vegetarians would conclude that since the son of God is a meat-eater, Christianity is incompatible with their beliefs and that they have an obligation not only not to become Christians, but to actively oppose Christianity. This, unfortunately, is what we sometimes see happening in the vegetarian and animal rights movements today.

The "orthodox" response to vegetarianism has been somewhat contradictory since the Council of Nicaea. The objection to meat consumption and the killing of animals has been taken as evidence of heresy when Christians have been faced with outsiders. When the Catholics attacked the Albigensian heresy in the middle ages, they would give suspected heretics some animals to kill, and if the suspects refused, they were determined to be heretics.[7]

This rejection of vegetarianism goes hand in hand, however, with a peculiar Christian embrace of vegetarianism—an embrace that is unmistakable and difficult to explain if the "orthodox" rejection of vegetarianism were really the original tradition. Vegetarianism met with a kinder reception among early Christian leaders and the monastic communities. Indeed, a list of those described as vegetarians reads very much like a Who's Who in the early church: Peter (*Recognitions* 7.6, *Homilies* 12.6), James (Eusebius, *Ecclesiastical History* 2.23), Matthew (Clement of Alexandria, *The Instructor* 2.1), and all the apostles (Eusebius, *Proof of the Gospel* 3.5). Clement of Alexandria, Origen, Basil, Gregory of Nanziance, Arnobius, Cassian, the Desert Fathers, Paul (the Hermit), Antony, Hilarion, Macharius, Columbanus, Arsenius, John Chrysostom, Jerome, and Tertullian were all probably vegetarians, based on writings by or about them. Many of these writers (such as Origen) concede that Christians are not required to abstain from meat, but they themselves are evidently vegetarian and can be counted on to say a few kind words about vegetarianism (see Origen, *Against Celsus* 8.28, 8.29).

This was not just the position of intellectuals. Augustine, while strongly arguing against any requirement that Christians be vegetarians, comments that the number of Christians who abstain both from flesh and wine are "without number"[8] —indicating a widespread acceptance of vegetarianism among ordinary Christians even as late as the fourth century. Eusebius recounts the story of a Christian martyr, a woman who initially denies under torture that she is a Christian. But when she is encouraged to make incriminating statements about the Christians, for example that they eat their own children, she reverses herself:

> But she recovered herself under the suffering, and . . . contradicted the blasphemers. "How," she said, "could those eat children who do not think it lawful to taste the blood even of irrational animals?" And thenceforward she confessed herself a Christian . . . (*Ecclesiastical History* 5.1.26)

In this case the response to the charge that Christians eat children is that Christians do not even eat the blood of animals. Now it is unlikely that this woman, under torture, was referring merely to not eating the blood of an animal, but accepting the flesh drained of blood—in this case, it is not a very good argument against the charge that Christians eat their children and this bit of theology is not likely to be the last words of a Christian martyr. The conclusion is inescapable that *she understands Christian nonviolence to include animals as well as humans*: Christians would not eat their own children, for they do not even eat animals.

Among the monastics, an impressive list of orders that restricted or eliminated meat consumption can be composed: ethical reasons for vegetarianism were eliminated, but health concerns were admitted as legitimate. Both Cassian and Jerome, early monastic leaders, recommended a vegetarian diet for their monks, and a number of rules favored vegetarianism: the rules of Benedict, Columbanus, Caesarius of Arles, Aurelian of Arles, the Carthusians, the Premonstratensians, the Grandmontines, the Cistercians, the Carmelites, and the Dominicans all either sharply restricted or completely prohibited the consumption of meat.[9] Vegetarianism sometimes was adopted by heretical Christian gnosticism. The Manicheans whom Augustine attacked with such vigor were vegetarians, as were the Bogomils, a neo-Manichean sect of the Middle Ages. The Cathars, who also flourished in the middle ages, advocated vegetarianism for those who reached the highest level within their religion.

While the church rejected the requirement for vegetarianism, it is indisputable that there were very large numbers of vegetarians in early Christianity. In fact, there are hardly any references to *any* early Christians eating meat. The view that Jesus ate meat creates a paradox: vegetarianism was practiced by the apostles and numerous early followers of Jesus, including Jesus' own brother, but not by Jesus himself! It is as if everyone in the early church understood the message except the messenger. The much more likely explanation is that the original tradition was vegetarian, but that under the pressure of expediency and the popularity of Paul's writings in the second century, vegetarianism was first dropped as a requirement and finally even as a desideratum.

Conclusions

The incident in the temple is the crucible in which the message of Jesus rests. The synoptic gospel accounts place the incident in the temple at the beginning of the quick succession of events that lead to his death. The accounts clearly identify his opponents as the leaders of the temple cult—the priests. The history of Jewish Christianity suggests an obvious hypothesis: Jesus opposed the temple sacrificial cult and his vegetarianism provided the moral basis for this opposition.

This point was resisted by the victorious party in early Christianity and competing traditions in the New Testament are clearly present. I believe that we can trace these competing traditions to the events following Jesus' death—the controversy over Paul, the struggle against gnosticism, and other events.

What these competing traditions all lack is a coherent explanation of why Jesus was killed. "Jesus was chasing the dishonest moneychangers out of the temple": the weakness of this theory is immediately apparent to anyone who has read the New Testament, where the conflict between the temple hierarchy and the Jesus movement is obvious. Yet scholars and religious leaders have not been able to provide a more convincing explanation. I seek to offer a coherent explanation not only as to what Jesus died for, but also for how his teaching was subsequently lost.

Part III
THE DISINTEGRATION
OF THE JESUS MOVEMENT

THE SPLIT IN THE EARLY CHURCH

10

THE CONFLICT BETWEEN PAUL AND JEWISH CHRISTIANITY

I N THE BEGINNING, THE FOLLOWERS OF JESUS WERE A single community. Acts states that after Jesus' departure from the earth, the believers were of "one heart and soul," even to the point of holding all their property in common (4:32). One of the most important of the mobilizing factors in the earliest church was the conviction that God had raised Jesus from the dead.

Ironically, the very force that propelled the followers of Jesus outward also split them into opposing groups. Soon, there were different visions of Jesus, and different interpretations of his message. With no living arbiter of Jesus-claims, the church was beset with factions—its existence suddenly split, with no clear authoritative voice to speak for all and to unify them.

Pentecost

All the gospels agree that Jesus was raised from the dead; but what precisely happened to bring this conviction to the primitive church? This is one of the hottest topics in the history of Christianity, a topic overlaid not only with countless layers of interpretation but also with a myriad of Christian expectations. Entire books have been written on the resurrection and it is impossible even to mention, much less to resolve, all the issues surrounding it. We can, however, safely say a few things.

A number of problems exist with the accounts of the resurrection. The earliest gospel account, by general consensus in some of the early manuscripts of Mark, ends with the shock of the discovery of the empty tomb (at Mark 16:8), with the rest of Mark 16 found only in later manuscripts. The gospel accounts are often contradictory. Mark indicates that after Jesus' ascension into heaven, the disciples immediately start preaching; but in Luke, they are ordered to wait for the holy spirit. In Matthew, Jesus appears to the disciples in Galilee; in Luke, Jesus appears in Jerusalem. Some of the descriptions of the resurrection are almost certainly later additions—for example John 21, which is patently "tacked on" to the rest of John, and the parts of Luke 24 that emphasize the physical nature of Jesus' appearance to the disciples, which are likely an addition (or a convenient memory) to combat the gnostic heresy that Jesus did not have a body.

The earliest account we have, and the only one by a contemporary who claimed to have seen the risen Jesus, is that of Paul. Paul states that Jesus appeared after his death to Cephas (Peter), the twelve, to more than five hundred at one time, to James, then to all the apostles, and finally to Paul himself (I Corinthians 15:3–8). Paul places his own vision of Jesus on a roughly equal basis (though later in time) with the appearance of Jesus to the others.

It is clear that *something* quite extraordinary happened. However, it staggers the imagination that any appearance of the risen Jesus could have been kept a secret for more than fifteen minutes by even the most fearful of disciples. Yet it was only *after* Pentecost that the Jesus community (now without Jesus) is impelled to take its message into the world. It is hard to resist the conclusion that the pivotal revelation was that at Pentecost—even though, by the account in Acts, the risen Jesus did not appear at Pentecost, having at this point already ascended into heaven. It is likely that Pentecost was really the appearance of Jesus to over five hundred mentioned by Paul.[1] Whether a vision, an appearance, or the "rush of a mighty wind," or "tongues of fire," or anything else— this was the moving force behind the energy in the primitive church. It gave the community the conviction that God had raised Jesus up and that he lived after his crucifixion.

The Jewish Christians accepted the reality of the risen Jesus. The *Recognitions* and the *Homilies* refer to it as a matter of fact, and Epiphanius would surely have mentioned any denial of the resurrection. It is also apparent in the first proclamation of the Christian message by Peter in Acts, which has a distinctive Jewish Christian flavor to it. Peter announces that God has raised Jesus up (Acts 3:22–26) and connects this with the prophecy of Moses that God would "raise up" a prophet, quoting the favorite Jewish Christian prophecy that Jesus would be the "true prophet" (Deuteronomy 18:15, quoted at Acts 3:22).

However, these appearances created an energy which could not be controlled. It propelled the primitive church outward, but also created serious divisions. For one of these visions was given to Paul, who took the message to a different audience and gave it a considerably different theological twist than that of the Jerusalem church.

The Letters and Beliefs of Paul

Paul's letters are moving documents for many Christians. They make an impression today on us and on anyone raised as a Christian who seeks to make sense out of the religion they have come to know. They also made a deep impression on those who read them in early Christianity. And they created a split in the early church the consequences of which we live with even today.

No one can read the synoptic gospels and the letters of Paul with an open mind without becoming aware of great differences in their pictures of Jesus. This is a point almost immediately apparent to modern Jews, though modern Christians, conditioned for centuries to a harmonizing theology that encompasses both the gospels and Paul's letters, usually have a more difficult time. For Paul, Jesus is the son of God raised from the dead as a sign of God's grace; faith in Jesus replaces the law of Judaism and transforms us into spiritual beings. For the synoptic gospels, Jesus is a miracle-worker and preacher urging the people to change their lives; living in accordance with the true law is the path to life.

Paul was a diligent and energetic missionary and, above all, an excellent writer. His style, rather than being logical, precise, and pedantic, is suggestive, rhetorical, and charismatic. The letters of Paul are the primary evidence we have for who and what Paul was. While this book is not an exposition of Paul's letters, some general things can be safely said about Paul's message.

1. Christ is the Savior and the means to salvation. "Christ died for our sins" (I Corinthians 15:3), as an atonement or payment for our sins (Romans 3:25), and then was raised so that all might live (I Corinthians 15:22). For Paul it is not Jesus' resurrection that brings us atonement, but his *death*. Jesus' death is very much like that of the sacrificed animals in traditional Jewish Temple worship: Jesus, in being killed, enabled us to achieve salvation. For Paul, Christ was designed by God to be the means of forgiveness of sins through his sacrificial death.

2. The law as a means to salvation is superseded by Jesus. "Before faith came, we were confined under the law," and the law was our custodian; but with Jesus, we no longer are under a custodian (Galatians 3:23–26). This does not mean that the law is invalid (Romans 3:31)—it does bring consciousness of sin (Romans 3:20)—but it does mean that we are not "justified" before God on the basis of the law. We are "discharged from the law," so that "we serve not under the old written code but in the new life of the Spirit" (Romans 7:6).

Here we have the most obvious contrast between Paul on the one hand and the synoptic gospels and the Jewish Christians on the other. In the first place, Jesus clearly expects his followers to keep the law, and complains because the Pharisees and scribes are rendering this law invalid. In the second place, there is the equation between the law and the "old written code"—an equation the Ebionites clearly would dispute, since they *attack* the written code but *defend* the law. The key element of Jewish Christian belief that made them "Jewish" was the binding acceptance of the law revealed to Moses; Paul, while he was at one time a Jew, rejects this premise and is, therefore, not part of Jewish Christianity.

3. Our natural material state is one of separation from God. We are prisoners of the flesh, the material world, and of demonic powers that seek to control us. In our "natural" state (in the flesh), we are sinners: "I can will what is right, but I cannot do it" (Romans 7:18); "I delight in the law of God, in my inmost self, but I see in my members another law at war with the law of my mind and making me captive to the law of sin which dwells in my members" (Romans 7:22–23). In order to find life, we must "put to death" all the base pursuits of the body (Romans 8:13).

We see in these passages the desperate condition of humanity, part of our created being, which in turn is the basis for the doctrine of "original sin." Paul also believes in the presence of supernatural and evil powers hoping to hold us in this condition, "the prince of the power of the air" (Ephesians 2:2), or Satan (e. g. II Corinthians 2:11, 11:14).

Apologists for Paul may argue that these themes do not contradict the synoptic gospels; but at the very least they present *very* different themes. Jesus' language does not suggest that he is to replace the law, and indeed he openly contradicts this idea. There are isolated passages where Jesus refers to his own death as an atonement (Matthew 26:28), but it is not a major theme. Jesus nowhere attaches a metaphysical quality to human error, and does not suggest (as does Paul) any concept of "original sin."

Paul makes a number of disturbing statements often quoted to justify the repression of women and slaves that contrast with the social egalitarianism evident in the words ascribed to and behavior of Jesus. Women should keep silent in church, should keep their heads covered, and obey their husbands; "wives, be subject to your husbands," says Paul, and follows this up with "slaves, be obedient to those who are your earthly masters"—two infamous statements that haunt Christianity to the present day (I Corinthians 11:3–16, 14:34–35, Ephesians 5:22, 6:5, Colossians 3:18–22). This is somewhat counterbalanced by that marvelous aphorism in Galatians 3:28: "There is neither Jew nor Greek, there is neither slave nor free, there is neither male nor female; for you are all one in Christ Jesus." Even given this, though, we have a significant contrast between the social egalitarianism of the synoptic gospels and Paul's concern to maintain precisely the social distinctions that Jesus apparently felt were unimportant.

Equally interesting is what Paul does *not* say, or says with a substantially muted tone. Gospel themes do not always make it into Paul's letters. Paul seemingly accepts, though he hardly dwells on, the principle of nonviolence and loving one's enemies, trusting in God to take any revenge necessary. "Never avenge yourselves, but leave it to the wrath of God," says Paul (Romans 12:19). This passage only asks the believer to renounce *acts* of vengeance, not the *hope* that vengeance will someday be taken—in contrast to the plea of the Sermon on the Mount that we should abandon anger as well as the acts that flow from anger. Paul does not discuss at any length the idea of nonattachment to material possessions, which is such a prominent feature of the synoptic gospels, though he does refer to "the contribution for the poor among the saints at Jerusalem" (Romans 15:26). He does say that we should not conform to the world (Romans 12:2), but this does not occur in a context of the rewards of righteous conduct in *this* world, but in a context of the rejection of *everything* in the world, including our own bodies, which we are to present as a living sacrifice (Romans 12:1).

There is an obvious problem here. Paul's emphasis and agenda is in a much different place than the program of Jesus in the synoptic gospels. He has introduced ideas that are only very weakly present in the synoptic gospels, while major themes of the synoptic gospels are only weakly present in Paul's letters. But who was Paul, and were Paul's ideas those of the first Christians?

Paul's Background

The accepted picture of Paul is that presented in Acts. Paul was born Saul, a Jew of Tarsus, and became a Pharisee. He was a persecutor of the church but then had a vision of Jesus on the road to Damascus where he had been intent on continuing his persecutions. After this vision, he converted to Christianity, changed his name to Paul, and became a devoted and effective missionary. He took the Christian message to the gentiles, just as the other apostles took this message to the Jews. He encountered some opposition from Jews who insisted that the new converts had to become full Jews as well as accept Jesus; but this was resolved when it was decided that this was not necessary. He was arrested on his third trip to Jerusalem, and appealed to Caesar as a Roman citizen. He was taken to Rome as a prisoner when Acts ends, though non-Biblical tradition has it that he became a martyr at Rome.

The account in Acts, however, differs both from the account in Paul's own letters and with the picture the Jewish Christians have of him. Specifically, Paul's letters show a *much* more abrasive relationship between Paul and other Christians than does Acts. Furthermore, the Ebionite picture of Paul also raises plausible questions about Paul and his relationship with the early church.

In Acts, Paul speaks Hebrew, is born a Jew and educated as a Pharisee (22:2–3, 26:4–5). Paul's being born a Jew and being a Pharisee is affirmed at only one point in the letters (Philippians 3:5). However, there are several problems with this view, which underscore an important fact: Paul's background was quite different from that of Jesus and that of primitive Christianity.

It can be seriously contested whether Paul knew Hebrew. When in his letters Paul quotes from the Old Testament, it is only possible to tell if he is using the Septuagint (the Greek version of the Old Testament) or the Hebrew Old Testament when the Septuagint and the Hebrew Old Testament are known to differ; and in each such case Paul uses the Greek of the Septuagint.[2] Why would Paul do this if he could speak Hebrew?

Paul's quotations from the Old Testament are fairly irrelevant anyway. Paul demonstrates a casual and rhetorical approach to the law, quoting texts out of context and giving idiosyncratic interpretations to illustrate his point. To give an example:

Now it is evident that no man is justified before God by the law; for "He who through faith is righteous shall live" [Habakkuk 2:4]; but the law does not rest on faith, for "he who does them

[the commands of the law] shall live by them" [Leviticus 18:5].
(Galatians 3:11–12)

Paul is using an Old Testament passage from Habakkuk to "prove"
that those who are righteous through their faith will live. But it is highly
doubtful that Habakkuk had the Pauline idea of justification through
faith. Habakkuk is not referring to "faith" but "faithfulness" or "being
faithful." Thus what Habakkuk is really talking about is more akin to
"loyalty"—indeed, probably loyalty to the law that Paul repudiates—
than to faith in God. This kind of treatment of the Old Testament is
typical of Paul's way of proceeding.

Paul's association with the Pharisees before his conversion is also
suspect. In Acts, Paul's persecution of the Christians is directed not by
the Pharisees, but by the high priest—an ally of the *Sadducees* (Acts
5:17–18). It is the high priest who accuses Stephen at his trial (Acts 7:1)
and the high priest who gives Paul his mission to persecute the
Christians in Damascus (Acts 9:1–2).

In fact, the Pharisees come out looking pretty good in Acts. It is the
Pharisee Gamaliel who urges toleration of the Christians (Acts 5:33–39)
and there are even some Christian Pharisees (Acts 15:5). There is no
account either in the synoptic gospels or in Acts of any deadly conflict
between the Christians and the Pharisees; it is the Sadducees and priests
who want Jesus killed. For all practical political purposes, therefore,
Paul is a Sadducee. If Paul was also a Pharisee (asserted at Philippians
3:5, Acts 23:6, Acts 26:5), perhaps he was an unusually conservative
Pharisee or was in that party largely by self-declaration rather than
because of any actual Pharasaic allies or ideology.

Acts tries to reconcile this situation by making all the disciples
equally "Jewish." Paul goes to the temple to keep a vow (Acts 21:26); the
disciples daily attend the temple together (Acts 2:46). Peter is wrapped
up in the laws about clean and unclean animals, and God needs to send
a vision to Peter to show him the path to not taking the Jewish
distinctions so seriously (Acts 10:9–23). These incidents, like the
statements that Paul was a Hebrew-speaking Pharisee who obediently

did what the Jerusalem church requested, sound very much like later gentile retrojections of what the early Christians, as Jews, "must have been" concerned with, rather than accounts of the early church. The gentile author or editor of Acts deals with the only Jews he knows— those who speak of the temple, avoid unclean animals, and are concerned with matters of ritual—and assumes that this was what primitive Christianity was like when it was still Jewish.

Many objective Jewish and Christian scholars believe that Paul's background was quite different from that of Jesus—including Samuel Sandmel,[3] E. P. Sanders,[4] and Geza Vermes.[5] Vermes asks rhetorically: "Is it an exaggeration to suggest that oceans separate Paul's Christian Gospel from the religion of Jesus the Jew?" We are faced with clear-cut differences between Paul and the environment, if not the doctrines, of Jesus. But how did this bring Paul into conflict with the church leadership, and what do these conflicts tell us about what Jesus really taught?

Opposition to Paul

Paul's Jewish Christian opponents contested Paul over at least three specific points: the Jewish law, Paul's claim to be an apostle, and vegetarianism. We see this both from Paul's own letters and from the Ebionite writings. While the Ebionites probably did not emerge as a distinct group until after the destruction of the temple in the year 70 CE, individual Jewish Christians with "Ebionite" views (views which would subsequently be adopted by the Ebionites) clearly existed well before then. Thus, the Ebionite writings and Paul's letters shed light on how some Christians approached these issues over a period of several hundred years.

The Ebionites detested Paul and considered him an apostate from the law. According to them, Paul was not born a Jew at all, but was a *convert* to Judaism. Paul fell in love with a priest's daughter, and it was in order to win the High Priest's favor that Paul (Saul) converted to Judaism and was circumcised. When he still could not marry the priest's daughter, only then did he begin to attack the law (*Panarion* 30.16.8–9).

Whether this story is true or not can be debated; though it must be said that if the Ebionites were fabricating a story to attack Paul's character, they would have done much better to fabricate a story about Paul's behavior *after* his conversion rather than before, when even by his own admission Paul was a terrible sinner. It agrees with the general picture we have drawn above of Paul as a Greek Jew more comfortable in a Hellenistic than a Palestinian world milieu.

Who more accurately reflected Jesus' own attitude toward the law—the Jewish Christians or Paul? In Galatians, Paul contends against "judaizers" who evidently think the law is still to be followed. But in the synoptic gospels, Jesus acts and talks as if the law *were* still valid. On the question of loyalty to the law, the "judaizers" appear to be closer to the Jesus of the synoptic gospels than Paul is. Thus, we can date this conflict over the law as an internal conflict in the early church, and the Ebionites can, on at least this point, claim as their spiritual ancestors many of those in apostolic times and even Jesus himself.

The second point of contention between the Ebionites and Paul was the latter's claim to be an apostle. "Am I not an apostle?" he protests (I Corinthians 9:1), emphasizing that he was called by God, not by humans (Galatians 1:1). Paul does not say in his letters who was questioning his claim to be an apostle. But the Ebionites contested this point vigorously. In the Clementine *Recognitions* and *Homilies* we see Peter debating his archenemy, the heretic Simon Magus. Simon justifies his views on the basis of visions he has had of Jesus. Peter counters that these visions cannot possibly be as authoritative as the teachings of Jesus Christ while he was on earth in the flesh, which he received from Jesus in person (*Homilies* 17.13–19). This is exactly the kind of thing the Ebionites would have said about Paul, because Paul squeezes in his claim to apostleship based on his own vision (or visions) of Jesus rather than on personal acquaintance with the earthly Jesus before his death (I Corinthians 9:1, 15:3–9). This was likely the Ebionite argument against Paul's claim to be an apostle and against all further claims to speak for Jesus on the basis of having "seen" him.

The third point of contention between Paul and the Ebionites was over vegetarianism. We know that the Ebionites were vegetarian and we also know that Paul attacked ethical vegetarianism in his letters (Romans 14, I Corinthians 10:25).

Paul appears to us as a Hellenistic Jew who did not know Hebrew and was out of place in Palestinian Judaism; and, as I have argued, he was allied with the priests and the Sadducees and not the Pharisees. The Ebionite portrayal of Paul as a Greek proselyte to Judaism is more plausible than the words that Acts puts in Paul's mouth about Paul being a Hebrew-speaking Pharisee. Moreover, if Paul was associated with the Sadducees and the priests, that would mesh with what we know of the opposition to Jesus.

Secondly, Paul's letters make it clear that some very early Christians held Ebionite views that the church later condemned as heretical. Paul's letters give evidence that some of his Christian opponents held that loyalty to the law was still valid; that some of his Christian opponents disputed his claim to be an apostle; and that some of his Christian opponents were vegetarians. The Ebionites held the law to be valid, disputed Paul's claim to be an apostle, and were vegetarians. This is incontrovertible evidence that the "Ebionites" (or those with views that would subsequently be adopted by the Ebionites) were thriving in apostolic times.

Confrontation at Antioch

The most celebrated dispute between Paul and others in the early church is the confrontation at Antioch. Galatians 2 gives Paul's version of this dispute. Peter at first ate with everyone in Antioch but, after "certain men came from James," he withdrew from table fellowship and ate apart from them. Paul confronted Peter and angrily denounced him to his face. Paul was not merely contending with nameless "judaizers" in the early church, but, startlingly enough, *with the leadership itself*: Cephas (Peter), James (the brother of Jesus), and John; the three of whom were "reputed to be pillars" of the early church. On the other side were Paul and Barnabas and the leadership of the Gentile churches. While Paul rails against Peter (Cephas), he is especially bitter about the "men from James" whose role seems to be to bring the wavering Peter in line. It must have been a united front against Paul, because he complains that "the other Jewish Christians showed the same lack of principle; even Barnabas was carried away" (Galatians 2:13).

Scholars have pointed out serious discrepancies between the accounts in Galatians and those in Acts. (Some, in fact, have suggested that they must be the account of two separate events altogether.) In Galatians, Titus is not compelled to be circumcised (2:3); in Acts, Paul circumcises Timothy (16:3). Now this is not an absolute contradiction—it is possible that Paul did circumcise Timothy, but that Titus was not compelled to be circumcised. Nevertheless, the difference between one picture of Paul indignantly refusing an act of judaization on principle, versus an agreeable, compliant Paul going along with the church leadership to maintain accord is significant.

In Galatians, Paul asserts that the law does not need to be observed (Galatians 2:16, 5:2), and even that it is wrong to observe it: "all who rely on works of the law are under a curse" (Galatians 3:10). In Acts, by contrast, he goes to the temple to spend seven days there in fulfillment of a vow (21:21–26)! In Galatians, Paul goes to Jerusalem after a revelation (2:2); in Acts, he goes to Jerusalem because he has been appointed by the local church officials (15:2). The contrast could not be greater. In Galatians, we deal with Paul the apostle from God, not men, standing alone against James, Peter, John, and Barnabas; in Acts we deal with Paul, the agreeable church brother without a trace of an attitude problem.

Which view is correct? Estimates of the date of the writing of Acts vary widely, from the mid-60s to the middle of the second century; but no one pretends that Acts was written before Paul's letters.[6] On the other hand, Galatians was written by a contemporary observer who actually participated in the events described. The image of conflict in Galatians has to be more accurate than the portrait in Acts many decades later of a church in harmony and resolving disputes in a spirit of concord.

Even the writer of Acts admits that there was "no small dissension and debate" (15:2). Was the issue at Antioch circumcision? In Galatians, it would appear not; Paul treats it as a settled issue that circumcision was not required of gentiles (2:1–4). Paul makes it clear that the church leadership had not made an issue of circumcising Titus, and that this was "urged only as a concession to certain sham-Christians" (Galatians 2:4, New English Bible).

If circumcision was a concession, then what was the real issue? Undoubtedly, circumcision had probably been an issue at some point, and Paul (sensing this was a conflict he could win) certainly wanted to pose the question in this light. But the precipitating event in Galatians was the withdrawal of Peter from table fellowship, and the real issue was *food*. There was in fact no Jewish law that prohibited Jews from associating or eating with Gentiles if the other food laws were met[7]; consequently, this was not an issue relating to Jewish practice as such. The problem was the *Christian* interpretation of the law of Moses, which was in this case *stricter* than normal Jewish practice relating to food. Acts 15 as a whole supports this view: the Christian Pharisees first raise the issue of circumcision, but when James pronounces the decision of the apostolic council, three of the four items relating to the matters of the law that all must abide by concern food. Moreover, what is more likely to have precipitated Peter's withdrawal from table fellowship—the marginal issue of circumcision or the issue of food? Obviously the food issue has everything to do with where Peter was eating and with whom.

Most interpreters have blandly assumed that the problem was that the Jewish Christians were insisting that kosher laws be observed. However, this view is *completely* without support in Paul's letters. *Nowhere* in Paul's letters does he attack the kosher laws as we commonly understand them (e. g. prohibition on pork, not mixing milk and meat). What he does attack is vegetarianism and the prohibition of eating meat sacrificed to pagan idols. Both of these merit comment.

> As for the man who is weak in faith, welcome him, but not for
> disputes over opinions. One believes he may eat anything, while

the weak man eats only vegetables. . . . Do not, for the sake of food, destroy the work of God. Everything is indeed clean, but it is wrong for any one to make others fall by what he eats; it is right not to eat meat or drink wine or do anything that makes your brother stumble. (Romans 14:1–2, 19–21)

Paul refers to how "clean" food is, which might be taken to refer to the kosher regulations; but in the same breath he speaks of *abstaining from meat and wine*; the "purity" alluded to pertains to vegetarianism rather than the kosher regulations as we understand them today. What is wrong is offending a fellow Christian who sincerely believes in vegetarianism; we should not place stumbling blocks in front of those who are weaker in the faith. Thus, "it is right not to eat meat or drink wine," if by our example we can avoid offending the "weak" vegetarians.

Paul rejects the idea that we have obligations towards animals. In an unrelated section in which Paul is arguing in favor of being able to earn a living, he comments on the Old Testament passage, "you shall not muzzle an ox while it is treading out the grain" (Deuteronomy 25:4). His question is: "Does God care for oxen?" (I Corinthians 9:9) Paul's answer: of course not! This is about as far as Paul goes on the subject of animals. The Jewish sages interpreted the saying about not muzzling the ox that treads the corn in just the way that Paul ridicules—as a commandment enjoining kindness to animals. Once again, we see the conflict between Paul's idiosyncratic interpretation of the Old Testament and that of the Pharisees—as well as Jesus' sayings about animals that assume precisely that God *does* care for oxen, and for sheep and sparrows, as well (Luke 12:6–7, 14:5, Matthew 12:11).

In I Corinthians, Paul deals with the problem of meat sacrificed to pagan idols. Once again, he concludes that there is nothing wrong with eating meat sacrificed to idols, but some who are "weak" do not understand this and will be lost by seeing others eat meat (I Corinthians 8:8–13). As in Romans, Paul pledges vegetarianism rather than offending the "weaker" vegetarian Christians: "I will never eat meat, lest I cause my brother to fall" (I Corinthians 8:13). But there is nothing intrinsically wrong with eating meat sacrificed to idols, or any meat at all—"eat whatever is sold in the meat market without raising any question on the ground of conscience" (I Corinthians 10:25). This sanctifies *all* meat, whether or not it was sacrificed to idols; Paul addresses the specific question about meat sacrificed to idols with a more general rule directed toward all meat.

Nowhere in these references is there the *slightest* evidence of concern for, or disputation with, the Jewish kosher regulations. *On the contrary, the concern is with meat consumption and meat offered to pagan idols.* The kosher regulations say nothing about meat consumption per se, and the objection to idolatry is much deeper than the kosher regulations. The food issues that are extensively discussed by *both* Paul and the Ebionites are far more explosive: meat consumption and table fellowship with those who eat meat or meat sacrificed to idols. A question of observance of ritual would not precipitate a conflict so divisive as that between Paul and the church leadership. A question of principle, deeply felt on both sides, would be required. It is these issues that likely initiated the confrontation at Antioch.

The Apostolic Council

We come finally to the verdict of the Apostolic council in Acts 15. Paul *never invokes the outcome of the meeting in Jerusalem in his disputes over food with other early Christians.* We are, therefore, left with three clues as to what the verdict was: (1) the account in Acts, (2) the fact that Paul never invokes it in support, and (3) the Jewish Christian discussion of the issue of table fellowship.

The account in Acts is fairly straightforward. James gives the judgment that the gentiles need to follow the law on only four points:

> . . . to abstain from the pollutions of idols and from unchastity and from what is strangled and from blood. (Acts 15:20)

This is repeated at Acts 15:29 and Acts 21:25. Even though the dispute is supposedly occasioned by the circumcision issue, when James finally gives his decision as head of the church, circumcision is not even mentioned. Instead we get the fourfold prohibition against what is sacrificed to idols (usually meat), blood, things strangled, and fornication.

Each of the three food items merits attention. To begin with, it is important that Paul's assertion that it is acceptable to eat meat sacrificed to pagan idols is *directly* contradicted by the apostolic decree, as well as by two passages in Revelation that attack such meat-eating (2:14, 20).

Commentators have generally been baffled by the prohibition against things strangled (in Greek, *pnitkos*). True, any strangled land animals would not be kosher, but there is no indication in the Old Testament or the Talmud that "strangled" animals were eaten by pagans or constituted any sort of issue; this kind of strangulation was virtually unknown in the ancient world and in ours. One kind of animal, however, that *was* commonly strangled, or denied air, was *fish*. This happened everywhere, is *not* prohibited by kosher regulations, but would be prohibited under a strict vegetarian ethic.

A second possible meaning of the term *pnitkos* is to a method of cooking rather than a method of slaughter. It can refer, that is, to the roasting, baking, or stewing of a piece of meat or cooking in a rich sauce.[8] However, this meaning also has strong vegetarian overtones and has nothing to do with kosher laws as such. The prohibition on *pnitkos* would seem to either directly imply, or recommend strongly, a vegetarian diet.

It is sometimes asserted that the prohibition against blood is a reference to a kosher rule, though if it were, it would concern *consuming* blood. Acts never refers to the prohibition as against eating or drinking blood, but just as against "blood." "Blood" could refer to violence against either humans or animals; and some early Christians thought of blood as referring to violence against *either* humans or animals.[9] The Christians whom Paul discusses in Romans 14 object to meat consumption, and the gospels report numerous pacifist sayings of Jesus. Does blood refer to animal blood, human blood, or both? We can't say for sure, but it is quite possible that it refers *both* to animal and human blood: a general prohibition against any kind of violence. The text of the decree in Acts is ambiguous, but directly contradicts Paul on one point (meat sacrificed to idols), and could be interpreted as contradicting Paul on the question of meat consumption as well.

There is another indication that the apostolic council did not go Paul's way: the fact that Paul never invokes this decree in his support. Most likely, Romans was written between Paul's second and third visits to Jerusalem and after the Jerusalem conference, because he mentions the collection that he is taking to Jerusalem (Romans 15:25, 30–31). Why then does he discuss vegetarianism at such length in Romans 14 without mentioning the Jerusalem conference? If, in fact, the Jerusalem conference as reported in Acts 15 had actually come to the conclusion that Acts proclaims, and these conclusions were given the interpretation they are today given (namely, that they concern certain minimal items of kosher laws), then why does he not invoke the conference decision in his favor? Why does this not definitely settle the "vegetarian" question, albeit with a minimal allegiance to not drinking blood, which shouldn't be too difficult for most Christians to cope with? Why couldn't Paul say: "Even my Jewish Christian opponents admit there is nothing wrong with eating meat as such"?

Arguments from silence can rarely be conclusive, but the simplest explanation for Paul's silence is that the decision of the conference was not in Paul's favor at all. The "minimal requirements" to be placed on the gentiles most likely required an abstinence from *bloodshed*, not merely from eating or drinking blood, and thus an abstinence from eating animals or warfare, as in fact the Ebionites believed. Thus, Paul never invokes the decree in his letters because in fact it did not support his positions. We know that this explanation is true on one point, the case of eating meat sacrificed to pagan idols: the apostolic decree specifically prohibits it, Paul specifically allows it. Paul's failure to refer to the apostolic decision is very much like the celebrated dog observed by Sherlock Holmes who did *not* bark in the middle of the night.

The three prohibitions mentioned by James that pertain to food all have a single tendency: to justify the rejection of meat consumption and the rejection of meat offered to pagan idols. Paul believes there is nothing wrong in principle with the consumption of meat, consumption of meat offered to idols, or table fellowship with those who eat idol meat or any other kind of meat. But what did Jewish Christianity say about these issues?

Sharing Meals in Jewish Christianity

There is a third indication of what the apostolic decree actually meant: the Jewish Christian discussion of "table fellowship," the issue that precipitated the crisis which Galatians describes in the first place.

Jewish Christian literature never specifically refers to the apostolic council, but table fellowship is extensively discussed. The *Recognitions* repeatedly refers to the necessity of being baptized before it is possible to eat at the same table as Christians (1.19, 2.71–72, 7.34, 7.36; see also *Homilies* 13.9, 13.11). This is not a reference to a kosher regulation or to some other Jewish food law, but rather to a *Christian* food law. Peter in the *Recognitions* declines table fellowship even with earnest seekers after the truth, before they have been baptized. There is a remnant of this attitude even in modern Christianity, in the celebration of communion or the Eucharist. This is a symbolic table fellowship only with other believers; it would not make sense to take communion with nonbelievers. The difference is simply one of intensity: for the Jewish Christians, *every* meal was treated like it was a communion meal and therefore to be eaten only with believers; whereas for modern Christians this restriction only applies to the occasional symbolic "meals" of communion or the Eucharist.

The rationale for this insistence on eating only with believers is interesting. The Jewish Christians believed that eating at the "table of devils" was a grave error because this act of eating gave the demons power over you. Demons are powerless over a person until that person becomes their table companion; the demons get power through food (*Homilies* 8.20, 9.9).

The "table of devils" is considered virtually any table with meat on it. Demons enter a person when one eats too much (*Recognitions* 4.16), or when one eats things sacrificed to idols (2.71). Demons are expressly allowed by God to take possession of a person who sheds blood, tastes dead flesh, or eats something cut or strangled (*Homilies* 8.19)—a list that contains two of the three prohibited food items in the decree of the apostolic council, and gives the demons permission to enter anyone who eats meat. God, by contrast, asks us not to eat meat:

> And the things which are well-pleasing to God are these: to pray to Him, to ask from Him, recognizing that He is the giver of all things, and gives with discriminating law; to abstain from the table of devils, not to taste dead flesh, not to touch blood . . . (*Homilies* 7.4)

A bit further down this is repeated, again with a prohibition of meat, along with a repetition of the forbidden items from the apostolic council:

> And this is the service He [God] has appointed: To worship Him only, and trust only in the Prophet of truth, and to be baptized for the remission of sins, and thus by this pure baptism to be born again unto God by saving water; to abstain from the table of devils, that is, from food offered to idols, from dead carcasses, from animals which have been suffocated or caught by wild beasts, and from blood; not to live any longer impurely . . . (*Homilies* 7.8)

Here all three of the food items prohibited by the apostolic council are mentioned explicitly and equated with the "table of devils." The fourth non-food item (fornication) is prohibited implicitly in the injunction not to live "impurely"—and all of this is in the same breath as the prohibition from the table of devils and from "dead carcasses."

The Jewish Christian interpretation would appear extreme even to most modern vegetarians. The Jewish Christians insisted not only that believers eat only at a table that did not contain dead flesh or food sacrificed to idols; they would not eat with anyone who was not already a believer. To draw an analogy, most modern vegetarians would not object to sitting at a table where meat was served, as long as the food they *themselves* ate was vegetarian. Some vegetarians might even refuse to eat at a table where any meat was served. But it is as if a modern vegetarian were not only to refuse to eat at a table where any meat was present—but to refuse to share any meal, even a vegetarian meal, with a nonvegetarian.

The Jewish Christians traced their rejection of any meat, blood, or dead flesh, back to the apostolic decree: the apostles themselves, led by Peter, counseled this very practice. Not only are we to be believers in God and the true prophet, said the Jewish Christians, we are to be vegetarians and refuse to eat with anyone else, except other believing vegetarians. *Every meal is holy* and therefore—like the modern symbolic communion meal of grape juice and crackers—is to be taken only with other believers.

While this position seems extreme to us, it nevertheless explains both the apostolic decree found in Acts (prohibiting blood, animals sacrificed to idols, and things strangled) *and* Peter's refusal of table fellowship that Paul protests so vehemently against in Galatians. In the Jewish Christian literature, we most likely have Peter's response to Paul's condemnation of him in Galatians 2. Perhaps Peter wavered initially before "certain men from James" (Galatians 2:12) came to him; perhaps he reasoned that as long as he ate vegetarian food, he could eat with nonbelievers. The "men from James," however, convinced him otherwise. And what the men from James brought was probably nothing less than the apostolic decree, a decree that outraged Paul and brought his passionate denunciation.

Conclusions

We do not wish to exaggerate the differences between the message of Jesus and Paul. Nevertheless, an objective reader cannot help but notice numerous differences between the message of Jesus given in the synoptics and the Christian message as articulated by Paul. Most conspicuously, the themes of the Sermon on the Mount—nonretaliation, rejection of property and riches, and the obliteration of social and class distinctions in the kingdom of heaven—are either sharply muted or completely absent in Paul. Conversely, the major themes of Paul's letters—salvation through faith, the misery of this physical world, the supersession of the law—are either muted, absent, or actually contradicted by the synoptic gospels. These differences should be understood in the context of the picture that Paul presents of a church sharply divided over the problem of food.

There was an angry dispute in the early church over food, which split the church's greatest missionary (Paul) with the leadership of the mother church, and especially James. Paul's opponents are vegetarians in the leadership of the church who raise a variety of issues in their campaign against meat consumption. The apostolic decree in Acts points more to vegetarianism than to kosher regulations. The Jewish Christians associated the prohibited items in the apostolic decree with the "table of devils" and with meat consumption—and this exactly explains the crisis that Paul writes about in Galatians.

This crisis initiated a split in Christianity with whose consequences we must reckon today. Ultimately, it was the views of Paul on these issues that prevailed, as the Jerusalem church and Jewish Christianity—until then the undisputed leaders of the Jesus movement—would shortly be fatally wounded in the wars between the Jews and Rome; while the gentile Christian churches, to whom Paul preached, would form the basis of the Catholic, Orthodox, and Protestant Christianity of today.

11 FROM CRISIS TO CATASTROPHE

JEWISH CHRISTIANITY UNTIL THE DESTRUCTION OF THE TEMPLE

T HE CONFLICT WITH PAUL WAS CERTAINLY A CRISIS OF the highest order for the Jerusalem church. However, two other crises were shortly to engulf the emerging church: the hostility and persecution of the church by the Jewish authorities and a war of national liberation they could neither join nor entirely escape. These three conflicts destroyed the authority of the Jerusalem church and with it the underpinnings of Jewish Christianity. Jewish Christianity became simply one of numerous different groups, and hardly the most prominent one, among those in early Christianity.

The Martyrdom of Stephen

The conflict between the Jesus movement and the Jewish authorities did not end with the death of Jesus. Both the first chapters of Acts, culminating in the martyrdom of Stephen, and the first chapter of the *Recognitions*, culminating in the attempted murder of James, show a continuing conflict. We may question the historical accuracy of both of these accounts: Was there ever a historical "Stephen," as appears in Acts? Did Paul actually attempt to murder James, as the Recognitions contends? What is striking is not just the stories of these two events, but the similarity of the themes presented in both of them.

These common themes include at least these elements: (1) Jesus is the prophet predicted by Moses; (2) the spirit is poured out on everyone willing to accept it; (3) there is conflict between the followers of Jesus and the priests in the temple. In fact, we do not even have to wait for Acts to get to the story of Stephen before all these themes have already come out. Peter cites the same text in Deuteronomy (18:15–18; at Acts 3:22–23) that the Ebionites use to justify their defense of Jesus as the "true prophet"—one of the most characteristically Jewish Christian views. Moreover, Jesus is "a man attested to you by God with mighty works," whom "God raised up" and "exalted at the right hand of God" (Acts 2:22, 32–33). Jesus' exaltation, therefore, appears as something *subsequent* to his appearance on earth—a straightforwardly "adoptionist" metaphor very similar to the adoptionist beliefs of the Ebionites.

In Acts, the holy spirit is spread around almost indiscriminately. In the Pentecost event, the power of the kingdom of heaven descends on many diverse individuals, just as it had earlier been poured out into Jesus: Peter quotes Joel as saying that the spirit of God will be poured out unto all people (Acts 2:14–21). This directly parallels the *Recognitions* when Peter declares that the *same* oil that anointed Jesus now anoints all believers (1.45)—and thus all believers have become Christs (another Ebionite theme).

The opponents of the Christians are named repeatedly: they are the priests and their allies, the Sadducees (Acts 4:1, 4:5–6, 5:21, 5:24, 5:27). It is only this small (though privileged) segment of the community that opposes the Jesus movement. The priests and their allies have the disciples arrested and brought before the council of elders, but the council dares not punish them "because of the people" (4:21). The high priest and the Sadducees again arrest the apostles (5:17), but they are restrained when a Pharisee named Gamaliel urges tolerance, warning the council they may be opposing God by persecuting the Christians (5:33–39). While the primitive church is violently opposed by the priests and the Sadducees, at least one Pharisee speaks out in opposition to killing the Christians—and the party of tolerance seems to have the upper hand, since the apostles are released.

Most striking of all is the speech of Stephen, the first Christian killed for his beliefs after Jesus, where these themes come out very strongly.

Stephen's opponents bring him before the council and accuse him of attacking the temple ("this holy place") and the law, saying that they have heard Stephen say that Jesus "will destroy this place" and change the laws of Moses to boot (Acts 6:13–14).

"This holy place" refers clearly to the temple, and the accusation made toward Jesus at his trial is repeated—that the intent of the Christians is to destroy the temple. As we have seen, Jesus in the gospels does not at all deny the charge that he wants to destroy the temple—in fact he makes predictions of its destruction. *The Gospel of Thomas* 71 actually has Jesus declaring that he *will* destroy the temple. The laws of Moses that Stephen's accusers think he wants to change would, in the context of Stephen's speech, clearly refer to the practice of sacrifice in the temple. It is as if Stephen's accusers had heard the saying that the Ebionites attributed to Jesus ("I came to abolish sacrifices," *Panarion* 30.16.5) and were framing a charge that would rely on this saying.

Now if the first Christians had been temple-worshiping Jews who brought animal sacrifices and whose only innovation was that Jesus was the Messiah, this would be the perfect place for Stephen to put their fears about the temple at rest. In fact, this kind of reassurance is just what we get later, when Paul goes to the temple to fulfill a vow (21:26–27)— almost certainly a complete fiction. Stephen, however, offers a speech that is anything but conciliatory.

Stephen's response to the charges is a long, rambling discourse on the history of Israel *that, in effect, affirms the charges against him.* He *does* want to destroy the temple and end the sacrificial system—he denies only that the sacrificial system came from Moses. The first part of Stephen's speech (Acts 7:2–34) is spent in talking about the history of Israel beginning with Abraham and going down to Moses. In this section the rootless nature of Israel in its state of purity before God is emphasized: Abraham, Joseph, and Moses were constantly wandering from place to place, yet God was everywhere with them. They had no temple, and yet were very holy.

The second part of Stephen's speech (Acts 7:35–53) emphasizes the rejection of Moses by the Israelites and attacks temple-worship as idolatry. Stephen quotes Moses' prediction that God will raise up a future prophet—again citing the Ebionites' favorite verse in Deuteronomy predicting the "true prophet." The Israelites rejected Moses, says Stephen, and sacrificed animals in the desert, but *this animal sacrifice was not offered to God, but to idols.* In support, he quotes part of a passage from Amos that is utterly opposed to animal sacrifice. God does not dwell in the temple anyway, Stephen says, quoting Isaiah in support: "Heaven is my throne, and earth is my footstool" (Isaiah 66:1). After attacking Solomon's construction of the temple, Stephen concludes: "As your fathers did, so do you" (Acts 7:51). Thus, Stephen likens the priests' practice of animal sacrifice in the temple to the idolatrous animal sacrifice in the desert! Stephen ends with more accusations against his listeners: they resisted the Holy Spirit, they betrayed and killed the "Righteous One," and they failed to keep the law. It is completely plausible that someone could be stoned after such a speech. We do not even hear a verdict in his case delivered; Stephen's opponents, enraged, simply seize him and have him stoned. As he is being stoned, the holy spirit descends on Stephen, and he prays for forgiveness of his enemies (Acts 7:55, 60), following the advice in the Sermon on the Mount.

The speech of Stephen is a striking affirmation of several Ebionite themes, including pacifism and rejection of animal sacrifice. In fact, there are remarkable parallels between Stephen's speech and *Recognitions* 1. In both places we have the justification of Jesus as the prophet predicted by Moses based on Deuteronomy 18:15; in both places we have the account of Israelite history from Abraham to Moses; in both places we have animal sacrifice and idolatry denounced in parallel; in both places we have the denunciation of Solomon's building of the temple; in both places we have the praise of the holy spirit poured out on all believers (*Recognitions* 1.45). Even the pacifist ending is kept the same: the Christians in the *Recognitions* do not offer any violent resistance to Paul's attempt to murder James due to their pacifist principles, while Stephen in Acts prays for his enemies as they stone him. The only difference is that Stephen is killed, whereas James in the *Recognitions* is attacked by Paul and left for dead but not killed. Because of these striking similarities, we have to wonder whether these are not really two different accounts of the same incident. Perhaps Paul really *did* attempt to murder James, but by the time Acts was written this was too shocking to be remembered and "James" had been turned into "Stephen."

When we turn from Stephen to the leadership of the primitive church, we find these same themes confirmed and expanded.

James as the First Leader of the Church

James, the brother of Jesus, was almost certainly the first leader of the church after Jesus' death. This is more than a historical quibble, because the Ebionites saw James as the first leader of the church after Jesus and traced their leaders through James rather than through Peter. Peter, in Ebionite thinking, was a great apostle but was not the leader. Moreover, James is described even by the orthodox in terms that emulate the Ebionite ideal: vegetarian, teetotaler, living a simple and righteous life.

The very phrase "brother of Jesus" causes trouble for many contemporary Christians because of the later traditions that grew up concerning the virgin birth of Jesus. If Mary was always a virgin and had only one child (Jesus), then James and Jesus would not be related at all. If Mary later had other children with Joseph, then James would be a half-brother. The Ebionites took the common sense position that Jesus was the son of Joseph and Mary (*Panarion* 30.20.5)—as Matthew and Luke also imply through their genealogies.

There is one significant countertradition that alleges that Peter, not James, was commissioned by Jesus to be the leader of the church. At Matthew 16:18, Peter declares Jesus to be the Messiah; and Jesus tells Peter that he is the rock on which he will build his church. However, this is highly questionable as history. Comparing the text in Matthew (16:13–20) to the parallel passages in the other synoptic gospels (Mark 8:27–30, Luke 9:18–21), we see in all three passages Peter's assertion that Jesus is the Messiah—but *only* in Matthew does Jesus mention Peter as the "rock" of the church. If this really were part of the original story, there would be no reason for Mark or Luke to leave this important declaration out; and nowhere else in the synoptic gospels does Jesus seem overly concerned about the church. Most likely, this is a convenient later insertion into the original text. A second countertradition exists in the gospel of John, which refers to the "beloved disciple" as the one who best understood Jesus; but this, again, is unsupported in the New Testament except in John. Aside from Matthew 16:18 and the ambiguous references to the beloved disciple in John, the consistent testimony in the New Testament—both from Acts and from the letters of Paul—is that James was the leader of the early church.

James' leadership is evident at several points. At the Jerusalem Council (Acts 15), in which the extent of the gentile converts' adherence to the law of Moses is discussed, Peter, Barnabas, and Paul all speak; but it is James who delivers the "verdict." He begins with the phrase, "therefore my judgment is" (15:19), words certainly suggestive of one having authority. He then voices the celebrated "apostolic decree," forbidding things sacrificed to idols, blood, things strangled, and unchastity. James speaks last, he gives a judgment that includes items not heretofore mentioned by Peter, Paul, or Barnabas, and it is accepted by "the apostles and the elders, with the whole church" (15:22). Later, in Acts 21:18, Paul is described during his third visit as paying a special visit to James when "all the elders" are present. That Paul is talking to James when all the leaders of the church are present certainly suggests that James was the person to talk to about important matters in the church.

The letters of Paul also speak of James in a leadership role. Galatians 2:9 speaks of the trio of James, Cephas (Peter), and John as the "pillars" of the church. James is evidently in the leadership role here. He is listed first in this list of three; moreover, Paul relates that Peter was taking his meals with the gentiles until "certain men from James" arrived—and thus Peter answers to James.

According to Eusebius, James assumed his position of leadership immediately following Jesus' death (*Ecclesiastical History* 2.1.2, 7.19), and received leadership of the Jerusalem church directly from his brother, Jesus. Eusebius has already put in the interpretation that James was only the leader of the "local" church in Jerusalem, but Hegesippus (whom Eusebius quotes) speaks of the Jerusalem church as if it *were* the church; he states that James "succeeded to the government of the Church in conjunction with the Apostles" (*Ecclesiastical History* 2.23.4).

The Ebionites believed that James, rather than Peter, was the leader of the church. The *Recognitions* present Peter as receiving his commission and instructions from James. Peter is instructed to send back an account to James each year (*Recognitions* 1.72), and cautions those he instructs not to believe any teacher unless they have been certified by James or one of his successors (*Recognitions* 4.35). These writings in the *Recognitions* may not be literally true, but they nevertheless reflect a memory that it was James who was the first leader of the church.

The Gospel of Thomas also makes James the first leader after Jesus:

The disciples said to Jesus, "We know that you are going to leave us. Who will be our leader?" Jesus said to them, "No matter where you are, you are to go to James the Just, for whose sake heaven and earth came into being." (*Gospel of Thomas* 12)

The importance of James goes deeper than just a "genealogical" dispute about through whom to trace apostolic succession. James is acknowledged by orthodox sources to be the Ebionite ideal: vegetarian, teetotaler, and living a simple and honest life. Eusebius quotes Hegesippus to illustrate what kind of person James was:

James . . . was holy from his mother's womb; and he drank no wine nor strong drink, nor did he eat flesh. No razor came upon his head; he did not anoint himself with oil, and he did not use the [public] bath. He alone was permitted to enter into the holy place; for he wore not woolen but linen garments. (Eusebius, *Ecclesiastical History* 2.23.5–6)

Epiphanius, who could surely be relied upon to report any anti-vegetarian tradition about James, agrees: he says twice that James did not eat meat (*Panarion* 78.13.3, 78.14.2). Even more astounding, though, Hegesippus not only describes James as a vegetarian and a teetotaler, but strongly implies that James was *raised* as a vegetarian and a teetotaler (through the use of the phrase, "holy from his mother's womb").

Eusebius also mentions in this same passage some other intriguing details. James did not cut his hair; he did not wear wool, but only linen garments; he did not use the public baths; and he did not use oil. *All of these items of practice are shared with the Pythagoreans and/or the Essenes.* This quotation from Hegesippus—while not conclusive—is still the single most striking piece of evidence that the Essenes and the Pythagoreans had some influence on early Christianity. The first four items are shared with Pythagoras or the Pythagoreans, who also did not eat meat or drink wine, cut their hair,[1] wear wool, or frequent public baths. The fifth item, the refusal to use oil, is something shared with the Essenes (Josephus, *Wars* 2.8.3). Moreover, it is likely that the Essenes did not eat meat or drink wine, since Josephus says that the Essenes practiced the same way of life as the Pythagoreans (*Antiquities* 15.10.4).

Even more significant than the resemblance between James and the Essenes and Pythagoreans are the similarities between James and other early Christians. Eusebius makes some of the same assertions about Jesus and the apostles that were made about James. Jesus is said to have rejected animal sacrifice, just as Porphyry and Apollonius of Tyana had done, citing two famous pagan philosophers who were also vegetarian (*Proof of the Gospel* 3.3). Eusebius also comments on the character of the twelve apostles, mentioning in passing that they "embraced and persevered in a laborious and strenuous life, with fasting and abstinence from wine and meat" (*Proof of the Gospel* 3.5).

The apostles—*all* the apostles, and not just James—abstained from both meat and wine, thus making them vegetarians and teetotalers, just like James. Would it not be plausible to assume that James came from the same environment as his brother? If James was raised as a vegetarian and a teetotaler, would it not be plausible to say that his parents raised Jesus in the same way? Why would Jesus' parents raise James one way and Jesus another? Would it not also be logical to say that the lifestyle of the leader of the community sets the tone for the entire community? These are obvious questions which all point toward the Ebionites as the bearers of the tradition passed down from Jesus.

The Martyrdom of James

James was the leader of the Jerusalem church for several decades, but a few years before the first Jewish revolt against Rome (probably in 62), James was stoned by a lynch mob. In the death of James we once again see evidence of the opposition of the Jesus movement to the priests and the temple—but this time the evidence is outside the New Testament.

Who was responsible for killing James? We have accounts from Hegesippus and from Josephus. Hegesippus (quoted by Eusebius) gives an account of James' martyrdom, in which the "scribes and Pharisees" are blamed for his death, though he also confusingly attributes the initiating and mysterious question asked of James just before his martyrdom ("What is the gate of Jesus?") to the sects that do not believe in the resurrection—that is, the Sadducees (*Ecclesiastical History* 2.23.8–9). Josephus, however, straightforwardly blames the high priest. The high priest, Ananus, was newly appointed and very bold and insolent. He brought James the brother of Jesus and some of his companions before him, accused them of breaking the law, and had them stoned to death (*Antiquities* 20.9.1).

So who was most likely responsible for James' death? It appears highly likely that the account in Josephus is correct and that the high priest is to blame—once again showing the continuity of opposition between the followers of Jesus and the priests in the temple. Josephus does not appear to have an axe to grind. He is much closer to these events chronologically (he was alive at the time) and, being Jewish, had a clearer grasp of the complicated politics of the day. In Josephus' account, the murder of James fits closely into his overall narrative; the murder, which did *not* meet with popular approval, explains why Ananus was dismissed as high priest after a very brief term of office. In Hegesippus, we have an explanation that could easily come from the later dim memory of gentile Christians who might not have easily distinguished between priests, Sadducees, Pharisees, or scribes, but tended to lump all of them together as "the Jews."

There is also a surprising point of agreement in the various accounts: the killing of James was an action that did *not* have the support of most of the Jews. Josephus, Eusebius, and Origen all agree on this point. Origen and Eusebius, incidentally, both attribute to *Josephus* disapproval for the murder of James: Josephus states that Jerusalem was destroyed as punishment for the murder of James, an innocent man (*Against Celsus* 1.47, *Ecclesiastical History* 2.23.19–20). It is more likely that the Sadducees rather than the Pharisees would have precipitated such an unpopular action; the Sadducees had a much narrower political base than the Pharisees.

Finally, there is the question of motive. Eusebius describes James as a vegetarian who would not even wear wool (*Ecclesiastical History* 2.23.5–6), implying that James was perhaps less than enthusiastic about the slaughter of animals in the temple. This would provide a motive for the high priests and the Sadducees to dislike James; it would not provide a motive for the Pharisees. This makes it very likely that the death of James, like the deaths of Stephen and Jesus before him, was orchestrated by a high priest who saw the chance to finally, and brutally, "settle a score"—the memory of which had persisted for three decades.

The Destruction of Jerusalem

The destruction of Jerusalem in the year 70 was a pivotal event in the history of Rome, the history of the Jews, the history of the world, and the history of the Jesus movement. Had this revolt not occurred, it is conceivable that the Roman Empire would have converted to a more pacific type of Judaism—perhaps even a Judaism influenced by the Jesus movement—instead of to gentile Christianity. Had the revolt actually succeeded, we can imagine that a militant Judaism might have overrun the Middle East in much the same way that Islam did six centuries later. In any event, the history of the world would have been much, much different.

The revolt followed a number of unsettling incidents that had raised tensions between the Romans and the Jews. The most ominous of these events had occurred nearly twenty-five years earlier during a crisis brought about by the Roman emperor Caligula. Some Jews had torn down some pagan altars and in retaliation Caligula had ordered a statue of himself put up in the temple—a plan which, to say the least, could scarcely have been better calculated to inflame Jewish opinion against Rome. Caligula, however, died before the plan could be put into effect. Since in this case the temple was saved from desecration by an apparent divine miracle (the death of the hated emperor), this event may have been a significant setback for the followers of Jesus who had anti-temple sentiments.[2]

When a full-scale revolt finally did occur in 66, the Jerusalem church was caught up in the violence along with everyone else. The big question for us, of course, is what happened to the followers of Jesus. There is one thing that is without doubt: the war caused incredible suffering. It lasted for nine years and was accompanied by repeated wholesale massacres of peoples of various religious views by their opponents. War was not civilized. Often, upon the capture of a city by its enemies, all the inhabitants were slaughtered—men, women, and children. If they were lucky, the women and children would be sold into slavery instead. The Jewish war was interrupted by a Roman civil war. In 69 CE Nero was killed and his successor usurped by yet another general. Vespasian, the general who was prosecuting the war effort in Judea, was persuaded to declare himself emperor and return to Rome to defeat his enemies and end the civil war. This he did. Thus the year 69 is sometimes known as the "year of four emperors." This led to a temporary respite during the actual siege of Jerusalem itself, but Titus (the son of Vespasian) then resumed the effort against the Jewish insurgency.

Jerusalem held out for a long time, with the inhabitants suffering incredibly (Josephus describes cannibalism). To prosecute the siege in the face of the Jewish tactics that destroyed the Roman siege works, the Romans had to chop down every tree within ten miles of Jerusalem. However, in the end, the Romans captured Jerusalem, destroyed the temple, and slaughtered the inhabitants. This was for all practical purposes the end of the revolt, though in isolated pockets some Jewish rebels held out for several more years—Masada, the last, only falling in 73 or 74. It also ended the practice of animal sacrifice, though not in the way which the Jewish Christians would have liked. The Jews never rebuilt the temple, and after a subsequent revolt sixty years later, were expelled from Jerusalem altogether.

Obviously, any Christians in Jerusalem—or, for that matter, anywhere else in Judea—were at risk at this time. If they were not killed by the revolutionaries for failing to support the war effort, and if they were not lucky enough to be in a city or location that surrendered peacefully to the Romans (or did not resist them in the first place), they most likely would be killed by the Romans. There is no doubt that this Jewish revolt against Rome adversely affected the position of Palestinian followers of Jesus.

Conclusions

The history of the church up to the great catastrophe of the year 70 underscores a number of points that support the Ebionite point of view, on which both the orthodox accounts (in Acts, Eusebius, and Epiphanius) and the Ebionite accounts (in the *Homilies* and *Recognitions*) agree. First, the primitive Christian rejection of animal sacrifices is not only found in the speech of Stephen and in *Recognitions* 1, but it is expressed in much the same way—in terms of the return to the ideal of the children of Israel in the wilderness, when there was no temple to act as a focal point for all worship. Secondly, the opponents are clearly defined: the Jesus movement on the one hand, the priests in the temple on the other. Thirdly, James is the leader of the church, just as the Ebionites described, and is a vegetarian and teetotaler (along with the rest of the apostles)—the Ebionite ideal.

It is practically indisputable that the Ebionites—whatever one may think of their later development—captured a number of essential points about the history of early Christianity. The themes of the rejection of animal sacrifice, endorsement of vegetarianism, and adherence to the leadership of James were not later sectarian quibbles from the second and third centuries. All of these appear at the very earliest stages of

Christian history and are acknowledged as such, even when they are opposed by Paul and by later orthodox writers. The Ebionite portrayal of the history of the church has a power that cannot be denied.

However, the forces at work here permanently ended the authority of the Jerusalem church. The evidence is circumstantial, but compelling: before the year 70, Jerusalem is the universally acknowledged center of Christian activity; after this year, the Jerusalem church practically disappears from the scene.

DISINTEGRATION

THE DECLINE OF
JEWISH CHRISTIANITY

A FTER THE FAILURE OF THE JEWISH REVOLTS AGAINST
Rome, gentile Christianity continued to grow and prosper with
only episodic and generally ineffective persecution from the
Romans. Jewish Christianity, however, was decimated by war, seriously
and effectively persecuted by its opponents, and isolated politically; it
stood outside both mainstream Judaism and mainstream Christianity. It
continued this sectarian existence for at least another three centuries,
mentioned chiefly in long lists of heretical sects. It broke up into
numerous smaller groups due to causes that are practically invisible to
us, and it was never able to seriously challenge mainstream Christianity
or mainstream Judaism after this point.

The Flight to Pella

What happened to the Jerusalem church after the failure of the first
Jewish revolt and the destruction of the temple? Unfortunately, we don't
have a clear answer to this question. The period from the destruction of
the temple to the beginning of the second century is perhaps the "black
hole" of Christian history. We may not have hard historical information
about the historical Jesus and the primitive church up to the revolt
against Rome, but even the most hardened skeptic has to admit that we
have at least an abundance of legends and stories. But for the few decades

following the destruction of the temple, we have almost no information at all, not even legendary.

We do know what the results of this historical period were: the Jerusalem church and Jewish Christianity disappear as major factors in the history of Christianity. Jewish Christianity also disappears as a factor in the history of Judaism; probably around the year 85 CE, Jewish Christians were finally excluded from the Jewish synagogues as well and condemned as Jewish heretics. Suddenly, within the space of a few decades, Jewish Christianity becomes a sect excluded by both Jews and Christians. It is during this time that the Ebionites probably first emerged as a distinct group, to preserve the religious views they felt had been passed down to them from Jesus himself through James and his spiritual descendants.

After the Roman suppression of the second Jewish revolt (in 117 CE, in Alexandria) and the third Jewish revolt (the Bar Cochba revolt of 132—135 CE), all Jews were excluded from Jerusalem, including the Jewish Christians. The Romans made no subtle distinctions between the various sects, even when these sects were themselves violently opposed to each other. The Jewish revolt was politically as well as physically devastating for Jewish Christianity. To many gentile Christians, the catastrophic destruction of Jerusalem and the temple appeared as a divine judgement against all Jews;[1] to other Jews, the Jewish Christians now appeared as traitors to Israel.

Nevertheless, Jewish Christianity established itself in a significant area just east of the Jordan river, from Mt. Hebron north of Galilee to the regions just east of the sea of Galilee, the river Jordan, and the Dead Sea, and as far south as Nabataea and northern Arabia.[2] Eusebius (*Ecclesiastical History* 3.5.3) tells the story that the Christian church in Jerusalem was saved from the general destruction of the year 70 when the community and the leaders of the church fled to Pella. Pella was a city just on the "other" (the east) side of the Jordan river, southeast of the sea of Galilee in northern Judea. Epiphanius also repeats and elaborates on this tradition—noting, however, that the regions east of the Jordan were just where the heretical Ebionites and Nazoraeans were found (*Panarion* 29.7.7–8, 30.2.7, 30.18.1)! The irony of this coincidence seems to have been lost on Epiphanius, who is oblivious to this devastating admission: any true successors to the Jerusalem church must have come from exactly the area in which the heretics were strongest.

There is another contrasting account in *Recognitions* 1.39; it does not explicitly refer to Pella but says that the believers will be saved from the destruction of the war.[3] Could the area east of the Jordan be the place to which the believers escaped? There are several references in Matthew's gospel to Palestine that imply that Matthew was written on the *east* side of the Jordan. Matthew speaks of Jesus dwelling in Capernaum (by the Sea of Galilee) and this as being "across the Jordan" (Matthew 4:15) and later speaks of Jesus as entering Judea "beyond the Jordan"(Matthew 19:1). This, of course, would imply a frame of reference on the *east* side of the Jordan, as both Capernaum and Judea are on the west side; otherwise one could not speak of these locations as being "across" or "beyond" the Jordan river. This would place the perspective of Matthew in the general vicinity of present-day Syria and Jordan—in exactly the place where the Ebionites were strongest—and strengthens the Ebionite claim to have the original version of this gospel.

It is hard to dismiss the flight to Pella as Ebionite propaganda, as Eusebius and Epiphanius are contemptuous of Jewish Christianity. Despite the testimonies both from Ebionite Christianity and from orthodox sources, some scholars have maintained that the flight to Pella was not historical, though the import of their denial is different. Some, like S. G. F. Brandon, would like to maintain that Jewish Christianity was completely destroyed in this war and that consequently the flight to Pella was entirely a myth. Others, such as Gerd Lüdemann, have said that a flight may have really occurred, but not necessarily to Pella. Regardless of the exact location, the area east of the Jordan would have been a logical escape route for Jewish Christians hoping to escape the catastrophe.

The reality is probably somewhere in between that of the church escaping almost intact and that of the church completely destroyed. It seems inescapable that the blow was severe and is a primary reason that the Jerusalem Church virtually disappears from the historical scene after 70 CE. The Jewish Christians suffered simply because everyone suffered, and they were part of the general catastrophe.

No matter how devastating the blow, however, it is hard to believe that *all* the followers of Jesus in Judea were killed. *Someone*—including some of the leaders and relatives of Jesus—must have survived out of the tens of thousands of Christians who had lived and actively promoted their views for over three decades. Sepphoris, the largest town in Galilee, which sided with the Romans in the war (and thus was spared destruction), probably had a large Ebionite congregation after the war, descended from the pre-war Christians.[4] Josephus gives numerous accounts of many people escaping from Jerusalem during the siege, right up until the last days, sometimes thousands at a time. So it is quite plausible that a number of Christians, including the leadership, could have gotten out no matter how late the "revelation" to leave Jerusalem came.[5]

We can, therefore, reasonably assume that some Christians in Palestine must have survived the war, and they are likely to have eventually reconstituted themselves in Pella or elsewhere on the east bank of the Jordan. It is simply too great a coincidence that the church decided to flee to the very area that then became the stronghold of Ebionism. Thus, it is plausible that it is precisely these "heretics" who became the spiritual heirs of the primitive Christian church.

The situation of the surviving Jewish Christians after the war was, as we have seen, quite difficult. Because of their opposition to the war, the Jewish Christians were likely to be regarded by many as traitors to Israel; also the temple was destroyed, thus removing their chief grievance. The temple the Jewish Christians had preached against was destroyed by a hated enemy, the Romans, thus perhaps linking in Jewish minds the Jewish Christians with the hated Roman enemy. Perhaps that is why Jewish protest of the sacrifices, so intense and bitter in Isaiah and some of the other prophets, almost completely disappears in the Talmud (largely written down after the destruction of the temple).⁶ There was no point in belaboring an issue that was dead.

Jewish Christianity was dealt another, and perhaps even more severe, blow as a result of the third great Jewish revolt against Rome, the Bar Cochba revolt of 132—135 CE. (The second revolt, in 117, took place outside Judea.) At the time of the Bar Cochba revolt, the Jews specifically targeted Jewish Christians for destruction. Bar Cochba was declared to be the Messiah and there was no room for a competing Messiah, Jesus; moreover, the pacifist tendencies of Jewish Christians did not lend themselves well to the spirit of the revolt. It must have been a deadly, possibly a surprise, assault on Jewish Christianity, as the Jewish Christians who fled back to Pella left behind one of their most precious relics, the chair of James.⁷ Justin Martyr remembers the Bar Cochba revolt and he says that the leader of the revolt, Bar Cochba himself, ordered that the Christians should be tortured unless they renounced Jesus (*First Apology* 1.31).

Perhaps the Jews were trying to learn from the mistakes of the first revolt, and remembered the factionalism that so weakened the Jewish revolutionaries in the previous conflict (the Jews in Jerusalem, while besieged by the Romans, were also in armed conflict with one another). Unfortunately, the Romans also had learned from their own mistakes in the first revolt, and when after much difficulty they finally subdued the Bar Cochba rebellion after three years of struggle they expelled all Jews from Jerusalem, which then became an exclusively gentile city (Aelia Capitolina). These events seriously weakened the leadership of Jewish Christianity and killed many of its followers. It also removed the Jewish Christians from Jerusalem. Because the Romans did not distinguish between different kinds of Jews, the Jewish Christians were not permitted to return any more than any other kind of Jew.

While these heavy blows were being dealt to Jewish Christianity, gentile Christianity remained almost entirely untouched. It is true that there were persecutions of the gentile Church as well, but these were largely episodic, unsystematic, regional, and ineffectual in nature. The martyrdom of Ignatius is very revealing of the nature of the persecutions the Christians faced. After his arrest, Ignatius was allowed to meet with Polycarp and to write letters to his friends; one of those letters was to Christians in Rome warning them not to come to his "rescue," but to allow him to be martyred. It was not until much later that the most serious persecutions of the gentile Church occurred—beginning under Diocletian, at the end of the third century. Jewish Christianity, by contrast, had to deal with a multitude of extremely serious problems. The net result of the destruction of Jerusalem was the destruction of the authority of the Jerusalem church.

The Family of Jesus

James was killed in Jerusalem in about the year 62 and his successors were all of Palestinian origin. In fact, if we follow the succession of church leadership from James, *we find that it goes to other relatives of Jesus*, the "desposynoi" ("those who belong to the Master," referring to the relatives of Jesus), who become the founders of Ebionism.

The successor of James was Simeon, who was a cousin of Jesus, according to Hegesippus (Eusebius, *Ecclesiastical History* 4.22.4). Hegesippus (quoted by Eusebius) also reports that other relatives of Jesus were active in the church and were leaders, evidently at a high level. Hegesippus tells the story of how some of the grandsons of Judas (another brother of Jesus) were arrested and brought before Domitian, who after interrogating them released them as harmless; Hegesippus remarks in passing that these grandsons "ruled the churches," both because they were relatives of Jesus himself and because they were witnesses to the faith (*Ecclesiastical History* 3.20.1–8).

Eusebius also quotes Julius Africanus on the relatives of the Lord, and how they had genealogies they had carefully kept for many years. These relatives lived both in Nazareth (in Galilee) and in Cochaba, a town on the *east* side of the Jordan river (Eusebius, *Ecclesiastical History* 1.7.14). Epiphanius reports that two groups of Jewish Christians (Ebionites and Nazoraeans) *also* lived in the town of Cochaba (*Panarion* 29.7.7, 30.2.7–8), and indeed that Ebionism began in Cochaba. Once again, we have a striking geographical coincidence: the relatives of Jesus settle in precisely the village where the heretical Ebionites originated.

There do not appear to be competing traditions on this point: Jesus' relatives form a community; this community inherits the traditions of the Palestinian church; it settles in precisely the area that the Ebionites settle in. *If one tried to draw a true line of "apostolic succession" from Jesus to James and his successors, this line goes directly to the Ebionites.*

This may also explain why Jesus' relatives are sometimes depicted in such hostile terms. The canonical gospels relate that the relatives of Jesus were actually hostile to him during his lifetime. Jesus is quoted as saying that "a prophet is not without honor, except in his own country, and among his own kin, and in his own house" (Mark 6:4). This is part of a general theme pursued in the gospels—especially Mark and Luke—that Jesus was rejected by those closest to him. The disciples are pictured as unable to understand what Jesus has to say, even when it is clearly and explicitly laid out for them. They do not understand simple parables, they argue among themselves about who is the greatest, they do not understand clear predictions by Jesus, and so forth (see for example Mark 7:17, 8:21, 8:31–33, 9:31–32, 10:13–16, and Luke 9:46, 22:24).

What is the point of all these stories? One possible interpretation is simply that the stories relate historical fact: those closest to Jesus, including his relatives, disciples, and fellow countrymen, really *did* reject him. But an equally possible interpretation also suggests itself: this is a convenient gentile myth and part of the gospel-writers' polemic against Jewish Christianity; you just can't trust Jesus' relatives. It is quite possible that these passages in Mark, which were most likely written in the period after the destruction of the Jerusalem temple, were specifically aimed at the *desposynoi*, by way of saying: those in the area in which Jesus grew up, and those related to him, are not truly following him.

Mark's account of Jesus' relatives flies in the face of well-established facts. James the brother of Jesus was the leader of the church and was eventually martyred for his testimony on behalf of his brother; and two grandsons of Judas, another brother of Jesus, likewise witnessed for

Jesus before Roman officials. Even Acts relates that on the day of the Pentecost both his mother and his brothers were present in the upper room (Acts 1:13–14). Any apostasy or doubts on the part of Jesus' relatives must have been over by the Pentecost, even by orthodox accounts. The most obvious explanation is that Jesus' family was part of the earliest Christian church, and that some of the relatives of Jesus, the successors of James, then became the leaders of the Ebionites.

The Fragmentation of Jewish Christianity

Jewish Christianity after the Bar Cochba revolt was fragmented and sectarian. All of the various forms of Jewish Christianity, however, were similar in their basic orientation and it is hard for us to grasp why they split into different groups. Modern-day sectarian groups often splinter into different factions, even when their views to outsiders seem almost identical, so this phenomenon is not implausible.

Epiphanius, that hostile critic of Jewish Christianity, describes the founder of Ebionism as like a "many-headed Hydra" (*Panarion* 30.1.1). It was probably the factionalism in Jewish Christianity that led to this description. There are other groups that are usually classified as "Jewish Christian," namely the Elchasaites, Nazoraeans, and Ossaeans; and there is another Jewish group which seems to be closely allied to them: the Nasaraeans. The Nasaraeans and the Nazoraeans have names that are very similar to each other, and their names are also very close to the term "Nazarene" (resident of Nazareth).

The Ebionites were almost certainly the most important Jewish Christian group; however, all of the Jewish Christian groups seemed to agree on essentials. Most of the information we have about the non-Ebionite Jewish Christians comes from the *Panarion*, which indicates that they were very similar to the Ebionites in their most prominent doctrines. Both the Ossaeans and the Elchasaites accepted the teachings of the prophet Elchasai; in fact, it is not clear they were two different groups at all. They were Jews who rejected animal sacrifices and meat-eating (19.3.6); they kept the "whole Law" but rejected the writings commanding sacrifices (19.5.1); they acknowledged Christ as the "great

King" (19.3.4). The Ossaeans could have been the same group as the Essenes of Philo and Josephus, due to the resemblance of the name and the doctrines; they both rejected the sacrificial cult and embraced vegetarianism.[8]

The Nasaraeans are described as a Jewish cult that existed *before* Jesus (*Panarion* 29.6.1), whose views are startlingly close to those of the Ebionites. According to Epiphanius, they acknowledged the patriarchs (Abraham, Isaac, Moses, etc.), kept the Jewish law, but specifically rejected the sacrificial cult. They believed it *contrary* to the law to eat meat or to make sacrifices, and that the patriarchs never instituted such practices (*Panarion* 18.1.3–4).

All of these ideas, however, are essentially the same as those of the Ebionites. We are left then with just one group that does not fit the above typology, the Nazoraeans. (The Nazoraeans are not to be confused either with the "Nasaraeans" just discussed or with "Nazarenes," residents of Nazareth.) In the New Testament, it is affirmed that Jesus was a "Nazoraean" (Acts 3:6, 4:10) thus identifying Jesus as a member of a group later condemned as heretical! Epiphanius, faced with this problem, says that all Christians called themselves Nazoraeans in early Christianity and that the "heretical" Nazoraeans differed in that they never changed their name when everyone else did. This explanation defends Jesus against the charge of heresy, but causes even more damage: he has to admit, in the first place, that the Nazoraeans were a first-century phenomenon, and secondly, that it was they—at least on this one point—who remained the same while the orthodox church of Epiphanius changed.

The problem of the Nazoraeans is that Epiphanius states they adhere to the Jewish law in *all* respects. He does not specifically say they accepted animal sacrifice, though some have made this assumption. The law and the prophets were accepted by the Nazoraeans, rather than rejected as they were by the Ebionites and Nasaraeans (*Panarion* 29.7.2, 29.7.5). On the basis of this statement, some scholars have concluded that the Nazoraeans were an orthodox Jewish sect, deviating from strict Judaism only in that they also thought that Jesus was the Messiah.[9] Thus, they would have accepted the sacrificial cult and the entire Old Testament, including the "false texts" that the Ebionites rejected.

Now it is certainly possible that there was such a Jewish Christian group that accepted the sacrificial cult; and this would not affect the conclusions of this book. However, there are warning flags everywhere that this is a poorly supported thesis. In the first place, if the Nazoraeans were a Jewish Christian group that accepted the sacrificial cult, they were the *only* such Jewish Christian group. All the other "Jewish Christian" groups and their Jewish predecessors or allies deviated from orthodox Judaism and orthodox Christianity in a predictable pattern: (1) they all rejected the sacrificial cult, (2) they were all vegetarians, (3) they all rejected the Pentateuch on the question of the laws of sacrifice.

Secondly, the Nazoraeans did not necessarily accept animal sacrifice just because they accepted "the whole law." It would only mean that they rejected the Ebionite doctrine of false texts. The *Recognitions* in fact suggests an alternative to the idea of false texts: animal sacrifices *were* commanded by Moses but only as a concession to human weakness (because Moses wisely saw that it would take time to wean the people from the ways of Egypt) and Moses specifically predicted a future prophet to correct the rest of this error (*Recognitions* 1.36). The *Recognitions*, therefore, suggests that we could accept the texts about animal sacrifice but deny that God wants us to sacrifice animals *now*.

Moreover, Epiphanius knows astonishingly little about the Nazoraeans. He has not read their literature, has not met any of them, and does not know the most basic features of their viewpoint. He does not even know whether or not the Nazoraeans rejected the virgin birth, the very first heretical doctrine which he attributes to the Ebionites. Klijn and Reinink comment that Epiphanius "knows very little about them [the Nazoraeans], except that they lived according to the Jewish law and accepted some orthodox beliefs about Jesus."[10] This lack of knowledge is a thin reed indeed to support the idea of a Jewish Christian group accepting animal sacrifices.

Moreover, what little Epiphanius does say actually supports the idea that the Nazoraeans, like the Ebionites, rejected the sacrificial cult. The

Nazoraeans are very similar to the Ebionites, their vegetarian friends. *Both* the Nazoraeans and the Ebionites accept the Gospel of Matthew in Hebrew (*Panarion* 29.9.4, 30.13.2). This Hebrew version of Matthew is quoted and attacked by Epiphanius because (among other things) it represents John the Baptist as a vegetarian (30.13.4–5), and Epiphanius attributes to their "so-called Gospel" the celebrated statement of Jesus: "I have come to abolish sacrifices" (30.16.5). If the Nazoraeans and the Ebionites had the same Hebrew version of Matthew before them, then the Nazoraeans would need to accept that Jesus came to "abolish sacrifices." Interestingly, Eusebius—writing over a half-century earlier— also described a Hebrew version of Matthew, but without the same denunciations as Epiphanius; he mentions it matter of factly as the original version of Matthew, and quotes Origen in his support (*Ecclesiastical History* 3.24.6–7, 3.39.16, 5.8, 5.10, 6.25).

The Nazoraeans also were strong in some of the same areas that the Ebionites and Nasaraeans lived: Bashanitis, Pella, and Cochaba (Panarion 18.1.1, 29.7.7, 30.2.7). Epiphanius acknowledges that many of the Nazoraean ideas are the same as those of the other Jewish Christian sects. He says that the Ebionites' founder held "opinions like" the Nazoraeans (*Panarion* 30.1.1), that he held "the doctrine" of the Nazoraeans, Ossaeans, and Nasaraeans (30.1.3), and that he was "with" the Nazoraeans (30.2.1). The book of Elchasai was accepted by not only the Nazoraeans, but also by the Ossaeans and Ebionites (53.1.3). This means the Nazoraeans had opinions like, had the same doctrine as, and accepted the same writings as four groups which *all* agreed in rejecting the sacrificial cult and in accepting vegetarianism. Indeed, several other writers think that the Nazoraeans and the Ebionites were two names for the same group; this is what Theodoret evidently thought,[11] as well as Jerome (*Letter* 112).

The evidence indicates that the Nazoraeans—if in fact they were different from the Ebionites at all—were doctrinally similar to the Ebionites, Elchasaites, Nasaraeans, and Ossaeans. The one *possible* difference they may have had with the Ebionites was that they rejected animal sacrifice for different reasons than their other Jewish Christian friends. They may have held that sacrifice was indeed permitted for a time as a concession to human weakness, but that with Jesus this time has ended. This would explain how the Nazoraeans could have the same "doctrine" as the Ebionites on vegetarianism and animal sacrifice, accept a gospel in which Jesus came to "abolish sacrifices," and could also accept "the whole law." All of the Jewish Christian groups, though splintered into rival sects, agreed with the Ebionites on the fundamental points of favoring vegetarianism and rejecting animal sacrifice.

Conclusions

Neither Judaism nor Christianity had a place for Jewish Christianity. That is what underlies the weakness of Jewish Christianity. That Jewish Christianity was able to maintain a front against both religions for four centuries is the true index of the power of its ideas. The Jewish Christians had Jesus' own relatives among their number, and thus an unbroken chain of tradition extending back to Jesus himself. As time progressed, Jewish Christianity shattered, breaking down into numerous diverse factions, whose true differences elude us. On the essentials, though, all of these factions were in agreement.

For better or worse, Judaism defined itself in terms of its unsuccessful revolts against Rome, and this was something which was incompatible with the message of Jesus in any of its forms. Judaism also correctly saw that the Christian message had become largely a gentile message which was incompatible with the revelation given to Moses, and which *substituted* the authority of the Church for the law of Moses. There was also the bitter memory of the "betrayal" of Israel by the Jewish Christians in both of the Palestinian revolts against Rome. For these reasons, Jewish Christianity could find no home in Judaism, and the prayers of Judaism included a request that the heretics (namely, the Jewish Christians) be speedily destroyed.[12]

Gentile Christians also had no room for Jewish Christianity. Gentile Christianity, for a variety of reasons, became antagonistic toward *all* Jews. From the point of view of gentile Christianity, the Jews had rejected Jesus, and the destruction of the temple and of Israel was God's judgement on them. The literature of Christianity evolved to reflect this growing antagonism towards the Jews, with the myth of Judas and of the Jewish mob crying "crucify him, his blood be on us and on our children" creeping into the New Testament, enabling Christians to conveniently backdate the Jewish rejection of Jesus to the time of Jesus himself.[13] For gentile Christianity, Jesus was a divine redeemer whom "the Jews" had rejected. The Christology of gentile Christianity evolved into a form that was as anti-Jewish as possible while still conceding that Jesus was a Jew. This anti-Jewish polemic evolved into an anti-Semitism that has had such tragic consequences down through history.

Thus history was rewritten by both sides and the Jews and Christians took separate paths—both sides ignoring the religion of Jesus. There was "no room at the inn" for the message of the Jewish Jesus in either Judaism or Christianity. The words of the Jewish Jesus were hereafter sown, not among the lost sheep of Israel to whom Jesus and James preached, but in a foreign land.

13 THE GOSPEL OF THE STRANGER GOD

THE FOLLOWERS OF PAUL CHALLENGE AND REMAKE THE CHURCHES

E ARLY IN THE SECOND CENTURY, A MAN NAMED MARCION
began preaching a version of the Christian gospel that depended
heavily on Paul. To some, Marcion was the epitome of evil, the
"first born of Satan" (Eusebius, *Ecclesiastical History* 4.14.7). To others,
Marcion expressed the original Christianity of Jesus and Paul.

Marcion is a very important figure in the history of Jewish
Christianity: he is its arch-nemesis. Marcion was largely responsible for
popularizing the letters of Paul and hoped to separate Judaism and
Christianity altogether. Marcion and the gnostics were rejected by the
orthodox churches, but they greatly influenced Christianity by pushing
it ever further from its Palestinian roots.

Marcion saw a fundamental dichotomy between Jesus and the Old
Testament: the God of the Old Testament, while very real, was *not* the
same God who was the Father of Jesus. Marcion's radical break with
Judaism spoke to something within early Christianity, because he
quickly acquired many followers. Marcion was a central figure in the
history of Christianity and his impact on Christianity was dramatic. As I
have pointed out, at the time of Marcion there was no clearly defined
"canon" of New Testament writings. Marcion, though, *did* have such a
group of writings: he brought a version of the gospel of Luke, plus ten of
Paul's letters, to Rome. This innovation was wildly successful; the letters

of Paul were permanently etched in Christian memory and the idea of a "canon" of writings became part of the Christian strategy.

Marcion and the reaction to Marcion and other gnostics created yet another major crisis in the history of Christianity. Marcion was condemned by the church as a heretic in the middle of the second century; but Marcionite churches continued, and battled the "orthodox" churches for more than a century after. Marcion took up two themes present in Paul: the despair felt concerning this world of misery and death, and the opposition between Jesus and the Old Testament. Christianity rejected Marcion, but had to accept Paul as part of the bargain, and in the heat of the struggle it was forged into something no one in the first century—neither James, Peter, nor Paul—could have foreseen or would have recognized: a religion that had some elements of Paul, some of Jewish Christianity, and some of neither.

Marcion's Stranger God

Is God a stranger to this world? Are we also strangers in this world, passing through a foreign land—a land of sadness, misery, and death? Are we returning to our true home in heaven when we die? These ideas, while we may disagree with them, do not seem foreign to us at all. Indeed, they are an integral part of much of Protestant thought, which speaks of the comfort of another, better world awaiting us after we get through the trials and tribulations of this one. And doesn't the God of the Old Testament seem at times to be a strange character—a vengeful, bloodthirsty being? How does one square the God of the Old Testament with the kind, loving God who is the father of Jesus? This problem is also familiar to many Christians.

Marcion solved these problems in a single, daring stroke: the God of Jesus and the God of the Old Testament were two different Gods altogether. The God of the Old Testament actually created the world; but the God of the Old Testament and the God of Christianity—the father of Jesus—were completely different. The true, highest God—the God we should worship—was a *stranger* to the creation of the world of flesh, misery, and death. The Creator God, sometimes called the "Demiurge," created the world, but was not the same as the Stranger God who was the father of Jesus. The Old Testament described the actions of the Creator God, not the Stranger God; thus to become a Christian meant rejection of the Old Testament (and Judaism) altogether.[1]

Marcion was one of the earliest and best known of the gnostics; however, there were many others also. Valentinus, who like Marcion flourished in the second century CE, held many of the same ideas that Marcion did: the depravity of the flesh and the material world, the rejection of our animal nature in favor of our higher or spiritual self, and the idea of the "docetic" or completely spiritual Christ who never truly incarnated in the world but only seemed to do so. The writings of the early church fathers testify to the strength of gnosticism: Irenaeus, Tertullian, Origen, and Epiphanius literally wrote volumes against the gnostics. It was a very real historical possibility that gnosticism might have triumphed and the nature and history of Christianity been completely different from what it was.

The struggle with Marcion left a deep imprint not only on Christianity but also on the New Testament. There are many texts in the synoptic gospels and Acts that seem specifically directed against this heretic. Indeed, three additional "letters of Paul" were put in the New Testament, over and above the ten that Marcion helped popularize. These letters (I and II Timothy and Titus) are generally acknowledged to be letters not written by Paul at all, but written sometime in the second century.[2] One of the reasons that these letters were included is doubtless that it is so difficult to refute Marcion on the basis of the other ten letters. It is unlikely that a force sufficiently powerful to introduce three new forged "letters of Paul" into the canon, would have left the rest of the New Testament untouched. Paul's authentic letters lend a great deal of support to Marcion. Indeed, Marcion could very plausibly claim to be a true disciple of Paul—perhaps the *only* true disciple we know of in early Christianity.

The Old Testament for Paul and Marcion

For Marcion, Jesus had *nothing* to do with the God of the Old Testament. The Old Testament was, therefore, "true" as far as it went but only told part of the story. The Creator God, the God described by the Old Testament, did give laws and a kind of "justice," but this came from the same source as a world of misery, suffering, and death—a thoroughly bungled creation.

Paul had earlier faced a similar fork in the road—and hesitated. For Paul, the law had been *superseded* by Christ. The law no longer had validity for those in Christ: "he annulled the law with its rules and regulations" (Ephesians 2:15, New English Bible); for Paul his own former allegiance to the law was "so much garbage" (Philippians 3:8, New English Bible). Paul, therefore, does not quite embrace Marcion's solution. He denigrates the law in the Old Testament and says that it does not apply to Christians; but he never says that the God of Jesus was not responsible *at all* for the Old Testament. However, while Paul's words do not explicitly support Marcion on this point, they do provide far more support for Marcion's wholesale rejection of the Old Testament God than do the synoptic gospels. Paul and Marcion are important testimonies that the later almost casual acceptance of the Old Testament was not a given to the early church.

The Jewish Christians also rejected the orthodox Christian claim for the Old Testament, though for completely different reasons than the gnostics. *For the Jewish Christians, the Old Testament was the imperfect story of the true God; for Marcion and many gnostics, the Old Testament was the true story of the imperfect God.* The Jewish Christians were strict monotheists and rejected the idea of two Gods. Thus, though the Jewish Christians and the gnostics were opposed to each other, they did agree that the world the Old Testament described was fundamentally flawed. They placed the blame for the imperfection in two different places: the Jewish Christians blamed a faulty text, Marcion blamed a faulty god.

The World and the Flesh for Paul and Marcion

We turn next to another question on which Paul more directly supports Marcion: the nature of the material world, our own bodies, and the resurrection. Gnosticism is strongly dualistic; matter is bad, spirit is good. As we have already seen, there is abundant support in Paul for the idea that the physical world—and attachment to it—is evil. How else are we to interpret passages such as "those who are in the flesh cannot please God" (Romans 8:8), "if you live according to the flesh you will die" (Romans 8:13), and "the desires of the flesh are against the Spirit" (Galatians 5:17)?

In Marcion, this theme is taken up in two ways: that Jesus did not come "in the flesh"—that is, he existed only as a spirit; and that Jesus (and we ourselves) will at the resurrection continue to exist, but spiritually and not physically. Why did Marcion hold these views? We don't have an account from Marcion himself, but it is obvious that these Marcionite extrapolations *are logical extensions of Paul's attack on the "flesh" and the material world.* If the flesh "cannot please God," it is hard to explain why our flesh will be resurrected and saved on the last day, or why Jesus, who was supposedly perfect and the incarnation of God, would come in a physical body.

Paul never says that Jesus had a physical body. He says that Jesus came "in the likeness of sinful flesh" (Romans 8:3), which leaves the door open just slightly. It's possible that there are two different kinds of flesh—sinful, and not sinful—and that Jesus had the latter type. But based on everything else Paul says, the most obvious interpretation is that *all* flesh is sinful and that Jesus only *appeared* to have sinful flesh. This is an interpretation that gnostics doubtless seized upon, since Tertullian feels called upon to respond to it (*Against Marcion* 5.14).

Those seeking to defend Paul's orthodoxy may try to say that Paul felt that not all flesh is sinful; that when Paul speaks of "flesh" he really means "fleshly thinking or actions," or "works of the flesh" as Tertullian says (*Against Marcion* 5.10). This is, I think, twisting the context and words of Paul to conform to an orthodox perspective; it's clear that Paul does not like the "flesh," but favors the "spirit." Paul sometimes makes statements that seem to imply that our resurrected physical bodies will inherit the kingdom of God, for example, Romans 8:11: "He who raised Christ Jesus from the dead will give life to your mortal bodies." But when he starts getting into specifics, he immediately adds qualifications that seem to bring into question what, precisely, will be resurrected. "All flesh is not the same flesh," says Paul, distinguishing between men, beasts, sun, and stars:

> So it is with the resurrection of the dead. What is sown in the earth as a perishable thing is raised imperishable. Sown in humiliation, it is raised in glory; sown in weakness, it is raised in power; sown as an animal body, it is raised as a spiritual body. (I Corinthians 15:42–44, New English Bible)

These verses have the effect of qualifying the term "body" so that it does not necessarily mean a "physical body": there are spiritual bodies and animal bodies. Thus, when Paul is speaking elsewhere about the resurrection of the "body," he undoubtedly means that a *spiritual* body" has been raised. This is made explicit a few verses further when Paul says emphatically:

> I tell you this, brethren: *flesh and blood cannot inherit the kingdom of God,* nor does the perishable inherit the imperishable. (I Corinthians 15:50, emphasis added)

Generations of commentators have twisted and turned to avoid the obvious and heretical conclusion: that what is good in us (and will be resurrected) does not consist *in any part* of flesh and blood. Irenaeus (*Against Heresies* 5.9) and Tertullian (*Against Marcion* 5.10) struggle with these key verses trying, unconvincingly, to deny that Paul meant what he clearly said. What is good in us is our spiritual selves; and on the last day, it is this spiritual self that will be raised, and given a *spiritual* body. Whatever our "spiritual bodies" are, they do not (for Paul) consist of flesh and blood. Yet for the orthodox, by contrast, it is our physical bodies, our flesh and blood, that will be recreated for us on the last day.

Paul provides a lot of comfort for anyone looking for such a gnostic view in the scriptures. He first states that the flesh is bad and then that the resurrection is of the spirit, not of the flesh. Even at best (from the orthodox point of view), Paul is not orthodox; at best he is inconsistent, sometimes saying one thing and sometimes another. At every point where flesh and spirit are contrasted, spirit is regarded as higher and better.

On this point, Paul and Marcion are in substantial agreement. It does not take much of an imagination to see that Marcion could have understood Paul's statement that "flesh and blood cannot inherit the kingdom of God" to mean, in fact, that flesh and blood cannot inherit the kingdom of God.

The "God of This World" for Marcion and Paul

Paul contrasts the "letter" of the law with the "spirit" of Jesus Christ. The letter kills, the spirit gives life. Could the same God who sent the "killing" letter also have sent the "living" spirit? Could the same God who created this world of fleshly misery also have sent his son to redeem us? Who, in brief, created the world—a world of flesh, misery, and death?

Paul nowhere explicitly answers this question in a way that would clearly either confirm or refute Marcion. He does, however, lend support and comfort to those looking for gnostic views. He states there are supernatural and evil powers abroad in the universe and that the unhappy condition of the universe has been imposed from without. Paul refers to Satan (II Corinthians 11:14, 12:7) and to our enslavement to "the elemental spirits of the universe" (Galatians 4:3). At some points he even refers to these spirits as gods:

> For indeed, if there be so-called gods, whether in heaven or on earth—*as indeed there are many 'gods' and many 'lords'—yet for us* there is one God, the Father, from whom all being comes, towards whom we all move . . . (I Corinthians 8:5–6, New English Bible; emphasis added)

Their unbelieving minds are so blinded *by the god of this passing age*, that the gospel of the glory of Christ, who is the very image of God, cannot dawn upon them and bring them light.(II Corinthians 4:4, New English Bible; emphasis added)

Paul says that "for us" all being comes from one God, but after all he has said about this passing and temporary world, it's not clear if that means God is really responsible for creating the world or whether the world was created by the "god of this passing age." This is reminiscent of the gospel of John, which quotes Jesus as speaking of the "prince of this world"—not God, but the devil (John 12:31, 16:11). It is only one step from saying that a supernatural evil power is "prince of this world" to saying that this same supernatural power actually created the world. Marcion in fact did take this step: he claimed that when Paul referred to the "rulers of this age" (I Corinthians 2:8), the "god of this passing age" (II Corinthians 4:4), or the "prince of the power of the air" (Ephesians 2:2), that Paul was really referring to the Creator God—so the gnostics quoted such passages with considerable relish (*Against Marcion* 5.6, 5.17).

Paul does not attribute the sinfulness and suffering of the world to a supernatural being like Marcion's Creator God. Paul *does* say, however, that the condition of the universe was imposed from without, rather than from within:

For the created universe waits with eager expectation for God's sons to be revealed. It was made the victim of frustration, not by its own choice, but *because of him who made it so* . . . (Romans 8:19–20, New English Bible; emphasis added)

Paul does not tell us who it is that "made it so"—that made the created universe the victim of frustration. Some commentators have tried to say that Paul meant to say that humans (perhaps through Adam's sin) "made it so,"[3] because making *God* responsible for this frustration would involve us in serious theological problems. We would then have to say that God and Jesus were working at cross-purposes—God to frustrate the world, and Jesus to redeem it. However, Paul seems to suggest exactly such an interpretation, for he implies that the frustration comes from a source *outside* the universe; the condition of the universe was *not* a choice. If God is not the source of this frustration, then it must be some other evil supernatural spirit. While Paul is not consistent here, he does on this point appear to support gnostic dualism.

Who made Paul a "miserable creature . . . doomed to death" (Romans 7:24)? Marcion could easily name the responsible supernatural power: it was the Jewish Creator God. The prison of this world was created by an ignorant or evil supernatural spirit—either Satan or a Demiurge along the lines of Marcion's Creator God. This makes Marcion a radical, but consistent, disciple of Paul.

The Ebionite Rejection of Gnosticism

Both the orthodox church and the Ebionites rejected gnosticism. This shows that "heresy" was by no means a uniform commodity; we should not always expect one set of heretics (the Ebionites) to be allied with another set (the gnostics). The rejection of gnosticism came only after a fierce battle that modified Christianity substantially; it is possible that the Ebionite opposition to gnosticism may have tipped the balance against gnosticism in this struggle.

The debates in the *Recognitions* and *Homilies* between Peter and Simon Magus, a figure who is presented as having gnostic views, make the Ebionite response clear. Simon Magus, like Marcion, argues that the Creator God of the Jews is not the highest God (*Homilies* 18.1–4, *Recognitions* 2.39), and Peter (speaking for Jewish Christianity) argues against this view. Jesus came in a physical body, and God and his creation are seen in a positive light. In this sense, the Ebionites seem to side more with the orthodox than with the gnostics.

Interestingly, however, the Ebionites seem to side with Paul and the gnostics on one point—the nature of the resurrection. The Jewish Christians, if we take the *Recognitions* and *Homilies* as our guide, did accept the resurrection, but saw this resurrection in much the same way as Paul did, as a resurrection of the spirit. Thus Peter comments:

Whence also angels, who are spirits see God; and therefore men, as long as they are men, cannot see Him. But after the resurrection of the dead, *when they shall have been made like the angels*, they shall be able to see God. (*Recognitions* 3.30; emphasis added)

At first this seems like something from a gnostic author whose writings somehow got into the *Recognitions*. It, of course, leads to an obvious question: If the Ebionites think that world and the flesh created by God is "good," then why is the resurrection only a resurrection of the spirit? Simon Magus, Peter's opponent, in fact asks this very question. Peter's answer, however, is very un-gnostic; instead of demeaning the physical world as a world of misery and death, he answers that this material world is good *despite* its being transitory:

As I might say, by way of illustration, however fairly and carefully the shell of the egg may seem to have been formed, it is yet necessary that it be broken and opened, that the chick may issue from it, and that may appear for which the form of the whole egg seems to have been molded. So also, therefore, it is necessary that the condition of this world pass away, that that sublimer condition of the heavenly kingdom may shine forth. (*Recognitions* 3.28)

This is probably tied back to the original resurrection experience, which both the Ebionites and Paul took to be a revelation of the *spirit* of Jesus rather than a revelation of his reconstructed flesh and bones. The experience of the resurrection of Jesus is in this respect a piercing of a "veil of illusion" that in fact is the substance of this transitory world. But this veil is necessary and prepares us for the next stage of reality; the world is thus not simply a depraved and miserable existence from which we must escape. Indeed, in Matthew, Jesus suggests such a "spiritual" view of the resurrection; in response to the Sadducees who present the question of whose wife a woman with seven husbands will be at the resurrection, Jesus responds that in the resurrection people do not marry but are like angels in heaven (Matthew 22:30). "Angels" would seem to be spiritual, not physical beings, both in Matthew and in the *Recognitions*.

It is often difficult to draw black and white distinctions between the various Christian groups. Despite some similarities, the Ebionites differed from the gnostics on two critical points: the Ebionites accepted the law of God as the law of the Creator of the universe, and thought of the creator and the creation as fundamentally good. Because Paul also appears to side with the gnostics on these points—by attacking the law and describing our existence as depraved—the Ebionites insisted on branding Paul as an apostate from the law of God and rejected Paul as well.

The Orthodox Rejection of Gnosticism

The emerging orthodox church, like the Ebionites, rejected gnosticism. But their response to Paul was different. Whether by choice or because they had no choice, they accepted Paul—but only after "modifying" Paul's views ex post facto in the pastoral epistles and in the book of Acts.

The Ebionites did not follow the lead of the church on Paul. They knew Paul and what he stood for; instead of modifying Paul to make him acceptable, they rejected his views altogether. This sealed the fate of Jewish Christianity; after this point it is difficult to see how a reconciliation between Jewish Christianity and orthodox Christianity was possible. The orthodox had canonized the writings of the man who was the Ebionites' enemy, who had rejected vegetarianism, and who (in their view) was an apostate from the law and thus from true Christianity.

The ten letters of Paul that Marcion promoted did not constitute the end of Marcion's impact on the New Testament. The most important repercussions were reactions *against* Marcion that can be found throughout the New Testament. The most obvious are the three "pastoral" epistles attributed to Paul: I and II Timothy and Titus. "Paul" can discuss such issues as the proper behavior of a bishop and a deacon (I Timothy 3:1–13), the status of elders and preachers (I Timothy 5:17–22), and the place of the Christian in the social order (Titus 3:1–2;

I Timothy 2:1–15). These matters were scarcely a concern to the historical Paul, who fully expected to live to see Jesus come again (I Thessalonians 4:13–18); but they were concerns for the church a hundred years after Paul lived—the most likely date for their composition.

The "pastoral" letters also specifically repudiate many of the gnostic doctrines that Marcion attributed to Paul. "Paul" explicitly says that Jesus came in the flesh (I Timothy 3:16), that there is only one God (I Timothy 1:17), and that the world of the creator is a glorious and good thing (I Timothy 4:4–5). No despair about a world of misery and suffering waiting for deliverance here! "Paul" even delivers an endorsement of the Old Testament: "every inspired scripture has its use for teaching the truth and refuting error" (II Timothy 3:16–17).

Acts, which was written later than either the authentic letters of Paul or the synoptic gospels, also bears the imprint of the struggle with Marcion. As we have seen, Acts emphasizes the harmony of Paul with the "Jewish leadership" in the early church and downplays the disharmony at every opportunity. Obviously, a strong polemical purpose against Marcion is being served if everyone in early Christianity, including Paul, is portrayed as being more "Jewish"; in the eagerness of orthodox writers to refute the Marcionite idea that Jesus repudiated the Old Testament God, the "Jewishness of Jesus" suddenly came back into fashion in second century Christianity. Samuel Sandmel aptly describes the situation: "What Acts does in its anti-Marcionism is to change Paul from being a religious genius into being just one more missionary."[4]

There is a tendency among scholars to equate anything "Jewish" in Christianity with the idea that it must be early, from the first century, and probably from Jesus or those close to him. This is most definitely not the case. It is most obvious in the case of Acts, where Paul—the same Paul who said that Jesus had annulled the law with its rules and regulations—is shown going to the temple to make a sacrifice! There are many other examples of this tendency;[5] their evident intent is to demonstrate that Jesus, his family, and his followers all scrupulously followed the Old Testament ritual observances. The introduction of such "rabbinic" details suggests that editing of Acts and the synoptic gospels may have continued many years after the books were initially written down, as details and incidents were modified to show their applicability to changing circumstances.

The history of early Christianity shows abundant evidence that there *were* Jewish Christians, but that they were uniformly opposed to animal sacrifice and had a fundamentally different character from the rabbinic Jews that Christians encountered in the second and succeeding centuries. It is a subtle trap because it is so easy to argue from Jesus' Jewishness to his being an orthodox Jew just like those described in the Talmud; and modern scholars have almost uniformly fallen for it as well. Most of these details come from the anti-Marcionite struggle in second-century Christianity and have no reference to anything in the primitive church.

The "Original Sin" Debate

"Christ died for our sins" (I Corinthians 15:3) says Paul, in one of his most widely quoted aphorisms. Why is the blood of Jesus necessary for our sins to be forgiven? The answer to this question created the biggest theological problem in Christendom: the doctrine of "original sin"—that Christ died for our sins, because we are born sinners and are inherently sinful—which plagues the church to this day.

Original sin is a controversial and complex topic. Paul is usually blamed for the idea of original sin, with Augustine cited as an accessory after the fact. However, whether Paul really intended to say that we were born sinners, rather than that we have all sinned just because we are imperfect, is unclear. The fifth chapter of Romans, on which the doctrine of original sin is based, is suggestive; but it is also one of the murkiest passages that Paul ever wrote, and many very intelligent people from Augustine on have spent long hours analyzing it and still have come up with different answers.

It is unlikely that *any* interpretation of Paul can make everything Paul says both clear and consistent. However, a gnostic interpretation of Paul on this point would at least be clear. A gnostic could simply say that we are sinners because we were *created* sinful, not because we ever chose sin. We are inherently sinful, not through our own choice, but because of the evil (or ignorant) power that made us sinful. We are liberated by the freeing power of the highest, good God, who redeems us from the evil or ignorant power that enslaves us.

This dualistic answer is supported by some of what Paul says. Understanding Paul is made complex because "sin" can be confused with a "sinful state." The actions *producing* a depraved existence in which we are separated from God are clearly different from this depraved existence itself. But the question is whether our own actions (or even Adam's actions) produce this sinful state? Or is the situation the reverse: the sinful state, or depraved existence, is the cause of sinful actions? Paul implies that it is our sinful state that produces sin, rather than vice versa. He says, for example, "If I do what I do not want, it is no longer I that do it, but sin which dwells within me" (Romans 7:20), emphasizing that Paul believes it is not an act of desire for evil that brings about sinful actions, but that sin *already* dwells in us, prior to our actions. One obvious interpretation of Paul is that there are competing powers in the universe—for good and evil—and that it is the evil power that made the universe a victim of frustration. Paul's idea of sin is in many ways closer to Marcion than to Augustine.

Jewish Christianity rejected all ideas of "original sin," simply because Jewish Christians accepted the Jewish framework in which humans are created in the image of God and are, therefore, not inherently depraved or sinful. Indeed, even the devil himself may be saved, for he has the capacity to become good (*Homilies* 20.3)! The *Recognitions* addresses the question of evil by blaming it, in Platonic/Pythagorean fashion, on lack of knowledge rather than on human depravity. It is ignorance that is the "mother of almost all evils" (*Recognitions* 4.8); it is ignorance "which is the worst of all demons" (*Recognitions* 2.25).

The Jewish Christians retold the story of the Garden of Eden in accordance with this idea. The Ebionite interpretation of Genesis, as related in the *Homilies* and *Recognitions*, removes sin from the Garden of Eden completely; in fact, Adam was without sin, having the spirit of

Christ within him (*Homilies* 3.20). The first sin is not due to eating a mythical "apple" but rather due to the consumption of meat, among other things, long after the Garden of Eden.

In the *Recognitions*, the first seven generations of humans are righteous, unlike Genesis where Adam and Eve (the first generation of humans) are expelled from the garden. It is in the *eighth* generation in which sin enters the world, through illicit sexual relations; in the ninth generation giants are born and the great flood occurs, which Noah escapes in his ark. It is because humans taste blood (among other things) that the flood is sent (*Recognitions* 1.29–30). This chronology places the "fall of man," the first eating of meat, and the great flood all in the eighth and ninth generations of humanity. The *Homilies* provides more elaborate details, specifically stating that angels and human women had intercourse and their offspring longed for blood, and then the first killing of animals for food occurred (8.15). It was this violence that was the occasion for the flood.

What, precisely, was the sin of Adam and Eve? Christians have answered this question in many different ways. Some would say that their sin was simply disobeying God's command. While eating of the tree of the knowledge of good and evil seems innocuous enough, God knows best, and Adam and Eve should have obeyed. Others, such as the gnostics, interpret the story as darkly suggesting that the serpent was right: the God who created the earth was not the highest God, but a jealous, spiteful being, and not the Highest Power in the universe after all.

The Ebionite explanation undercuts any possibility of a dogma of "original sin" by rejecting the idea that sin occurred in the Garden of Eden at all. The tasting of blood, the "fall of man," and the great flood, all occur in quick succession after eight righteous generations have already come. For the Ebionites, we are not inherently sinful and anyone can follow the same path as Jesus: just as oil from the tree of life anointed Jesus as the Christ, similar oil anoints the believers when they come to the kingdom of God (*Recognitions* 1.45). The Ebionites affirmed that they themselves were "able to become Christs" (Hippolytus, *Refutation of all Heresies* 7.22), and thus proclaimed the Christhood of every believer.

Even in the New Testament, Jesus expresses every confidence that his followers can achieve spiritual realization, insisting that his followers be "perfect" (Matthew 5:48), and predicting that those who follow him will not only do what he did, but even greater things (John 14:12). Instead, however, orthodox Christianity is preoccupied with guilt and sin—something that has been part of orthodoxy since the time of Augustine. "Original sin" in its modern form had no place in the teachings of Jesus or in Judaism, paganism, Jewish Christianity, or probably even in Paul. It originated in the need to twist Paul's dualistic ideas into a non-dualistic framework and achieved its final form with Augustine.

Conclusions

In the second century, it was Marcion who understood Paul the best. It is not without reason to suppose that he brought forward the letters of Paul to defend his Gospel of the Stranger God. Like Paul, Marcion disparages the Jewish law and the Old Testament, while acknowledging a certain legitimate place for it in the creation. Like Paul, Marcion sees a duality between the flesh (bad) and spirit (good). Like Paul, Marcion sees strong supernatural powers (other than the one highest God) in charge of our world. Marcion, despite his strangeness for modern Christians, is closer to the doctrine of Paul than most ancient or modern writers.

The struggle with gnosticism was another step in the dissolution of primitive Christianity. Despite its failure, gnosticism modified Christianity beyond recognition. The writings of Paul, the enemy of the Ebionites, were accepted as scripture; and even as sanitized by the orthodox, they were too much for the Jewish Christians to swallow. Many passages in Acts, the synoptic gospels, and elsewhere throughout the New Testament are more the consequence of anti-Marcionite polemic than an accurate record of the words and deeds of Jesus and his first followers. Paul was not consistently gnostic, and following a line from Jesus to Paul may not get us all the way to gnosticism. However, we can say this: *the trajectory from Jesus to Paul ends logically in gnosticism.*

NO GOD
BUT ALLAH

HOW ISLAM ABSORBED
JEWISH CHRISTIANITY

W HAT FINALLY HAPPENED TO JEWISH CHRISTIANITY? Jewish Christian sects continued to exist until at least the fifth century, falling prey to divisions among themselves concerning issues that are largely obscure to us. We don't know whether the various Jewish Christian groups were really distinct groups marked by some sort of leadership and organization, or just vague tendencies in certain Christian communities. We can only speculate based on our knowledge of sectarian groups in modern times: groups that to outsiders seem nearly identical in their viewpoint will sometimes be fiercely divided over issues that are practically invisible to us.

Jewish Christian thought, like that of the orthodox, underwent change and development during this time. Like the orthodox and the gnostics, Jewish Christians too probably distorted the teachings of Jesus and the primitive community. We see this, for example, in the evolution of the concept of the "true prophet." In the beginning, this may have involved nothing more than the conviction that Jesus was the prophet predicted by Moses (Deuteronomy 18:15–18). But it progressed to a more elaborate and exalted view—somewhat analogous to that of the orthodox—of the "eternal Christ" who manifested himself to Adam, Abraham, and Moses. Despite the opposition between Jewish Christianity and gnosticism, some gnostic tendencies infiltrated Jewish Christianity, apparent in the conclusion that the present world has been given to the devil (*Homilies* 20.2, *Panarion* 30.16.2). This pessimistic view may have been a consequence of the Jewish Christians' perception of their own declining influence within Christianity.

Jewish Christianity might have continued as an obscure group of sects for many more hundreds of years, but then yet another unexpected blow fell: Christianity became the religion of the Roman Empire.

Constantine and the Disappearance of Jewish Christianity

In the year 312, Constantine became emperor and Christianity underwent yet another pivotal change—from a persecuted minority to a state-supported religion. Just fourteen years prior to Constantine, Diocletian had initiated the most severe and effective persecutions ever directed against the early church. Then, in 303, Diocletian ordered all copies of the Bible burned and all churches demolished. These persecutions fell on all Christians, regardless of sect, and continued until almost the very day when Constantine marched into Rome as emperor in 312.

Constantine probably had several motivations in supporting the Christian church. To begin with, he evidently sincerely believed in one God; based on his own public statements, Constantine was a monotheist. He, therefore, saw something of the truth in Christianity, and he saw more truth in the church than he saw in paganism. His own personal belief in Christianity beyond that, though, is open to question. While he supported the churches with his imperial power, at the beginning he also supported paganism. Moreover, he did not actually convert to Christianity, despite all the support he gave the church, until he was dying.

Of course all this affected the church. Most importantly, it became an important interest to the Roman Empire to maintain a strong, united church. This meant that points of view that were "inconvenient" from the point of view of the Empire were weakened or discarded, such as the emphasis on pacifism. It also meant that heresies were not tolerated. After Constantine, the number of Christians in the Empire probably doubled or tripled in a relatively short period of time. Countless soldiers, for example, were baptized in the new religion, thus insuring the status of the military in Christianity. Christianity changed almost as dramatically in a few short decades as it had in its entire history up to that point.

Constantine certainly helped the orthodox cause, because he helped suppress the non-orthodox forms of Christianity.[1] Thus, Jewish Christianity had to suffer persecution twice—first under Diocletian, and then under Constantine. On the other hand, Constantine's support for orthodoxy was largely motivated by his political desire to see the church united and strong. Thus, he did not see very much virtue in either side in the celebrated Arian controversy, which was the occasion for the Nicene Council, and ordered Arius (who had been excommunicated) to be readmitted to the fellowship (Arius died before this could happen).[2]

The idea of the virtue of supporting the Roman social order in exchange for support from that same order would probably have evoked words like "betrayal" in the middle of the third century. The Donatist controversy in North Africa in the early fourth century—one of the first of the "church crises" to be dealt with by Constantine—involved just this issue. This controversy revolved around, in essence, whether those who denied the faith for reasons of expedience during the great persecution prior to Constantine could serve in positions of church leadership. The Donatists said that, in effect, they should not, and refused all appeals from Constantine to join with the great church. The Donatist split was never resolved, and ended only when Christianity (both orthodox and Donatist) in North Africa was wiped out. Evidently, the Donatists felt that testifying to the faith was not something that should be lightly abandoned or tolerated on grounds of expediency. Yet, by the middle of the fourth century, expedient cooperation with the state had become a virtue because it enabled the church establishment to flourish.

Epiphanius, who wrote the *Panarion* just over 50 years after the Council of Nicaea, is the last person to give any substantial historical evidence about Jewish Christianity. Hans-Joachim Schoeps concludes that Jewish Christianity disappears sometime in the fifth century CE.[3] This should be the end of the story; but it isn't. There is remarkable evidence of a continuing influence of Ebionite ideas in Islam, the religion that exploded into existence early in the seventh century CE—an influence which continues down to the present day. The Ebionites left an impact, and perhaps even a line of teachers, in the religion that eventually triumphed in the areas where Ebionism was the strongest.

The Emergence of Islam

Early in the seventh century a camel driver in Mecca named Mohammed had a vision and heard the command: "Recite! Recite!" When he began reciting, the words he produced became the *Qur'an*, or the "recitation" that is the basis of Islam. "Islam," the religion announced by Mohammed, literally means "surrender," that is, surrender to God. It was a strict monotheism, rejecting any polytheism as well as the Christian "trinity" and even any ascription of divinity to Mohammed himself. The followers of Mohammed, armed with the slogan "there is no God but Allah (God)" (Qur'an 2:163, 23:91, etc.), opposed the idolatry and the feuding clan-wars that pervaded Arabia at that time. Within Mohammed's lifetime, Islam had been firmly established in Arabia. A hundred years later, Islam had swept westward through northern Africa into Spain and had spread eastward to the border of India.

Today, most westerners think of Muslims as a militant and aggressive, hardly the picture of pacifist vegetarians living in abject poverty. This view is a distortion; religions often incorporate many different cultural streams into the river of faith. One of these streams was the remnants of Ebionism, which influenced Islam and the development of Sufism, the mystical dimension of the religion.

There is no unequivocal evidence that links Ebionite Christianity to Islam: nowhere do we find early Sufi or Islamic writers discussing by name the Ebionites or Jewish Christianity. By the seventh century, Ebionism might not have been significant enough even to record as a tendency by those who chronicled the history of Islam—if indeed Ebionism still existed at all at that time. Nevertheless, Ebionite tendencies in Islam are striking and, in sum, support my belief that Ebionism was absorbed into Islam.

Ebionite Tendencies in Islam

Orthodox Islam differs from orthodox Christianity in endorsing some distinctively Ebionite positions. Just as the Ebionites rejected all alcohol, Islam also rejects the use of alcohol, and has rejected it from the beginning (Qur'an 5:90–91). Also, the Qur'an endorses the Ebionite idea that the scriptures have been tampered with and extends it from the Old Testament to the New Testament as well. According to Islam, the Jews broke their covenant; and, moreover, they "change words from their context and forget a part of that whereof they were admonished." Allah made a covenant with the Christians as well as the Jews, but they too forgot part of what they were told; and as a consequence Allah has "stirred up enmity and hatred among them till the Day of Resurrection" (Qur'an 5:12–5:14).

Thus, according to Islam, both the Christians and the Jews have distorted the message that God sent to them. The Christians have not only forgotten the revelation they received but—by divine decree!— cannot even agree among themselves on what the message is. All this sounds very similar to the Ebionite depiction of history, though there is the additional suggestion not only that false texts have been inserted ("change words from their context") but also that true texts have been deleted ("forget a part of that whereof they were admonished").

There are many favorable references to Jesus in the Qur'an. Jesus is said to have performed many miracles, including healing the sick, raising the dead, and creating birds from clay—a miracle not in the New Testament (Qur'an 5:110; see also the Christian account in the *Arabic Gospel of the Infancy of the Savior* 36). This, however, does not imply that Jesus was a divine being, only that he enjoyed divine favor. Jesus in the Qur'an himself rejects his own right to be exalted to the status of being a "partner" with Allah (Qur'an 5:116) and the Christian belief in the Trinity is explicitly rejected (Qur'an 5:72, 5:73). Those who ascribe "partners" to Allah are repeatedly denounced in the Qur'an, and this denunciation includes not only the polytheistic idolatry with which Mohammed had to contend in Arabia, but also the Trinitarianism (Father, Son, and Holy Ghost) of the Christians. However much orthodox Christianity rejects the charge of polytheism, Islam sees the ascribing of "partners" to Allah, with however much subtlety it is done, as wrongheaded. We have here an echo of Ebionite unitarianism, with Jesus as the True Prophet. There is, however, one significant difference: Islam accepts the idea of the virginal conception of Jesus by his mother Mary through a divine power of some sort (Qur'an 19:17–22). As with the other miracles relating to Jesus, this does not imply that Jesus himself was divine, only that divine favor was bestowed on him and his message.

There is, finally, in Islam a constant emphasis on the need to support the poor. The Islamic summary of the Law of Moses in Qur'an 5:12 gives three elements: establishing God's worship, supporting God's messengers, and giving to the needy (the poor, orphans, and widows). The command to support the poor is repeated often in the Qur'an (e. g. 2:43, 2:215, 24:56). The refrain to give to charity occurs almost as often as the command to support the messenger of God (i. e., Mohammed), and in the same context: as one of the pillars of Islamic belief. It does not occur in quite as radical a manner—the poor are to be supported, but there is no suggestion that one must join them.

Thus, the Ebionite themes of the rejection of Trinitarianism, support for the poor, the rejection of alcohol, and the corruption of Jewish scripture are all echoed in orthodox Islam. It may be objected, however, that the support for the poor occurs in a relatively mild form present in almost all religions; and that, notwithstanding these similarities, the most obvious and distinctive Ebionite beliefs—namely, pacifism, the rejection of animal sacrifices, and the acceptance of vegetarianism—are not found in Islam at all. It might further be added that Islam is a religion that began among pastoral nomads—people who kept and herded animals as their primary means of livelihood. Islam spread through warfare at its inception and retains that image to its day. The Qur'an itself says:

Warfare is ordained for you. (2:216)

The beast of cattle is made lawful unto you (for food), except that which is announced unto you (herein). (5:1)

These kinds of passages are found throughout the Qur'an and seem to be intrinsic to Islam; meat-eating and warfare clearly have a divine sanction. Further, of the three major Middle Eastern religions emerging in this period of history (Judaism, Christianity, and Islam), Islam is today the only one that still practices animal sacrifice. Thousands of Islamic pilgrims converge on Mecca and slaughter animals in the belief that this is ordained by their religion and with the approval of the Islamic authorities. The purpose is not forgiveness of sin or appeasement of God; the animal sacrifice is specifically so that the meat can be donated to the poor.[+] Among Moslems today you will find scant evidence of vegetarianism or pacifism, or concern for animals either—except, ironically, in the Qur'an itself.

Islam in some ways seems to be the least likely of all religions to harbor Ebionite beliefs. The Islamic "environment" not only does not contain pacifist vegetarian elements; it seems to be positively hostile to such elements. This makes the discovery of precisely these factors in Islam even more striking.

Animals in Islam

Notwithstanding the approval of meat consumption and animal sacrifice in Islam, animals have a status in the Qur'an unequaled in the New Testament. According to the Qur'an, animals are manifestations of God's divine will, signs or clues for the believers provided by God (45:3-4). The animals, in fact, all praise and worship Allah (17:44). The beasts pay adoration to God, and the birds in flight praise him as well (22:18, 24:41). Allah has given the earth not just for human domination but for all his creatures (55:10). Animals have souls just like humans, for we read:

There is not an animal in the earth, nor a creature flying on two wings, but they are peoples like unto you. We have neglected nothing in the Book (of our Decrees). Then unto their Lord they will be gathered. (6:38)

Indeed, it would appear that animals can be saved on the Day of Judgment; for if people in the nations are summoned to judgement (45:28), and the animals are a "people" just like humans, then it would seem that the animals, too, will be there on that day.

Sufism

There is one Islamic tendency that merits special mention, and that is Sufism—usually thought of as a form of Islamic mysticism. "Sufism" is a broad label within Islam, much like identifying a Christian as a "Protestant." It does not denote a formal order, but rather a tendency of thought that has several different branches; there are different Sufi orders, but no single organized hierarchy.

Sufism picks up and develops the central facet of Islam, namely the meaning of "Islam"—surrender. There is in Sufism an echo of the theme that the Ebionites took up, namely that of intensification of the law, going beyond what the tradition requires. Sufi asceticism goes beyond renouncing what is unlawful—all good Muslims were supposed to do that—but includes renunciation of what is lawful, and finally, renunciation of everything else except God. Thus, many Sufis identify with the poor and practice poverty.[5] Others have lived communally, in such a way that a Sufi practitioner is ordered to have no private property at all, something we should recognize from the communalism practiced by the first Christians.[6] This is exactly the same rationale given by the Ebionites for their own "poverty"—that they owned everything in common.

Rabi'a al-Adawiyya, an early Sufi saint (died 801 CE), also embodied this desire to go beyond the requirements of the Qur'an. A celebrated story about Rabi'a is that she prayed that her motivations would exclude even the hope of reward in Paradise or fear of hell: "O Lord, if I worship you out of fear of hell, burn me in hell. If I worship you in the hope of paradise, forbid it to me. And if I worship you for your own sake, do not deprive me of your eternal beauty."[7]

For Rabi'a, this includes vegetarianism, as a famous story about her demonstrates. Rabi'a had gone to the mountains, and all kinds of animals surrounded her—goats, gazelles, and others. She is approached by an acquaintance of hers, Hasan al-Basri, whereupon all the animals scatter. Hasan is disturbed by this and asks Rabi'a why the animals make friends with her but not with him. Rabi'a asks him what he has eaten, and after Hasan replies, she counters: "Well, you eat of their flesh, why shouldn't they be afraid of you?"[8] Rabi'a must have been a vegetarian for this story to have any meaning: the animals are friends with Rabi'a because they recognize that she does not eat animals.

Not all Sufis were vegetarian, but this was a pronounced tendency. Some vegetarian Sufis, like Hamiduddin Nagori, might have become vegetarian after contact with Hinduism; but Rabi'a did not come from India, and other Islamic saints from North Africa were not only vegetarian but even avoided killing insects.[9] Indeed, there are many stories about Muslim saints that show the friendly relationship between those who were holy and the animals, similar to stories told by Christians and Buddhists about their heroes. As Annemarie Schimmel says: "For the Muslim mystic, this close relationship with the animal world is not at all amazing, since every creature praises God in its own voice and he who has purified his soul understands their praise and can join them."[10]

The poetry of Kabir, a fifteenth-century Islamic mystic and poet whom the Sufis also invoke, contains some of the most intense condemnation of meat-eating found anywhere:

> They're morons and mindless fools
> who don't know Ram in every breath.
> You rampage in, knock down a cow,
> cut her throat and take her life.
> You turn a living soul to a corpse

and call it a holy rite. . . .
Pandits read Puranas, Vedas,
Mullas learn Muhammed's faith.
Kabir says, both go straight to hell
if they don't know Ram in every breath.[11]

Fast all day,
kill cows at night,
here prayers, there blood—
does this please God?[12]

Of course, many Sufis were *not* vegetarian, including one of the most famous of the Sufis, al-Ghazali—and thus his testimony about Jesus is most interesting.

Jesus in al-Ghazali

Jesus is not an unknown figure in Islam, but the Sufis express an extraordinary interest in Jesus and have sayings of Jesus and stories about Jesus found nowhere in Christianity. Especially interesting and significant is the treatment of Jesus by al-Ghazali, an eleventh-century Islamic mystic who wrote prodigiously on religion and who is widely credited with making Sufism respectable within Islam.

For al-Ghazali, Jesus looks amazingly like the Ebionite Jesus; he lives in extreme poverty, disdains violence, loves animals, and is vegetarian. It is clear that al-Ghazali is drawing on a tradition rather than creating a tradition, because some of the same stories that al-Ghazali relates are also related by others both before and after him, and also because al-Ghazali is not himself a vegetarian and clearly has no axe to grind one way or the other. Thus, these stories came *from a pre-existing tradition that described Jesus as a vegetarian.*

In *The Precious Pearl* al-Ghazali relates this story about Jesus:

Learn a lesson from the Messiah [Jesus], for it is said that he had no purse at all, that he was dressed in the same woolen garment for twenty years, and that in his travels he had only a small mug and a comb. One day he saw a man drinking with his hand, so he threw the mug from his hand and never used it again.[13] Then he passed by a man running his fingers through his beard, so he threw away the comb from his hand and never used it after that. He used to say, "My feet are my riding animal, my houses are the caves of the earth, and my food is its plants and my drink its rivers. What riches are greater than this, O sons of Israel? Eat barley and wild onions, but beware of bread made from wheat, for you will not be grateful for it."[14]

In this one passage al-Ghazali emphasizes both the extreme poverty and simplicity of Jesus and his vegetarianism. The simplicity of Jesus' lifestyle and his vegetarianism is stated on several other occasions:

Said Jesus (on him be peace): "Verily I say unto you, whosoever seeketh heaven let him eat barley bread and sleep on the dunghill with the dogs. This is enough for me."

Jesus was accustomed to say, "O children of Israel, let the water of the brook suffice you and the vegetable of the field and the barley loaf; and beware of the white loaf for it will keep you from worship."

Said Jesus (on him be peace): "My food is hunger; all my thoughts are fear of God; my dress is wool; my warming place in winter is the rays of the sun; my candle is the moon; my steed is my legs; my food is fruit that springs from the ground; I go to bed and have nothing and arise without anything; and yet there is no one richer than I am."[15]

Jesus also appears to have pacifist tendencies. Al-Ghazali quotes Jesus almost verbatim from Matthew 5:38–41, the Sermon on the Mount, saying "do not return evil for evil."[16] At another point, Jesus says that one's own anger brings about God's anger towards oneself.[17] Jesus does admit to John the Baptist that he cannot completely avoid anger as he is only human. John responds, "then do not desire property"; to which Jesus replies, "that is possible."[18] Avoiding property was apparently developed by Jesus into an art form:

> It is related that Jesus one day was pillowing his head on a stone; and the devil passed by and said, "O Jesus, now you have shown your love for the world!" Then Jesus picked up the stone, threw it at him and said, "Take it and the world."[19]

Even the possession of a stone for a pillow is something that Jesus can live without. Other Sufi stories show Jesus being kind to animals. Jesus carefully takes care of a gray donkey; when his disciples question him, he replies: "Nobility is no more than humble service to the Creator and kindness to all creatures."[20] When he finds a dead dog and his disciples comment on the stench, Jesus responds by praising the shining whiteness of the dog's teeth and declaring: "Say nothing about God's creatures except that which is in praise." A pig passes by, and Jesus greets the pig saying: "Pass in Peace." When those around him ask him why he spoke to the pig in this way, he replies that he finds it unpleasant to speak bad words.[21]

The Sufi image of Jesus is that of someone used to extreme poverty, abstaining from violence, eating only the roughest kind of plant foods, and full of respect and kind words for animals. Except for the wool garment, it is compatible with the Jewish Pythagoreanism of the Essenes. Indeed, there are almost as many "words of Jesus" from Sufism that express Ebionite ideals, as from the *Recognitions* or *Homilies* or any other "Jewish Christian" source.

The stories and sayings of Jesus from the Sufis show a Jesus who is much more like the Ebionite Jesus than the Jesus of Christian orthodoxy. The Ebionites were active in Nabataea, which extends into northern Arabia, before the time of Mohammed (see Panarion 30.18.1, 30.2.9). Perhaps some individual Ebionites, still preserving the tradition handed down to them from the master, in turn gave these traditions to the Sufis or actually joined the Sufis—and thus Jewish Christianity was absorbed into mystical Islam.

Conclusions

How could a religion of pastoral nomads in a warlike, meat-eating society, come to have positive views about pacifist vegetarianism and admiringly describe Jesus as a pacifist vegetarian living in poverty? It seems unlikely these views came from Mohammed himself or any of his known early disciples.

A tantalizing hypothesis is that these features came from the last vestiges of Jewish Christianity. Mohammed did not hesitate to incorporate features from Judaism and Christianity when he felt these were from God. The Christianity that Mohammed knew was not orthodox Christianity but those "heretical" Christian sects that had fled the Byzantine Empire.

In Islam, we have many of the major features of Ebionism such as poverty, vegetarianism, and pacifism, incorporated into the favorable Sufi image of Jesus—ideals the Sufis in some cases themselves adopted. Indeed, many Ebionite beliefs were incorporated into Islam, such as unitarianism, the rejection of alcohol, and the idea of the corruption of the scriptures. The teachings of Jesus, Jewish in their origin, in the end became elements of Islamic mysticism.

15 THE TRUTH OF EBIONITE CHRISTIANITY

RESTORING THE LINK BETWEEN JESUS AND OURSELVES

TWO THOUSAND YEARS HAVE PASSED SINCE JESUS WALKED on the earth. What does it mean for someone to say, "I am a follower of the religion of Jesus"? Could such a statement actually refer to the religion of the historical Jesus?

This book has attempted to answer these questions by looking at the early Jewish Christians. Some of Jesus' followers were Jewish and continued to identify themselves as Jews; others were gentiles and either failed to identify themselves as Jews or were actually hostile to Judaism. Gentile Christianity defined what Christianity eventually became; but, as I hope I have shown, the Jewish Christians were closer to Jesus' first century roots.

Christianity is best understood not as a gradual expansion and development of the teachings of Jesus, but as the result of a succession of crises in Christianity. These crises, over time, changed Christianity from a Jewish sect seeking the radical original interpretation of the Jewish law, to a new gentile religion that rejected the necessity of obeying the Jewish law at all. The New Testament is best understood against the background of this historical fact.

Jewish Christianity sought to intensify allegiance to and understanding of the Jewish law; gentile Christianity sought to replace the Jewish law with the church. I believe that not only did the gentile church misunderstand where Jesus was coming from, but that it also misunderstood where he was going—as the simple living and nonviolence that Jesus saw as the basis of the law disappeared from Christianity except as ideals for those aspiring to sainthood.

Early Christians were sharply divided in their views about Jesus. Any view on the historical Jesus must rely on some idea of early Christian history, and any idea of early Christian history must come to grips with Jewish Christianity. My hypothesis is that the Ebionites understood Jesus better than any of the other groups in early Christianity and that conclusions about the historical Jesus need to be adjusted accordingly.

What was the religion and message of Jesus? Why was Jesus baptized? Why was Jesus killed? Why was there controversy over Paul? Why did the church move from Jerusalem to Rome? Why was the early church so divided? As I have argued, the answer to these questions lies in the history of Ebionite Christianity.

An Ebionite View of History

If the Ebionites were around today, they would give a version of early Christianity much different from the accepted church histories. Instead of a story of the triumphant march of a new message across the Roman Empire, it would be a story of how a new message was slowly weakened the further it got from its Palestinian origins. The Ebionite view of history would go something like this:

Jesus, inspired by a group of Nasaraeans who are vegetarian and attack animal sacrifice, is baptized by John the Baptist. He proclaims a Jewish gospel based on a radical interpretation of the universal law of God—a gospel based on simple living, pacifism, and vegetarianism. He goes to Jerusalem where he protests against the animal sacrifice business in the temple. He is brutally crucified by the Romans as a troublemaker at the instigation of the priests in the temple.

His followers come together at the Pentecost and, after powerful revelations, declare that Jesus has appeared to them. The priests in the temple still violently oppose Jesus' followers, arrest the apostles, try to kill James the brother of Jesus, and kill at least one other prominent follower (Stephen). They are checked by the more moderate Pharisees. The sect survives and grows.

The Jesus movement gains adherents and a new twist with Paul. Paul, on the basis of his own visions and independently of the other followers of Jesus, preaches adherence to a Jesus who is more than a prophet—a Jesus who does not merely proclaim the law but actually replaces it. Controversy is introduced to the early church. Paul and the Jewish followers of Jesus disagree over the Jewish law and over various food issues (eating meat, eating food offered to idols). Prominent members of the followers of Jesus, including his brother James and all of the apostles, are vegetarian; but the question of whether vegetarianism is required is sharply disputed by Paul (Romans 14). Many of the followers of Jesus are "zealous for the law" (Acts 21:20), but Paul denies that this is necessary at all. The disputes grow and divisions deepen.

A number of blows shatter the Jesus movement within Judaism. In the year 62, James the brother of Jesus is killed by a lynch mob at the instigation of the high priest. In the year 66, the Jews rise up in revolt against Rome. In the year 70, the Romans capture Jerusalem, butcher its inhabitants, and destroy the temple, which is never rebuilt. The last Jewish resistance ends in the year 74. The followers of Jesus are irrevocably identified as traitors to Israel: late in the first century, followers of Jesus are expelled from the synagogues. Sixty years later, Judea again revolts against Rome and violently persecutes the followers of Jesus, but the revolt is again savagely put down by the Romans. Jewish Christianity has to suffer twice, both politically and physically: first from the Romans because they are Jews, and second from other Jews because they follow a rejected prophet.

By contrast, gentile Christianity escapes almost untouched. There are persecutions, but they are sporadic and isolated. Over the succeeding decades, it is the gentile Christian communities that grow and expand while Jewish Christianity remains stagnant as a sect within a religion that has condemned it.

Gentile Christianity, lacking any central point of origin, is highly diverse. The gnostics, including Marcion, almost take over the church and declare that the God of the Jews and the God of the Christians are two distinct Gods altogether. The gnostics fail, but the writings of Paul that

Marcion champions are so popular that they are embedded in the Christian Bible and do more to shape the definition of Christian theology than anything in the gospels. In 312, Constantine becomes Roman emperor and begins a policy of first tolerating and then favoring Christians. In 325 the Council of Nicaea establishes what we know as Christian orthodoxy. In succeeding years, the church condemns and persecutes all rival sects, including both the gnostics and the Jewish Christians.

This "Ebionite" view of history explains a number of things the orthodox view of Christianity—maintaining that Christianity is simply an outgrowth of Jesus and his first followers—does not. It first of all explains a fundamental fact about Jesus: that Jesus was a Jew and that all of his first followers were Jews. The whole subsequent development of Christian theology is an effort to explain away this obvious and embarrassing fact—that Christianity should by all rights be a Jewish sect. In this Ebionite view, true Christianity *is* a Jewish sect; it is Jesus' Jewish followers who best understood him and Jesus' gentile followers who rejected the Jewish law made a fundamental mistake.

Secondly, this view explains the death of Jesus and the conflicts between the primitive Jesus movement and the priestly hierarchy in Jerusalem. The conflict was over animal sacrifice. Jesus chased those who sold animals out of the temple and predicted its destruction, while Stephen compared temple worship to idolatry. The priests were behind the arrest of Jesus, the arrest of the apostles, the stoning of Stephen, and the killing of James the brother of Jesus three decades later. Why would Jesus have risked and given his life for something not central to his message? Yet the Jewish Christians are virtually alone among early Christian groups in emphasizing Jesus' attack on the temple and the practice of animal sacrifice.

Thirdly, this Ebionite view of history explains with devastating simplicity why there was so much heresy in early Christianity. *The first heretic was Jesus himself.* Why else is Paul confronted so early with opponents who seem to be ensconced in positions of leadership in the Jerusalem church? Why else, centuries later, does orthodoxy still have to contend with such a bewildering diversity of sectarian opponents and have such difficulty asserting itself, finally needing the assistance of the Roman Empire to achieve its purpose? The historical problem is not accounting for the existence of heresy, but accounting for the existence of *orthodoxy*—a relative latecomer in church history. I believe that the growth of the gentile mission under Paul, the destruction of Jerusalem in the Jewish revolts, and the failure of Marcion's protest explain most of these problems.

The Jewishness of Jesus, the conflict over the temple, and early Christian diversity are the three central issues that both Christian scholars and practitioners have failed to grasp. Unless we come to grips with the religion of Jesus, the cause for which Jesus died, and the nature of his early followers, we have not understood Jesus. The Ebionites did this; modern Christianity, even after two millennia, still has not.

To evaluate this "Jewish Christian" view of history, we need to evaluate the conflicts between Jewish Christianity and Paul, and the divisions which this created in the early church.

The Disputes With Paul

The Jewish Christians were caught off guard by Paul's theology and the development of gentile Christianity. Neither Jesus in the synoptic gospels nor evidently the very earliest Jewish followers of Jesus felt the immediate need to establish a systematic theology. As a sect within Judaism, they simply took the broad context of Jewish theology for granted: God revealed his law to the children of Israel through Moses. Since there was no need to document this thesis—all the Jews around them accepted it as a matter of course—there was no perceived need to establish dicta on this subject.

The gentiles to whom Paul preached did not already accept this context, though. Paul in his letters rushed in to fill this theological vacuum, and supplied the gentile converts to the Jesus movement with an explanation of what they were supposed to believe. The Jewish followers of Jesus only prepared themselves for spiritual "battle" with other Jews. The one who told them that the mission was only to the "lost sheep of the house of Israel" (Matthew 10:6) had given them no directions on how to deal with gentiles. The Jewish followers of Jesus sought to defend what they saw as essential to his teachings; they agreed that circumcision was unnecessary (Galatians 2:3), but drew a line when it came to food issues (Galatians 2:11–14).

Jesus, even in the synoptic gospels, presented himself as a loyal follower of the law. Jesus was a Jew, and any concept of the historical Jesus that does not come to grips with this fact has lost its hold on reality. It is hard either to read the gospels or to make sense of Christian history except by recognizing that Jesus was a Jew and did not do anything that obviously took himself or his followers beyond the pale of first-century Judaism.

Yet a hundred years after Jesus' death, we find that the Jesus movement is having a major identity crisis. Most of the followers of Jesus are not Jews, live far from Galilee, do not speak or understand Aramaic or Hebrew, and are circulating gospels that ridicule Jesus' relatives as not having understood him. A series of crises have left the followers of Jesus without clear leadership, yet those claiming to be his followers are experiencing continued success. Perhaps this movement does not need leaders, one might say; but there is really not just one movement, but multiple forms of Christianity all emerging and growing, often having little in common except reverence for Jesus. Many different sects are emerging, and when one of these viewpoints (usually called "orthodox") finally wins out, it has many elements that were never present at the beginning at all.

When we look down the road three centuries after Jesus we find on the one hand a small minority of Jesus' followers who still think of themselves as Jews and intend to remain Jews, notwithstanding their rejection by rabbinic Judaism. On the other hand we find that the large majority of Jesus' followers have renounced Judaism. Which group would we expect to best understand Jesus?

We know from Paul's responses to his opponents that there was a vegetarian faction in earliest Christianity. This is *not* a later development that Jewish Christian sects retrojected into their version of Jesus. The letters of Paul, written in the first decades after Jesus' departure from the earth, speak openly and straightforwardly on this topic. "One believes he may eat anything, while the weak man eats only vegetables" (Romans

14:2)—how else are we to interpret this except as a reference to vegetarianism? "Eat whatever is sold in the meat market without raising any question on the ground of conscience" (I Corinthians 10:25)—how can we read this except as (among other things) a condemnation of ethical vegetarianism? And, of course (according to Paul), God does not care for oxen (I Corinthians 9:9–10).

These are *Christian* vegetarians, otherwise Paul's further counseling of a diplomatic diet makes no sense: "It is right not to eat meat or drink wine or do anything that makes your *brother* stumble" (Romans 14:21, emphasis added). Food was a divisive issue, even more divisive than the pseudo-issue of circumcision. In Galatians, it is not circumcision that provokes the crisis at Antioch—Titus is not compelled to be circumcised—but rather Peter's refusal to share in table fellowship.

Paul's opponents are therefore vegetarians and also Jewish Christians. These two factions are not explicitly linked—two different sets of opponents might be posited—but the hint is strong that the vegetarians are also Jewish Christians. When we look at the later history of the church, we find *Jewish Christians who despise Paul and are ethical vegetarians.* They did not eat meat because "Christ revealed it to me," in the words of one Jewish Christian (Panarion 30.18.9), thus tracing vegetarianism back to Jesus himself. The logical conclusion of ethical vegetarianism is that the animal sacrifices in the Jewish temple in Jerusalem are wrong *in principle* and are to be condemned. The Jewish Christians condemned the animal sacrifices and kept the memory of this grievance alive long after the temple had perished.

The Divisions in the Early Church

The Jewish Christian version of history not only better explains Jesus' own position on the law, it also better explains the emergence of the myriad varieties of Christian belief in the first four Christian centuries. Why was the early church so divided? The Jewish Christian account suggests an obvious answer: because the Jewish Christian authority was fatally weakened at an early stage.

Based on surviving Christian literature, the opposition of the heretics was much more serious than the opposition of the pagans. Why did heresy leave such a deep impression on both the doctrines and the literature of the early church? For the orthodox, heresy is a mysterious, pervasive, and powerful force, without a clear origin. Tertullian says that an abundance of heresies was inevitable and they were sent to test us (*The Prescription Against Heretics* 1). Polycarp's answer to Marcion, that Marcion was the "first born of Satan," is telling here: Polycarp can only attribute this heresy to the father of evil himself. Polycarp doesn't want to confront the divisions that were present in early Christianity, of which Marcion was one of the logical results, and is unable to account for the strength of Marcion's following except to attribute it to the devil himself.

The divisions in the church are also related to the question of why the church moved from Jerusalem to Rome. The orthodox explanation is that the church moved to Rome because Peter came to Rome and founded the church there: it was part of the divine plan. Most historians accept that this is a relatively innocent myth. No one not in the stranglehold of church dogma thinks that the historical Peter came to Rome to deliberately move the church away from the place of its origins. Yet the myth is not so innocent; it was necessary in order to legitimize the primacy of the church in Rome. If not Rome, then Jerusalem, or the successors to the Jerusalem church in Pella and east of the Jordan, would otherwise have been the obvious choice; but this was excluded because of the rejection of Jewish Christianity, which dominated the Christian churches in this area. Jerusalem is the center of the early church, but after the revolts against Rome Jerusalem is scarcely heard of again, except as a travel destination for pilgrims.

Divisions existed in the early church because "heresy" was present from the beginning. The church was divided into Jew and gentile at an early stage, and the two sides were never reconciled. Paul's cry for a church that was neither Jew nor Greek (Galatians 3:28) was a call for a church in which Jews abandoned the primacy of the law of Moses. Some of Paul's followers took this premise to its logical conclusion—the church should not only abandon the law of Moses but the God of Moses as well. This created a centuries-long diversion for gentile Christianity as it struggled with gnosticism. Gnosticism arose in the first place because there was no clear Christian leadership that could have dealt with the crisis at an early stage. The rise of gnosticism is due in no small part to the fact that the leadership of the church late in the first century was non-existent.

The divisions in early Christianity cannot be tossed aside as misunderstandings that only came along much later. Both the gnostics and the Ebionites saw the origin of error as lying in the controversies in which Paul was involved. In this case, they were both right: the church had to choose between Paul and Jewish Christianity. Instead, it simply "averaged" their views. It accepted Paul but turned him into a dutiful follower of the Jerusalem church. It produced a mishmash theology with bits and pieces from Judaism and paganism. It produced a mishmash ethics in which simple living and nonviolence were only necessary for those aspiring to sainthood. The strength of orthodoxy was not due to its being early in the history of Christianity, but to its attractive political position.

The Basis of Jesus' Message

The Ebionite view of history explains the content as well as the history of Jesus' message better than the orthodox or gnostic versions. Look at the "Nicene creed" or the so-called "Apostle's creed" and you will see no ethical content at all: you will see simply a succession of theological and mythological statements. Their content is scarcely more than this: Jesus is God's son, was born of a virgin, was crucified, rose on the third day, and will come again to judge the world; we believe in the authority of the church and the resurrection of the dead. There is no mention of simple living and nonviolence and no mention of the need to completely change one's life. What happened to the *message* of Jesus in the creeds of the later church? The answer is simple: *it has been eliminated.* Modern Christianity has given us a Messiah without a cause.

In the beginning, the core of Jesus' message was ethical, not theological. Jesus' message did not begin with "believe," but "repent." When Jesus talked to those Jews who approached him—whether they sought healing, debate, or the path to eternal life—Jesus did not attempt to direct them away from the religion they were in. Those who opposed Jesus were labeled hypocrites: they would be saved by actually following their professed precepts. The one seeking life was told: "If you would have life, keep the commandments." The ones who sought healing were told: "Your faith has healed you." In each case—even that of the "hypocrites"—the seeker is *already* in possession of the means to salvation.

Jesus' radical acceptance of the law of God is echoed in gentile Christianity, but in a much weakened form. There is somewhat a rejection of materialism, as we are advised to help the poor. There is somewhat a rejection of violence, though soldiering eventually becomes an accepted occupation. There is even a weak endorsement of vegetarianism, with the Catholic abstention (until very recently) from red meat on Fridays and the abstention from meat by many saints and church leaders. The ethical aspect of Jewish Christianity was dissipated and diluted by larger questions of social order and theology under the emperor Constantine and beyond. This social order in many cases allows, or even encourages, the very materialism and violence that Jewish Christianity attacked.

All of these themes are tied in with incidents deeply embedded in Christian consciousness. Jesus was crucified after a confrontation in the temple in which he outraged the priests. The entire Jesus movement brought forward their property and gave it to the apostles. Jewish Christianity rejected bloodshed, whether of human beings or of animals. The whole thrust of Jesus' teaching in Jewish Christianity was to strengthen the Jewish law and make it *stricter* than the tradition of the day seemed to teach—not, as in Paul, to explain why no one needed to follow the Jewish law anymore. The Ebionite explanation of history is better suited to explain both the content of Jesus' message, in that the Ebionites continued to stress simple living and nonviolence, as well as the fact that Jesus had an ethical message at all—a message that today has disappeared into an endless series of formulas of belief.

The books seeking to understand the Jewishness of Jesus are now legion. Yet almost no one wants to confront the problem of Jewish Christianity. The reason for this reluctance is not hard to find; the views of Jewish Christianity are not those of most Christians. The theology is of course unacceptable, being in essence a form of Jewish monotheism; and the moral teachings, with the strong emphasis on the necessity for a simple lifestyle and the objection to bloodshed of either animals or humans, are much too awkward for modern ears.

Simple Living and Nonviolence Today

Given all of this concerning ancient Christianity, how can we reconnect with Jesus *today*?

Should modern Christians dash down to the local synagogue and present themselves as Jewish converts? This *might* make sense if we could sweep away the last two thousand years of human history. Many modern Jews would regard all talk of "Jewish Christianity" as just another attempt to convert the Jews. Two thousand years of following separate religious and cultural paths, plentiful doctrinal issues, and a natural suspicion of anyone proclaiming a prophet in whose name there has been so much persecution of Jews—all of these would make any kind of reunion of this sort a highly uneasy one.

Any modern "Ebionites" would meet an equally chilly reception in contemporary Christianity. There is no easy path to retrace two thousand years of church dogma, to go back to the first century and rethink such fundamental Christian ideas as the trinity, the divine inspiration of the scripture, and original sin—let alone the meaning of simple living and nonviolence in the teachings of Jesus. Some Christian churches, to their credit, *are* rethinking these ideas, so the follower of Jesus might be able to find a spiritual home there.

However, helping us to find the right church or spiritual group is not the primary concern of Jesus' message. Jesus did not come to found an organization or to promote a new theology, but rather to proclaim the kingdom of God; we should change our *lives* so that it accorded with the divine will. The world of Jesus was different from our world today; moreover, our knowledge of Jesus is not always complete. Nevertheless, those who became followers of Jesus in first-century Palestine appear to manifest two characteristic changes—toward simple living and nonviolence. Reconnecting with Jesus, for those who still choose to follow this path, involves commitment to both simple living and nonviolence in some form.

Simple living and nonviolence are complementary. Violence usually occurs in order to appropriate something (or to retrieve something unjustly taken), whether it is property, territory, or a perceived social order. Simple living is the affirmation that there is a living presence in one's life that is more important than property, territory, or a perceived social order. Indeed, for Jesus, this living presence is more important than life itself.

Violence in Jesus' day was more openly brutal, and there was less need for apology about starting wars, killing civilians, or selling them into slavery. We read with horror of ancient warfare in which whole populations were butchered without mercy. But is our situation so very different? In both numbers and savagery, twentieth-century violence exceeds anything in the first century or any other century. Every generation seems to produce its own version of mass killings: the First World War, the Second World War, the Holocaust, Vietnam, Cambodia, and Rwanda, in which thousands, hundreds of thousands, or millions of innocents are slaughtered. Irrational violence is not just in faraway places, the Middle East or Africa; it is something suddenly all around us and even within us, in the schools and workplace. We need to resolve many problems based on our abuse of nature; not only are resources becoming scarcer, but conflict over these scarce resources is introducing yet more problems.

For both the Jewish and gentile followers of Jesus before Constantine, the Christian response to violence was nonviolence. Opposition to war was practically universal among Christians for centuries after Jesus. Faced with the commands to love one's enemies and to pray for those that persecute you, most early Christians declined the opportunity to serve in the Roman army. Pacifism is a characteristic common to both Jewish Christianity and much of gentile Christianity until after the time of Constantine. All Christianity understood Jesus' sayings such as "do not resist one who is evil" and "love your enemies" (Matthew 5:38–39, 44) in a straightforward way—as implying nonviolence in the face of evil. That is why, in the very first chapter of the *Recognitions*, the Jewish Christians refuse to use violence to defend themselves from the attacks of Saul and an angry gang of hooligans: martyrdom was preferable to violent self-defense. Their experience, and the experience of much of gentile Christianity as well, was that their own innocent blood was a more powerful tool than any number of weapons or violence.

The problem of violence is not just a problem of human violence toward other humans. Violence toward animals and the earth itself has increased exponentially as human population, development, and consumption have increased. Over nine billion animals are killed for food every year in the United States alone. If we each had to kill our own food, or even had to watch it being produced in our modern slaughterhouses, most of us would be vegetarians. We put it outside our mind: we don't want to be reminded of it; we don't want to have to think about it.

We are now experiencing *the greatest mass extinction of plant and animal species* since the mass extinction of the dinosaurs sixty-five million years ago. However, this time it is not due to a natural catastrophe such as the collision of a large meteor with the earth—it is due to human activity. Deforestation, soil erosion, habitat destruction, pollution, global warming—how can this ripping apart of the ecosystem fail to affect human beings at some point? How can we engage in activities that have the effect of causing extinctions at a hundred to a thousand times the normal rate and expect that life will continue for us much as before?

The past century, in which humanity in general and the rich countries in particular have experienced the highest standard of living in recorded history, has also witnessed some of the most devastating violence in history. Violence towards humans, violence towards animals, and violence towards the earth is all of one piece—it is all an endless appropriation of more and more. Everything and everyone becomes a "resource" that must be appropriated and exploited for human purposes. Jesus and the early Christians saw that the whole system of violence was madness, and that the answer was not to try to reform it, but simply to remove oneself from it entirely.

And how do we remove ourselves from this system of violence?

The emphasis on the poverty and simplicity of the disciples is one of the most striking features of the gospels. "We have left all that we ever had and followed you" (Luke 18:28), says Peter to Jesus. Jesus declares: "Whoever does not renounce all that he has cannot be my disciple" (Luke 14:33) and "It is easier for a camel to pass through the eye of a needle than for a rich man to enter the kingdom of God" (Matthew 19:24). The modern slogan of "simple living" is, if anything, insufficiently radical to convey the change that Jesus is advocating. If one just looks at the words—"sell everything you have," "renounce everything you have"—then it would at first glance scarcely leave any alternative except joining the homeless, and some Christian ascetics such as St. Antony took it upon themselves to do just that.

"Simple living," however, does capture the basic flavor of what Jesus is offering in at least one sense. Jesus in the New Testament is not asking for an ascetic renunciation. Except for the forty days and forty nights he voluntarily spends fasting in the wilderness, Jesus never appears to be without food. He is constantly surrounded by disciples and friends whom he describes as his "mother, sister, and brother" (Matthew 12:50). "Do not be anxious," Jesus says, about what you are to eat, drink, or wear; "a man's life does not consist in the abundance of his possessions" (Luke 12:15). In the first Christian community —the community which the Jewish Christians cited as their model for Christian poverty—"there was not a needy person among them" (Acts 4:34). Those who share in the community of Jesus gain a community of fellow believers who act as their true family, and who help each other with their physical needs.

What simple living means to us today may very well be somewhat different. Some exceptional individuals may actually voluntarily join the homeless. Peace Pilgrim, the name given to an otherwise anonymous woman who from the 1950s to the 1980s wandered across the nation preaching a message of peace, springs to mind; but most of us lack either the determination or the charisma to do this sort of thing consistently. Peace Pilgrim made a vow to walk 25,000 miles, fasting until she was offered food (she was a vegetarian), and wandering until she was offered shelter, carrying only a pen, a comb, and some notebook paper to write on. She traveled many more miles even than that before her death. But for most of us, even were we to summon the will to join the homeless, this action would simply make it much more awkward for ourselves and makes it much more difficult for us to either support ourselves or to help others. There is the possibility of joining a communalistic group, like the Hutterites or the Shakers. Yet culture, conditioning, practical problems, and ethical dilemmas (neither the Hutterites or Shakers are vegetarian, for example) make it problematic for many to enter into a community in which we literally share our possessions.

However, there is one relatively easy step for anyone interested in simple living, and that is to become a vegetarian. There is nothing in our current economy that causes more human and animal suffering or wastes more natural resources than the routine consumption of meat. Indeed, vegetarianism is actually advantageous. Vegetarians live longer and suffer less from heart disease, the most common forms of cancer, diabetes, and obesity than do meat-eaters. Meat production and animal food agriculture takes up about two-thirds of the cropland in the United States, and all of the grazing land; it contributes overwhelmingly to the soil erosion, groundwater depletion, and deforestation that now threaten the basis of human life on earth. And there is nothing that causes more suffering among animals than the systematic, unthinking annual slaughter of billions upon billions of innocent animals—animals who do not live easy lives, often crammed into tiny cages, and do not die easy deaths either. *If simple living and nonviolence mean anything, they mean vegetarianism.* It is no wonder the Jewish Christians quoted Jesus' saying: "I require mercy, not sacrifice."

The whole system of life on earth resembles a gigantic growing pyramid, with everyone scrambling to get to the top while everything beneath it is crushed. The lower middle class in the United States lives better than most people in less developed countries, who in turn fare relatively better than the animals who are killed for human appetites. We do not have the natural resources to sustain the world's current standard of living for that much longer, much less bring the entire world "up" to the destructive American level of development. Simple living is more than just a personal choice; it is a necessity in order to sustain life on the planet.

Jesus probably did not directly address the question of environmental destruction. Nowhere in the gospels are there commands to recycle, grow our own vegetables, take the bus, or compost our kitchen waste. Nevertheless, Jesus has *something* to say that is relevant to these subjects: we are to have compassion, mercy, and live simply with love for all. The pursuit of wealth is undermining the ecological system that supports us. It is not a question of whether but when we will have to change our ways—not simply as individuals or as a nation, but as a species.

Conclusions

The history of Jewish Christianity is a challenge both for the historian and for the Christian. It is a challenge to separate the ideal of the simple lifestyle of the primitive Christian community from the ideals of free enterprise, home ownership, a chicken in every pot, and two cars in every garage. It is a challenge to understand that the vision of Jesus is something that does not mesh easily with the easygoing and all-pervasive accumulation of worldly goods and exploitation of other humans and the earth.

This is a challenge the religion of Jesus can accept and meet. This religion takes no comfort in the view that an almighty Being supports and sustains the pillaging of the earth's resources, the annual slaughter of billions of innocent creatures, and a culture of domination—this was not, and is not, the religion of Jesus. This religion confidently expects the coming of the kingdom of God, in which

> They shall not hurt or destroy in all my holy mountain;
> for as the waters fill the sea,
> so shall the land be filled with the knowledge of the Lord. (Isaiah 11:9, New English Bible)

APPENDIX

Examples of Jewish Christian beliefs described in the *Panarion* of Epiphanius, compared to ideas in the *Recognitions* and *Homilies*.

PANARION	RECOGNITIONS AND HOMILIES
1. Vegetarianism:	
"They have spoken falsely about Peter . . . that he abstained from that which had life in it and from meats, even as they do; and from all other food prepared from flesh, they say, since also Ebion himself and the Ebionites abstain from these totally." (30.15.3)	"I [Peter] use only bread and olives, and rarely pot-herbs." (*Homilies* 12.6) "And the things which are well pleasing to God are . . . not to taste dead flesh . . ." (*Homilies* 7.4)
2. Rejection of animal sacrifice:	
"The gospel which they recognize contains the provision that 'I came to abolish sacrifices, and unless you cease from sacrificing, my anger will not cease from you.' " (30.16.5)	"He then [God] who at the first was displeased with the slaughtering of animals, not wishing them to be slain, did not ordain sacrifices as desiring them." (*Homilies* 3.45)
3. Jesus is the true prophet:	
"They say that the Christ is the True Prophet." (30.18.5)	"He [Jesus] therefore is the true Prophet, who appeared to us, as you have heard, in Judea . . . " (*Recognitions* 5.10)
4. Christ was in Adam, and appeared to the patriarchs:	
"[The Ebionites say] he [Christ] comes here when he wishes, as also he came in Adam, and appeared to the patriarchs clothed with a body." (30.3.5)	"If any one do not allow the man fashioned by the hands of God [i. e., Adam] to have had the Holy Spirit of Christ, how is he not guilty of the greatest impiety. . . ?" (*Homilies* 3.20) "Therefore Abraham. . . the true prophet appeared to him. . ." (*Recognitions* 1.33) ". . . the true prophet appeared to Moses . . ." (*Recognitions* 1.34)

PANARION	RECOGNITIONS AND HOMILIES

5. Poverty as a virtue:

"But they exalted themselves saying that they were poor because in the time of the apostles they sold their possessions and placed them at the feet of the apostles." (30.17.2)

"For we—that is, I [Peter] and my brother Andrew—have grown up from our childhood, not only orphans, but also extremely poor." (*Recognitions* 7.6)

6. False insertions into the Jewish scriptures:

"And neither do they receive the whole Pentateuch of Moses, but cast out certain passages." (30.18.7)

"For the Scriptures have had joined to them many falsehoods against God on this account." (*Homilies* 2.38)

7. Daily baptism:

"They have spoken falsely about Peter in many ways: that he baptized himself daily for purposes of purification even as they also do . . ." (30.15.3)

Recognitions: frequent references to Peter bathing, e. g. 4.3, 8.1; also *Homilies* 8.2, 11.1.

8. Acceptance of the Jewish Law:

"He [Ebion] relies on the law of Judaism with regard to the Sabbath, circumcision, and all other things . . ." (30.2.2)

"Meantime they came to Mount Sinai, and thence the law was given to them." (*Recognitions* 1.35)
"The only good God . . . appointed a perpetual law to all, which neither can be abrogated by enemies, nor is vitiated by any impious one, nor is concealed in any place, but which can be read by all." (*Homilies* 8.10)

9. Pacifism, objection to war:

Epiphanius does not mention pacifism in his descriptions of the Jewish Christians.

In a celebrated section of the *Recognitions* (1.70–71), clearly of Jewish Christian origin, a "certain enemy" (Paul) violently attacks James in the temple; from their fear of God, the followers of Jesus prefer to be killed than to kill, even when they were the superior force. Later, Peter draws the explicit conclusion that warfare is forbidden. (*Recognitions* 3.42).

|

10. Rejection of Paul:

"They [the Ebionites] are not ashamed with trumped-up charges of evildoing and deceit made by their false apostles accusing Paul . . ." (30.16.8).

In the *Recognitions* "a certain enemy" (who is clearly Paul before his conversion) attempts to murder James in the temple (*Recognitions* 1.70–71). Then, in the debates later between Peter and Simon Magus (a figure presented as a gnostic), many objections are made by Peter against the views of Simon Magus that sound very much like objections to Paul: for example, Simon Magus (like Paul) says that he is an apostle of Jesus on the basis of a vision, and Peter refutes this view (*Homilies* 17:13–19).

11. Avoidance of alcohol:

Epiphanius notes that the Ebionites take communion using water instead of wine (30.16.1)

The *Homilies* have Peter declaring, "According to the worship of God, the proclamation is made to be sober," and describes the drunken worship of pagan gods as being the opposite of this worship (*Homilies* 11.15).

12. Jesus is not God:

Rejection of the virgin birth is the very first doctrine that Epiphanius attributes to the Ebionites (30.3.1), with Jesus becoming the "son of God" by "the coming of the Christ into him from above in the form of a dove" (30.16.3). Epiphanius exclaims, "How do they define the savior a mere man from the seed of man?" (30.20.5).

There is no direct denial of the virgin birth, but Peter says that Jesus never proclaimed himself to be God (*Homilies* 16.15), and declares that an oil similar to that which anointed Jesus now anoints all believers (*Recognitions* 1.45), suggesting that whatever made Jesus special is in principle available to all. The reference to Jesus as a prophet (the "true prophet") also suggests someone who is an exceptional human being but not God.

NOTES

1. Broken Thread

1. The expression "orthodox Christianity" (using a lowercase "o") refers not to the modern Eastern Orthodox or Russian Orthodox churches, but rather to the Christianity that emerged from the Council of Nicaea in the year 325 CE—that Christianity which is the spiritual ancestor of all modern Protestant, Catholic, and Orthodox churches.
2. Helmut Koester in Petersen, editor, *Gospel Traditions in the Second Century*, p. 33.
3. Lüdemann, *Heretics*, p. 167.
4. Quoted in Dart, *The Jesus of Heresy and History*, p. 156.
5. Schoeps, *Jewish Christianity*, p. 3.
6. Funk, *Honest to Jesus*, p. 314.
7. Koester, *op. cit.* note 2, p. 19.
8. Funk, *op. cit.* note 6, p. 113.
9. James and Jude are mentioned as disputed in *Ecclesiastical History* 2.23.25; II Peter, at 3.3.1; and II and III John, at 3.24.17.
10. There are only a handful of books in English whose primary subject is Jewish Christianity. Among these are: Danielou, *The Theology of Jewish Christianity*, 1964; Jones, *An Ancient Jewish Christian Source on the History of Christianity*, 1995; Koch, *A Critical Investigation of Epiphanius' Knowledge of the Ebionites*, 1976; Lüdemann, *Opposition to Paul in Jewish Christianity*, 1989; Schoeps, *Jewish Christianity*, 1969; Skriver, *The Forgotten Beginnings of Creation and Christianity*, 1991; Vaclavik, *The Vegetarianism of Jesus Christ*, 1987.

2. The Followers of the True Prophet

1. *Recognitions* 1.45 uses "Christ" as a title and says that all believers who come to the kingdom of God are anointed, just as Jesus was anointed. This would imply that all believers are "Christs" since "Christ" has been explicitly defined in this passage as being due to being anointed. Epiphanius does not mention this, but Hippolytus confirms that, for the Ebionites, all believers are "able to become Christs" (*Refutation of all Heresies* 7.22).

2.   See Klijn and Reinink, *Patristic Evidence for Jewish-Christian Sects*. The Ebionites are mentioned by Irenaeus, Tertullian, Pseudo-Tertullian, Hippolytus, Methodius, Eusebius, and Epiphanius; the Nazoraeans are only mentioned by Epiphanius and a single sentence from Tertullian—a sentence that, however, creates doubt as to whether the Nazoraeans and the Ebionites were different groups. The Elchasaites are mentioned by Hippolytus, Eusebius, and Epiphanius.

3.   See for example Richard Friedman's excellent book, *Who Wrote the Bible?*

3. A Voice in the Wilderness

1.   See the excellent discussion in Crown and Cansdale, "Qumran: Was it an Essene Settlement?"
2.   Eisler, *The Messiah Jesus and John the Baptist*, p. 236–237.
3.   Quoted in Eisler, *op cit.* note 2, p.224–225.

4. Follow Me

1.   Origen, *Comment. In Matthaeum XV* 14; cited in Klijn, *Jewish Christian Gospel Tradition*, text III, p. 56.
2.   "A moment ago, my Mother, the holy spirit, took me by one of my hairs and brought me to the great hill." Origen, *Comment. in Johannem II* 12; *Hom. in Jeremiam XV* 4; Jerome, *Comment. in Micha* 7,5–7; *Comment. in Esaiam* 40, 9–11; *Comment. in Hiezechielem* 16,13. Cited in Klijn, *op cit.*, text II, p. 52.
3.   Corley, *A Place at the Table*, p. 208.
4.   Haskins, *Mary Magdalen: Myth and Metaphor*, p. 90.
5.   Countryman, *The Rich Christian in the Church of the Early Empire*, p. 76.
6.   Stark, *The Rise of Christianity*.

5. The Law and the Prophets

1.   Cadbury, *The Peril of Modernizing Jesus*, p. 58; he cites *Encyclopedia Judaica*, vii., col 1185 ff.
2.   E. g., Maccoby, *The Mythmaker*; Falk, *Jesus the Pharisee*; and Maqsood, *The Separated Ones*.
3.   Vermes, *Jesus the Jew*, p. 54.
4.   Neusner, *First Century Judaism in Crisis*, p. 59, 64.
5.   Horsley, "Jesus and Judaism: Christian Perspectives," in Attridge and Hata, editors, *Eusebius, Christianity, and Judaism*, p. 60, 72.
6.   Flusser, "Jesus and Judaism: Jewish Perspectives," in Attridge and Hata, p. 83.
7.   See chapters 10 and 13, where this point is explored in more detail. Most importantly, the letters of Paul show a much more abrasive relationship between Paul and the other church leaders than does Acts.

6. The Lying Pen of the Scribes

1.   The commonly accepted theory is that the "J" (Yahwist), "E" (Elohist), "D" (Deuteronomist), and "P" (Priestly) writings were contributed over time. See Friedman, *Who Wrote the Bible?*; Friedman maintains that virtually the entire book of Leviticus is part of the "P" writings, written sometime in the sixth century BCE.
2.   Schoeps, *Jewish Christianity*, p. 83–84.

3.   Indeed, in the version of the parable in Mark—which features a farmer sowing seed, without the enemy sowing weeds—this is exactly the interpretation suggested. Matthew's Jesus offers a slightly different interpretation, though—he suggests that the equation is not seed=word of God, but rather seed=followers of God. Matthew's interpretation may not have been the original meaning of the parable. In fact, the saying at Matthew 15:13 where the Father will root out every plant which he has not planted himself, seems to apply *perfectly* to this parable. That Matthew 15:13 may have belonged elsewhere, and not to the present Matthew 15, is supported by Matthew 15:15, "explain the parable to us"—despite the fact that at this point, no parable has been offered.

4.   See *The Bethany Parallel Commentary on the New Testament*. Matthew Henry, commenting on Matthew 15:3 (p. 127–128) begs the question by noting that the Pharisees' interpretation contradicts Exodus 20:12, the fifth commandment—overlooking that Jesus' interpretation contradicts Numbers 30:2. Adam Clarke, commenting on Matthew 15:2 (p. 127), equates "the tradition" that Jesus attacks with "the oral law." This argument also begs the question, since what Jesus puts forward in Matthew 15:1–6 is *also* a principle not found in the written code. It is an oral tradition either initiated by Jesus or someone before him. This tradition initiated or received by Jesus, incidentally, was eventually accepted by orthodox Judaism and thus became part of the "oral law" and incorporated into the Talmud, which thus agrees with Jesus on this issue.

7. Children of Peace

1.   Quoted in Wink, *Engaging the Powers*, p. 216.
2.   Brandon, *The Fall of Jerusalem and the Christian Church*, as well as Eisenman, *James the Brother of Jesus*.
3.   *The Apostolic Tradition of Hippolytus*, trans. Easton, p. 42.
4.   Cadoux, *The Early Christian Attitude to War*, p. 246.
5.   *Ibid.* p. 149.
6.   *Ibid.* p. 150.
7.   *Ibid.* pp. 246–247.

8. The Blood of the Lamb

1.   Sandmel, *The First Christian Century in Judaism and Christianity*, p. 14, note 22.
2.   The New International Version mistranslates this passage by inserting the word "just" in the phrase, "I did not [just] give them commands about burnt offerings and sacrifices." See J. R. Hyland.

9. Confrontation in the Temple

1.   Animal sacrifices are criticized at *Recognitions* 1.36, 1.37, 1.39, 1.54, 1.64, 4.36, 8.48, and Homilies 2.44, 3.24, 3.26, 3.45, 3.52, 3.56, 7.3 and 18.19. This does not include the many criticisms of pagan animal sacrifice found throughout the *Recognitions* and *Homilies*.
2.   *Pentateuch with Targum Onkelos, Haphtaroth and Prayers for Sabbath and Rashi's Commentary* (London: Shapiro, Vallentine & Co., 1946), commentary on Exodus 23:12, p. 125.

3. Harnick, *The Lord's Table*, p. 115, and Goodenough, *Jewish Symbols in the Greco Roman Period*, vol. 6, pp. 134–141.

4. Aland and Aland, *The Text of the New Testament*, p. 305.

5. Drinkwater, *Food in the Early Church*, p. 14.

6. For example, Augustine, *On Christian Doctrine* 3.19.

7. Bazell, *Christian Diet*, p. 164. The treatment of other vegetarian "heretics" is described in pp. 144–165.

8. Augustine, *On the Morals of the Catholic Church* 33.

9. Bazell, *op. cit.* note 7, pp. 71–131.

10. The Split in the Early Church

1. See Lüdemann, *The Resurrection of Jesus*.

2. Maccoby, *The Mythmaker*, p. 71.

3. Sandmel, *The Genius of Paul*, pp. 8–14.

4. Sanders, *Paul and Palestinian Judaism*, p. 553.

5. Vermes, *The Religion of Jesus the Jew*, p. 212.

6. Fitzmyer, *The Acts of the Apostles*, pp. 51–54.

7. Sandmel, *Judaism and Christian Beginnings*, p. 479, note 20.

8. Proctor, "Proselytes and Pressure Cookers." p. 472.

9. Eusebius, *Ecclesiastical History* 5.1.26, reports an early Christian martyr who interpreted the prohibition of the blood of animals to imply vegetarianism. Minucius Felix refers to bloodshed in the arena and the blood of animals in the same breath (*Octavius* 29.6). Tertullian points out that Christians are forbidden both human and animal blood (Apology 9). Sandmel states that blood could refer either to the blood of a sacrificed animal or to human violence: *Judaism and Christian Beginnings*, p. 408.

11. From Crisis to Catastrophe

1. Gorman, *Pythagoras*, p. 40: "The long hair of the Pythagoreans was proverbial in antiquity."

2. Theissen, *The Gospels in Context*, p. 232.

12. Disintegration

1. Eusebius concludes that "the judgment of God at length overtook those who had committed such outrages against Christ and his apostles, and totally destroyed that generation of impious men" (*Ecclesiastical History* 3.5.3).

2. Epiphanius mentions Nabataea, Moabitis, Bashanitis, Cochaba, Karnaim, and Astaroth in connection with the Ebionites (*Panarion* 30.2.7, 30.18.1); he mentions Cochaba and Pella in connection with the Nazoraeans (*Panarion* 29.7.7). Eusebius mentions Cochaba (*Ecclesiastical History* 1.7.14) in connection with the "Desposynoi." According to Schoeps, Cochaba is about 18 miles north of Pella (*Jewish Christianity*, p. 28), which would put it just southeast of the Sea of Galilee by a few miles. Since Astaroth is in Bashan, "Bashanitis" probably means Bashan and "Moabitis" means the Moab; both of these are regions in Palestine on the east side of the Jordan. Karnaim is a town east of the Jordan attacked by Judas Maccabeus (I Maccabees 5:26, 43 ff.). Nabataea is a region that extended southward from the

Dead Sea into northern Arabia. Epiphanius also mentions Banias, a town on the coast of the Mediterranean sea, and Cyprus, which is evidently as far west as the Ebionites went.

3. In the Syriac version of the *Recognitions*, *Recognitions* 1.37 includes the prediction that believers will saved from destruction after being led to a "fortified place of the land." See Jones, *An Ancient Jewish Christian Source on the History of Christianity*, p. 66. This "fortified place" could be a reference to Pella or Cochaba.

4. Schoeps, *Jewish Christianity*, p. 30.

5. Pritz, *Nazarene Jewish Christianity*, p. 122–127.

6. Sanders, *Paul and Palestinian Judaism*, p. 162–163.

7. Schoeps, *op. cit.* note 4, p. 35. Schoeps evidently bases this conclusion on the fact that Eusebius states that the chair of James still existed in the fourth century (*Ecclesiastical History* 7.19); since it is completely implausible that the Jewish Christians would have taken it with them and then given it to their sectarian opponents later, it must have been left behind and recovered later by gentile Christians (or alternatively, left behind and a "fake" chair later produced by gentile Christians).

8. Epiphanius does describe another group called the "Essenes" in a very unhelpful fashion: they are Samaritans, and are engaged in an obscure dispute over festivals with other even more obscure Samaritan groups.

9. Pines, *The Jewish Christians of the Early Centuries of Christianity According to a New Source*; and Pritz, *Nazarene Jewish Christianity*.

10. Klijn and Reinink, *Patristic Evidence for Jewish-Christian Sects*, p. 46.

11. Halton, *An Analysis of the Heresiological Method of Theodoret of Cyrus in the Haereticarum Fabularum Compendium*, p. 141–142.

12. Schoeps, *op. cit.* note 4, p. 131.

13. Maccoby, *Judas Iscariot and the Myth of Jewish Evil*; and Crossan, *Who Killed Jesus?*

13. The Gospel of the Stranger God

1. For a general description of Marcion, see Harnack, *Marcion*; Knox, *Marcion and the New Testament*; and Lüdemann, *Heretics*.

2. Early in the nineteenth century, German historians challenged the idea of Pauline authorship for I and II Timothy and Titus, and most scholars now accept their conclusions. These "pastoral" letters not only contain different ideas, but different vocabulary: out of the 901 words in the pastoral letters, 306 are not found in any other letter of Paul, and 335 are not found anywhere else in the New Testament. See on this point Hoffmann, *Marcion*, p. 281. Of the other letters, seven are generally accepted as genuine (Romans, I and II Corinthians, Galatians, Philippians, I Thessalonians, and Philemon); see Koester, *History and Literature of Early Christianity*, vol. 2, p. 52. Three others are disputed (II Thessalonians, Ephesians, and Colossians), but it is thought these were written after Paul's death by followers who shared his views.

3. E. g., *The Bethany Parallel Commentary on the New Testament*, p. 928.

4. Sandmel, *The Genius of Paul*, p. 155.

5. Jesus' parents offer an animal sacrifice after Jesus' birth (Luke 2:22–24); Jesus instructs the leper to offer the priest the gift that Moses commanded, namely an

animal sacrifice (Mark 1:44, Matthew 8:4); Peter slavishly follows the kosher regulations and needs a vision to correct his error (Acts 10:9–16). These incidents have been discussed in chapters 5, 9, and 10.

14. No God But Allah

1. Fredriksen, *From Jesus to Christ*, p. 7.
2. Jones, *Constantine and the Conversion of Europe*.
3. Schoeps, *Jewish Christianity*, p. 136.
4. Masri, *Animals in Islam*.
5. Smith, *The Way of the Mystics*, pp. 161, 165.
6. Schimmel, *Mystical Dimensions of Islam*, p. 230.
7. Sells, ed. *Early Islamic Mysticism*, p. 169.
8. Nurbakhsh, *Sufi Women*. Nurbakhsh states that Attar renders this tale in verse in his Book of Divinity.
9. Schimmel, *op. cit.* note 6, p. 358.
10. *Ibid.* pp. 207–208.
11. Šabda 83. Quoted in Hess and Singh, *The Bijak of Kabir*, p. 69.
12. Ramaini 49. Quoted in *The Bijak of Kabir*, note 10, p. 88.
13. Interestingly, this same story about throwing away the cup was also told about a cynic philosopher: Mack, *The Lost Gospel*, p. 116.
14. Al-Ghazali, *The Precious Pearl*, p. 77.
15. Zwemer, *A Moslem Seeker After God*, p. 283 and 284, citing *The Revival of Religious Sciences*, Vol. IV, p. 164.
16. *Ibid.*, p. 274, citing *The Revival of Religious Sciences*, Vol. IV, p. 52.
17. Nurbakhsh, *Jesus in the Eyes of the Sufis*, p. 79, quoting al-Ghazali, *The Revival of Religious Sciences*.
18. Zwemer, *op. cit.* note 15, p. 270.
19. Zwemer, *op. cit.* note 15, p. 262, citing al-Ghazali, *The Revival of Religious Sciences*, Vol. III, p. 26.
20. Nurbakhsh, *op. cit.* note 17, p. 107; quoting Auhadi Maraghi Esfahani.
21. *Ibid.* pp. 98, 93, quoting al-Ghazali, *The Revival of Religious Sciences*.

BIBLIOGRAPHY

Ancient Works

Al-Ghazali. *The Precious Pearl*. Jane Idleman Smith, translator. Missoula: Scholars Press, 1979.

Arnobius. *Against the Heathen*. In *The Ante-Nicene Fathers*, volume 6, pp. 413-540.

The Ante-Nicene Fathers. Alexander Roberts and James Donaldson, editors. 10 volumes. New York: Charles Scribner's Sons, 1905.

The Clementine Homilies. In The Ante-Nicene Fathers, volume 8, pp. 223–346.

Epiphanius. *The Panarion of Epiphanius of Salamis*, Book I. Frank Williams, translator. Leiden: E. J. Brill, 1987.

———. *Panarion 30*. In Glenn Alan Koch, *A Critical Investigation of Epiphanius' Knowledge of the Ebionites: A Translation and Critical Discussion of Panarion 30*. Diss. Abstr. International 37 (October 1976) 2253–A. Ann Arbor: UMI Dissertation Services, 1976.

Eusebius. *Ecclesiastical History*. In *A Select Library of Nicene and Post-Nicene Fathers of the Christian Church*, Second Series, Volume I, pp. 81–387.

———. *The Proof of the Gospel*. Edited and translated by W. J. Ferrar. Grand Rapids, Michigan: Baker Book House, 1981.

Hippolytus. *The Apostolic Tradition of Hippolytus*, trans. Burton Scott Easton. Ann Arbor: Archon Books, 1962.

Iamblichus. *On the Pythagorean Way of Life*. Translated by John Dillon and Jackson Hershbell. Atlanta: Scholars Press, 1991.

Irenaeus. *Against Heresies*. In *The Ante-Nicene Fathers*, volume 1, pp. 315–567.

Jerome. "Letter 112." In *The Correspondence (394–419) Between Jerome and Augustine of Hippo*. Carolinne White, translator. New York: The Edwin Mellen Press, 1990.

Josephus, Flavius. *The Antiquities of the Jews* and *The Wars of the Jews*. In *The Life and Works of Flavius Josephus*, William Whiston, translator. Philadelphia: John C. Winston, 1957.

Kabir, *The Bijak of Kabir*. Translated by Linda Hess and Shukdev Singh. San Francisco: North Point Press, 1983.

The Meaning of the Glorious Koran. Mohammed Marmaduke Pickthall, translator. New York: Mentor Books, 1953.

The New English Bible With the Apocrypha. Joint Committee on the New Translation of the Bible, editors. Oxford University Press and Cambridge University Press, 1970.

The New Oxford Annotated Bible: Revised Standard Version. May, Herbert G. and Metzger, Bruce M., editors. New York: Oxford University Press, 1973.

Origen. *Against Celsus.* In *The Ante-Nicene Fathers,* volume 4, pp. 395–669.

————. *De Principiis (On First Principles).* In *The Ante-Nicene Fathers,* volume 4, pp. 239–382.

————. *Homilies on Joshua.* In *Origen's Homilies on Joshua: An Annotated Translation.* Barbara June Bruce. Ann Arbor: UMI Dissertation Services, 1988.

Philo. "Every Good Man is Free." F. H. Colson, translator. In *Philo,* G. H. Whitaker and F. H. Colson, translators. 12 volumes. Cambridge, Massachusetts: Harvard University Press, 1941. Volume 9, pages 11–101.

The Recognitions of Clement. In *The Ante-Nicene Fathers,* volume 8, pp. 75–211.

A Select Library of Nicene and Post-Nicene Fathers of the Christian Church. Philip Schaff, editor. 14 volumes. Buffalo: The Christian Literature Company, 1886.

A Select Library of Nicene and Post-Nicene Fathers of the Christian Church, Second Series. Philip Schaff and Henry Wace, editors. 14 volumes. New York: The Christian Literature Company, 1890.

Sells, Michael A., editor and translator. *Early Islamic Mysticism.* Mahwah, New Jersey: Paulist Press, 1996.

Tertullian. *Against Marcion.* In *The Ante-Nicene Fathers,* volume 3, pp. 271–474.

————. "Prescription Against Heretics." In *The Ante-Nicene Fathers,* volume 3, pp. 243–265.

Theodoret. *Compendium of Heretical Fables.* In *An Analysis of the Heresiological Method of Theodoret of Cyrus in the Haereticarum Fabularum Compendium.* Thomas P. Halton. Ann Arbor: UMI Dissertation Services, 1990.

Modern Works

Aland, Barbara and Aland, Kurt. *The Text of the New Testament.* Grand Rapids: Eerdmans, 1987.

Attridge, Harold W. and Hata, Gohei (editors). *Eusebius, Christianity, and Judaism.* Detroit: Wayne State University Press, 1992.

Bauckham, Richard. "The Relatives of Jesus." **Themelios** 21(2): 18–21, January 1996.

Bazell, Dianne Marie. *Christian Diet: A Case Study Using Arnald of Villanova's "De Esu Carnum."* Ann Arbor: UMI Dissertation Services, 1991.

Brandon, S. G. F. *The Fall of Jerusalem and the Christian Church.* London: SPCK, 1951.

Cadbury, H. J. *The Peril of Modernizing Jesus.* London: SPCK, 1962.

Cadoux, C. John: *The Early Christian Attitude to War.* London, Headley Bros.: 1919.

Cansdale, Lena. *Qumran and the Essenes: A Re-evaluation of the Evidence.* Tübingen: J. C. B. Mohr (Paul Siebeck), 1997.

Corley, Kathleen. *A Place at the Table: Jesus, Women, and Meals in the Synoptic Gospels.* Ann Arbor: UMI Dissertation Services, 1992.

Countryman, L. Wm. *The Rich Christian in the Church of the Early Empire: Contradictions and Accommodations.* New York: Edwin Mellen Press, 1980.

Crossan, John Dominic. *The Historical Jesus: The Life of a Mediterranean Jewish Peasant.* San Francisco: HarperSanFrancisco, 1991.

———. *Who Killed Jesus? Exposing the Roots of Anti-Semitism in the Gospel Story of the Death of Jesus.* San Francisco: HarperSanFrancisco, 1995.

Crown, Alan D., and Cansdale, Lena. "Qumran: Was it an Essene Settlement?" **Biblical Archaeology Review** 20(5):25 ff., September/October 1994.

Danielou, Jean. *The Theology of Jewish Christianity.* Translated and edited by John A. Baker. Chicago: the Henry Regnery Company, 1964.

Dart, John. *The Jesus of Heresy and History: The Discovery and Meaning of the Nag Hammadi Gnostic Library.* Harper & Row, San Francisco, 1988.

Deakle, David Wayne. *The Fathers Against Marcionism: A Study of the Methods and Motives in the Developing Patristic Anti-Marcionite Polemic.* Ann Arbor: UMI Dissertation Services, 1991.

Dombrowski, Daniel. *Christian Pacifism.* Temple University Press, Philadelphia, 1991.

Drinkwater, G. N. *Food in the Early Church.* London: St. Alban Press, 1956.

Ehrman, Bart D. *The Orthodox Corruption of Scripture. The Effect of Early Christological Controversies on the Text of the New Testament.* New York: Oxford University Press, 1993.

Eisenman, Robert. *James the Brother of Jesus.* New York: Viking Penguin, 1996.

Eisler, Robert. *The Messiah Jesus and John the Baptist.* London: Methuen and Company, 1931.

Falk, Harvey. *Jesus the Pharisee.* Mahwah, N. J.: Paulist Press, 1985.

Fitzmyer, Joseph A. *The Acts of the Apostles: A New Translation With Introduction and Commentary.* New York: The Anchor Bible, Doubleday, 1998.

Flusser, David. "Jesus and Judaism: Jewish Perspectives," in *Eusebius, Christianity, and Judaism* in Attridge and Hata, pp. 000–000.

———. *Jewish Sources in Early Christianity.* New York: Adama Books, 1987.

Fredriksen, Paula. *From Jesus to Christ: The Origins of the New Testament Images of Jesus.* New Haven: Yale University Press, 1988.

Freyne, Sean. *Galilee from Alexander the Great to Hadrian.* Wilmington, Delaware: Michael Glazier, 1980.

Friedman, Richard. *Who Wrote the Bible?* New York: Harper and Row, 1987.

Funk, Robert. *Honest to Jesus: Jesus for a New Millennium.* San Francisco: HarperSanFrancisco, 1996.

———. Roy W. Hoover, and the Jesus Seminar, trans. *The Five Gospels: The Search For the Authentic Words of Jesus.* New York: The Macmillan Publishing Company, 1993.

Goodenough, E. R. *Jewish Symbols in the Greco Roman Period,* vol. 6. New York: Pantheon, 1956.

Gorman, Peter. *Pythagoras: A Life.* London: Routledge & Kegan Paul, 1979.

Harnack, Adolf von. *Marcion: The Gospel of the Alien God.* The Labyrinth Press, Durham, N. C., 1990.

———. *Militia Christi,* D. M. Gracie, translator. Fortress Press, 1981.

Harnick, Gillian Feeley. *The Lord's Table: The Meaning of Food in Early Judaism and Christianity.* Washington: Smithsonian Institution Press, 1994.

Haskins, Susan: *Mary Magdalen: Myth and Metaphor.* London: HarperCollins, 1993.

Hoffmann, Joseph R. *Marcion: On the Restitution of Christianity. An Essay on the Development of Radical Paulinist Theology in the Second Century.* Chico, California: Scholars Press, 1984.

Horsley, Richard: "Jesus and Judaism: Christian Perspectives." in Attridge and Hata, pp. 53–79.

Hyland, J. R., " 'Just' One Little Word," **Humane Religion**, January–February 1998, pp. 5–7.

Jones, A. H. M. *Constantine and the Conversion of Europe.* University of Toronto Press, 1978.

Jones, F. Stanley. *An Ancient Jewish Christian Source on the History of Christianity: Pseudo-Clementine Recognitions 1.27–71.* Atlanta, Georgia: Scholars Press, 1995.

Klijn, A. F. J. *Jewish-Christian Gospel Tradition.* Leiden: E. J. Brill, 1992.

———. and Reinink, G. J. *Patristic Evidence for Jewish-Christian Sects.* Leiden: E. J. Brill, 1973.

Knox, John. *Marcion and the New Testament.* Chicago: University of Chicago Press, 1942.

Koester, Helmut. *History and Literature of Early Christianity.* Two volumes. Philadelphia: Fortress Press, 1982.

Kyrtatas, Dimitris J. *The Social Structure of the Early Christian Communities.* London: Verso, 1987.

Lüdemann, Gerd. *Heretics: The Other Side of Early Christianity.* Trans. John Bowden. Louisville, Kentucky: Westminster John Knox Press, 1996.

———. *Opposition to Paul in Jewish Christianity.* Trans. M. Eugene Boring. Fortress Press: Minneapolis, 1989.

———. *The Resurrection of Jesus: History, Experience, Theology.* London: SCM Press Ltd, 1994. Translated by John Bowden.

Maccoby, Hyam. *Judas Iscariot and the Myth of Jewish Evil.* New York: The Free Press, 1992.

Maccoby, Hyam. *The Mythmaker: Paul and the Invention of Christianity.* San Francisco: Harper & Row, 1986.

———. *Paul and Hellenism.* Philadelphia: Trinity Press International, 1991.

Mack, Burton. *The Lost Gospel: The Book of Q and Christian Origins.* New York: HarperSanFrancisco, 1993.

Maqsood, Ruqaiyyah Waris [aka Rosalyn Kendrick]. *The Separated Ones: Jesus, the Pharisees, and Islam.* London: SCM Press, 1991.

Masri, Al-Hafiz Basheer Ahmad. *Animals in Islam.* Petersfield, England: Athene Trust, 1989.

Neusner, Jacob, *First Century Judaism in Crisis.* Nashville: Abingdon Press, 1975.

Nurbakhsh, Dr. Javad. *Sufi Women.* Khaniqahi–Nimatullahi Publications: New York, 1983.

———. *Jesus in the Eyes of the Sufis.* Khaniqahi–Nimatullahi Publications: New York, 1983.

Parrinder, Geoffrey: *Son of Joseph*. Edinburgh: T & T Clark, 1992.

Petersen, William L., editor. *Gospel Traditions in the Second Century: Origins, Recensions, Text, and Transmission*. Notre Dame, Ind.: University of Notre Dame Press, 1989.

Pines, Shlomo: *The Jewish Christians of the Early Centuries of Christianity According to a New Source*. Jerusalem: Israel Academy of Sciences and Humanities, 1966.

Pritz, Ray. *Nazarene Jewish Christianity*. Jerusalem: Magnes Press, 1988.

Proctor, John: "Proselytes and Pressure Cookers: The Meaning and Application of Acts 15:20," **International Review of Mission** 85(339):472.

Sanders, E. P. *The Historical Figure of Jesus*. London: Allen Lane, The Penguin Press, 1993.

————. E. P. *Paul and Palestinian Judaism*. Philadelphia: Fortress Press, 1977.

Sandmel, Samuel. *The First Christian Century in Judaism and Christianity*. New York: Oxford University Press, 1969.

————. *The Genius of Paul*. New York: Farrar, Straus, & Cudahy, 1958.

————. *Judaism and Christian Beginnings*. New York: Oxford University Press, 1978.

Schimmel, Annemarie. *Mystical Dimensions of Islam*. Chapel Hill: The University of North Carolina Press, 1975.

Schoeps, Hans-Joachim. *Jewish Christianity: Factional Disputes in the Early Church*. Philadelphia: Fortress Press, 1969.

Sells, Michael A. *Early Islamic Mysticism*. Mahwah: Paulist Press, 1996.

Siepierski, Paulo Donizeti. *The Liberating 'Leitourgia' of Basil the Great*. Ann Arbor: UMI Dissertation Services, 1990.

Smith, Margaret. *The Way of the Mystics: The Early Christian Mystics and the Rise of the Sufis*. New York: Oxford University Press, 1978.

Stark, Rodney. *The Rise of Christianity: A Sociologist Reconsiders History*. Princeton, New Jersey: Princeton University Press, 1996.

Theissen, Gerd. *The Gospels in Context*. Linda M. Maloney, translator. Minneapolis: Fortress Press, 1991.

Valantasis, Richard. *The Gospel of Thomas*. London: Routledge, 1997.

Vermes, Geza. *The Religion of Jesus the Jew*. Minneapolis: Fortress Press, 1993.

————. *Jesus the Jew: A Historian's Reading of the Gospels*. New York: Macmillan, 1973.

Wink, Walter. *Engaging the Powers: Discernment and Resistance in a World of Domination*. Minneapolis: Fortress Press, 1992.

Zwemer, Samuel M. *A Moslem Seeker After God: Showing Islam at its Best in the Life and Teaching of al-Ghazali, mystic and theologian of the eleventh century*. New York: Fleming H. Revell, 1920.

Works on Vegetarianism and Judaism and Christianity

Adams, Carol J. *Neither Man nor Beast: Feminism and the Defense of Animals*. New York: Continuum Publishing Company, 1994.

Akers, Keith. *A Vegetarian Sourcebook: The Nutrition, Ecology, and Ethics of a Natural Foods Diet*. Denver CO: Vegetarian Press, 1993.

Berry, Rynn. Food for the Gods: Vegetarianism and the World's Religions. New York: Pythagorean Press, 1998.

Hyland, J. R. God's Covenant with Animals: A Biblical Basis for the Humane Treatment of All Creatures. New York: Lantern Books, 2000.

Kalechovsky, Roberta. Vegetarian Judaism: A Guide for Everyone. Marblehead, MA: Micah Publications, 1998.

———. ed. Judaism and Animal Rights: Classical and Contemporary Responses. Marblehead, MA: Micah Publications, 1992.

Kowalski, Gary. The Bible According to Noah: Theology as if Animals Mattered. New York: Lantern Books, 2001.

———. The Souls of Animals. Walpole, NH: Stillpoint Publications, 1999.

Linzey, Andrew. Animal Gospel. Louisville: Westminster John Knox, 1999.

———. Animal Theology. Urbana, IL: Illinois University Press, 1995.

———. and Dorothy Yamamoto, eds. Animals on the Agenda. Urbana, IL: Illinois University Press, 1998.

McDaniel, Jay. Of God and Pelicans: A Theology of Reverence for Life. Louisville: Westminster John Knox, 1989.

Murti, Vasu. They Shall Not Hurt or Destroy: Animal Rights and Vegetarianism in the Western Religious Traditions. Available from 30 Villanova Lane, Oakland, CA 94611, 1995. Also www.jesusveg.org

Pinches, Charles, and Jay McDaniel, eds. Good News for Animals?: Christian Approaches to Animal Well-Being. Maryknoll, NY: Orbis, 1993.

Regan, Tom, ed. Animal Sacrifices: Religious Perspectives on the Use of Animals in Science. Philadelphia: Temple University Press, 1988.

Rosen, Steven. Diet for Transcendence: Vegetarianism and the World Religions. Badger, CA: Torchlight, 1996.

Rowe, Martin, ed. The Way of Compassion: Vegetarianism, Environmentalism, Animal Advocacy, and Social Justice. New York: Stealth Technologies, 1999.

Schwartz, Richard. Judaism and Vegetarianism. New York: Lantern Books, 2000.

Skriver, Carl Anders. The Forgotten Beginnings of Creation and Christianity. Denver: Vegetarian Press, 1991.

Spencer, Colin. The Heretic's Feast: A History of Vegetarianism. Hanover, NH: University Press of New England, 1995.

Vaclavik, Charles. The Vegetarianism of Jesus Christ: The Pacifism, Communalism, and Vegetarianism of Primitive Christianity. Three Rivers, California: Kaweah Press, 1987.

Webb, Stephen H. On God and Dogs: A Christian Theology of Compassion for Animals. New York: Oxford University Press, 1997.

Young, Richard Alan. Is God a Vegetarian? Christianity, Vegetarianism, and Animal Rights. Chicago: Open Court Publishing, 1999.

SUBJECT INDEX

SCRIPTURE INDEX

21.10–13, 39
22:4, 110, 131
25:4, 150
32:10–12, 110

I Kings
8:5, 104
Psalms
2:7, 46
145:9, 110

Proverbs
6:6–8, 110
12:10, 110
30:24–28, 110

Amos
5:14, 107
5:15, 107
5:18, 107
5:21–24, 107
5:25–27, 107

Ecclesiastes
3:19, 110

Isaiah
1:2–3, 110
1:11–13, 105

1:15–16, 105
2:3–4, 95
2:4, 110
11:9, 232
45:5–7, 81
66:1, 162
66:3, 106

Jeremiah
2:2–3, 107
7:9, 118
7:11, 118
7:21–22, 108
7:22, 118
8:8, 82

Ezekiel
20:25–26, 108

Hosea
2:18, 109, 110
6:6, 109, 114
6:9, 109
8:11–13, 109

Micah
4:2–3, 95
6:6–8, 108

Qur'an

2:43, 208
2:163, 206
2:215, 208
2:216, 209
5:1, 209
5:12–14, 207
5:12, 208
5:72, 207
5:73, 207
5:90–91, 207
5:110, 207
5:116, 207
6:38, 210
17:44, 209
19:17–22, 208
22:18, 209
23:91, 206
24:41, 209
24:56, 208
45:3–4, 209
45:28, 210
55:10, 209

**Rabbinic
Literature
Mishna and
Talmud**

B. Babia Mezi'a
32b, 110
B. Erubin
53a, 70
53b, 70
B Nedarim
18b, 70
B. Sanhedrin
59b, 110
B. Shabbath
31a, 65
P. Shabbat
16.8, 70